HIDDEN FORTUNES

*Two powerful men, **Carlos Salinas de Gortari**, President of
Mexico, and **John Reed**, head of Citibank, are supposedly ignoring
what the third man, **Raúl Salinas de Gortari**, did to accumulate an
enormous personal fortune in Swiss and British banks. As in the
times of Watergate, the press and society have to ask the tough
questions in order to know who knew what and when they found out.
The presidentof the bank, John Reed, and the adjunct president in
charge of Latin America, **Bill Rhodes**, have the fiduciary
responsibility of making sure that no money laundering operations
are executed under Citibank auspices.*

Mike Wallace, of the CBS program "60 Minutes."

HIDDEN FORTUNES

Drug Money / The Cartels
and
The Elite World Banks

Eduardo Varela-Cid
With
Fabian Baez

Hudson Street Press
New York – Miami

© 1999 by Eduardo Varela-Cid
cid@mail.com

Published by Hudson Street Press, *New York, NY*
Produced in Publishing Alliance with El Cid Editor, Inc., Miami, FL

Translated by: Michael C. Berman.
Additional Translation and Editing by John B. Jensen
and Jennifer L. Jensen

Cover Design: Public Image and Barbara Ward

ISBN: 0-935016-00-0
Library of Congress Catalog Card Number: 98-74722
HIDDEN FORTUNES, Drug Money / The Cartels & The Elite
World Banks
1. Money Laundering 2. Drug Traffic 3. Cartels
4.Mafia 5. Corruption 6. Post Law 7. War on drugs
8. Legalization 9. Latin America

Printed in the United States of America

Distributed by **BookWorld** Services, Inc.
1933 Whitfield Park Loop • Sarasota, FL 34243
Tel.: 800 444-2524   941 758-8094
Fax: 800 777-2525   941 753-9396

To Marcela,
my beloved wife, who has seen me
through the most difficult of times.
And to Lucas,
who came later.

.

To Eduardo Duhalde
and Domingo Cavallo
Two politicians fighting against the
Mafia

Acknowledgments

I would like to recognize Fabian Baez, who worked with me toward the completion of this book. We both began this work convinced that the solution was more than just a war on drug trafficking; but as I have gradually grown into this idea, he has been of this opinion all along. Let me also say that my opinions stated herein regarding the decriminalization of drug consumption are not always shared by Fabian. In sum, without his help as my advisor and his service on the Penal Legislation Committee when I was serving as a congressman, this book would not exist. Together we drafted and revised the current Argentine anti-drug trafficking legislation, which includes a whistle-blower provision. But again, over time, I have changed my mind on these issues.

CONTENTS

Preface

THE MAFIAZATION OF SOCIETY

"The problem is not so much that there are a lot of corrupt people, but rather that there are so many that the honest are scared of the corrupt." This is how Frank Serpico, an ex-police official in New York, began his narrative. They no longer hide out, but rather attack and accuse those who have not come to terms with them, an agreement they usually call " "loyalty."

What happens when corruption gets to the point where it controls the police, appoints judges, and runs congress? The corrupt even have their own armies of journalists and lawyers.

In Mexico, the brother of ex-president Salinas owns foreign bank accounts containing unexplained millions; he worked with partners in privatization deals carried out by his brother's government; and, to top it off, an undercover agent of the DEA has connected the accounts with money laundering for a drug cartel.

It is impossible to tell the whole story of what happens in Mexico. Let's just say that as the result of an investigation, all the Ministers of a particular state had to resign, all having been implicated in a cartel in the area. A drug trafficker was in prison, and after completing his sentence, he was made director of a bank. It would appear that requirements are not very strict for such a position.

In Colombia, there are eleven legislators in jail. Until recently, I had kept a count: one hundred one legislators dead and two hundred seventy journalists murdered. However, it is really impossible to keep a count of the workers who have died and those who are in jail, and those who are not, but who have been indicted. The hero of this story is ex-Minister of Justice, Rodrigo Lara Bonilla, the politician who wanted to extradite drug traffickers because he found himself powerless to fight against them in his own country. First, they deposited $12,000 in an account to finance his campaign for senator; then they harassed him for months in congress using their own journalists who accused him daily of corruption; finally, they murdered him. The corrupt have their problems, but anyone who fights seriously against drug trafficking gets killed. Mafia operations to discredit those who work against their interests are impressive and discourage even the most valiant.

In Peru, President Fujimori put the Armed Forces to work in the struggle against drug trafficking. First, an army captain asked for refuge and confessed that the army was charging smugglers $15,000 for each helicopter that left with drugs, and then they split up the proceeds. Top authorities denied the story. A short time later, an imprisoned drug dealer appeared before the prosecutor, and the charges against him were such that it took eight long hours just to read the indictment. A lot of people seemed to be involved. A few weeks later an Air Force plane was detained in Canada with 250 kilos on board, and a few days after that, two Navy boats were found to contain drugs.

In Bolivia, when ex-President Jaime Paz Zamora took office, he said that he himself did not have a quorum, but that the drug traffickers did have one. He said that he would govern honestly the part of Bolivia that he controlled, but that there was another part under the control of others.

In Brazil, I once visited a slum in the company of a legislator and a policeman. We had to ask permission of a gentleman who had a machine gun on a tripod and who let us through only grudgingly.

In Argentina, a non-producing country due to its climate, and until recently of low consumption and without cartels as they are known elsewhere, there was a businessman, Alfredo Nallib Yabran. Everybody was afraid of him, and both politicians and journalists were careful not to go against his interests. Some worked directly for him, and others simply wanted to survive. Many know the journalists who work for him; if someone should happen to go against his interests, they immediately attack mercilessly. There is proof of his press operative giving out money at a table in a bar.

Three important men of the financial world, a Swiss banker, a Spanish banker, and an ex-Minister of the Economy from Argentina, told me that in 1993 Yabran offered 800 million in cash to buy a majority share of stock in Aerolíneas Argentinas.

But this is not the most significant fact. Between 1994 and 1995, he managed to get so much control of parliament that he was having a law passed that would have privatized the post office, which he called a "custom-tailored suit." Everyone knew that Yabran would be the future owner of the post office, and the privatization law had a provision that would have authorized him to offer *secret monetary services.* This means money orders, transfers in Argentine pesos or any other currency, within the country or abroad, without limitation, with a legal prohibition against informing monetary authorities about who sends money to whom, and when it is sent (Article 4, paragraph 5).

In other words, in a country without bank secrecy laws, a businessman was going to have the ability, from the post office, to send and/or receive transfers from or to any part of the world, and monetary authorities were prohibited by law from exercising any control. Something like this: *Welcome Money Launderers. Come, criminals of the world.*

A good question would be: Who is the real author of the bill that would create such a singular law? It is actually known that it was one of Yabran's lawyers, but this has not been duly proven. The two senators who introduced the bill understood nothing of its subject matter and they were never even able to debate it.

No less strange is the attitude of the Radical Party (U.C.R.), which has been against all privatization's carried out by the Menem government (petroleum, gas, electricity, telephones, etc.), but supported without objection the privatization of the state-owned post office.

The internal workings of congress were also notable, in that one year before the attempt to pass the law, several members of the Communications Committee were removed, a necessary step for the bill to get to the floor without objection.

Finally, the law was not approved, thanks to the courage of a few legislators who opposed it even at the risk of destroying their political careers, Minister of the Economy Cavallo, who called things as he saw them, and the dignity of ex-President Raul Alfonsin, who, embarrassed by the orgy of corruption among parliamentarians, ordered a vote against it.

The climate of impunity and resignation is such that all those legislators continue enjoying high prestige as politicians, as if nothing had happened. Some time later, in January, 1997, news photographer José Luís Cabezas was killed, apparently on the orders of Yabran, and the radicals accused Menem supporters of being Yabran's partners. They may not have been very far off, for when the FBI brought in Excalibur, it was discovered that more than 500 telephone calls had been made between Yabran and various of Menem's ministers and legislators, including calls to the President's own residence.

Money gets laundered in all countries, but in few has criminal control of congress been so evident.

The United States makes reports, *certifies* or *decertifies*, in accordance with its belief regarding the way a country is cooperating in the war on drugs, but within its borders it shows just as many contradictions as the other countries mentioned. The Bank of Boston laundered $1.2 billion over five years, while at the same time it went through an inspection by a representative of the Treasury Department; the inspector was a fool. The bank pled guilty and paid a fine of $500,000. Now it has just been discovered that the money laundered by Raúl Salinas de Gortari went through Citibank of New York and its subsidiaries in London, Switzerland, and Mexico, using investment funds that lend out money to the very countries from which it has been collected.

If we divide the world between the winners and losers, without asking how, we create an unmerciful and amoral philosophy of life. In defense of this position, the road taken by a large segment of society is a nihilistic ethic. *"I don't get involved and I survive."*

What occurred during totalitarian periods under the communists and the Nazis is occurring again within the circles of corruption. Who would dare to have denounced Stalin or Hitler? Although totalitarianism does not reign today, the armies of corrupt politicians, journalists and lawyers can generate the same type of intimidation.

The lawyers of the Mafia write books in the United States and produce television programs which hail the United States as a great country. But those who die (the *losers*) in the clutches of their clients (the *winners*) write no such books. Meanwhile, publicly, this whole process is being framed as a war on drugs.

The residual discourse from this "war on drugs" has become a political exposition; however, none of the politicians in power explain what road we should follow to really exterminate this problem. Only between 5 and 10% of the drugs and between 2 and 3% of laundered money is seized. The problem of drugs and its resulting institutional corruption has been explained again and again. But what is the solution? More *war*?

There are 1,300,000 people in prison in the United States, 59% of whom are tied directly to drugs. How many people are we going to put in jail? To the above figure, we need to add 2,700,000 more who are either out on bail or on probation.

The Mafia bosses die of old age in their mansions; the prisoners are drivers, prostitutes, minor gunmen who cannot afford a good lawyer. But the lawyer of the BCCI was Clark Clifford, probably one of the most important lawyers in Washington, aide to President Truman (1948-1952), and Secretary of Defense under President Johnson.

Money laundering is going to be the most important political topic in the next few years. In a meeting of the Latin American Parliament in 1991, a Uruguayan lawmaker voted in favor of a proposal to fight drug trafficking, but against one that opposed money laundering. For that legislator, drugs were bad and he did not want them in his country, but let the money come.

The same discussion took place in the House of Lords in the United Kingdom. They would not allow opium to come in, but money from the sale of opium was welcome.

A famous Argentine journalist said repeatedly: "It doesn't matter where the money comes from, only where it goes," perhaps convinced that the traffickers were going to give it to him to buy radio stations to put on democratic programs criticizing corruption.

REAL POWER AND APPARENT POWER

Under capitalism, real power is concentrated in the hands of the few. Moreover, with the rise in technology, unemployment and gaps in opportunity have increased. The establishment wants neither to socialize nor democratize its power. However, drugs cannot become a vehicle of social mobility and power. The millionaires want politicians to remain in office only a short time, with no chance of threatening their fortune or their power; then they want another inexperienced politician to enter the political arena for another short while. Although the politicians can argue the newspapers, the real power, the permanent power, is money, which is something else entirely.

The debate over how to approach this situation is an important one. It is clear, however, that we cannot attempt to challenge the power of drug traffickers or money launderers by playing their game. That is, we cannot fight fire with fire, or in this case, money with money. Society would perish, strangled between the old establishment and the new Mafia.

The story of Robert Kennedy's struggle against the Mafia is noteworthy. Kennedy had the infamous drug trafficker of New Orleans, Carlos Marcelo, exiled for two years. There is now evidence that indicates that Kennedy was one of the persons whom Marcelo marked for death. Marcelo died of old age at 83 in his mansion. So was Bobby Kennedy a loser and Marcelo a winner? Marcelo's lawyer wrote a book (*Mob Lawyer*), in which he basically concluded that if you want to be a politician, first make friends with a crime boss.

Are politicians who adopt the alternative destined for transitory, unreal, and superficial power? Or to be cynical, must they be unscrupulous friends of the Mafia? Is this the only way to approach election campaigns? Where will this road of political incredulity take us? If a politician wants to be decent, how long before organized crime chokes him?

Is it possible that anyone in Colombia believed that the minister of justice could have been bought for $12,000? Nevertheless, Lara Bonilla passed the last months of his life declaring that he had not endorsed the check. The journalist who was attacking him was the spokesman of the cartel, with a direct line to Pablo Escobar.

This book will perhaps shed light on events that perhaps you were not familiar with. It supports the view that if we do not rethink this war on drugs, we will never win, or that there really never has been such a war, only maneuvers to increase prices. In sum, if we know we are in a war in which we know we will not win, why don't we try another approach to the problem?

This *war* is full of heroes who have sacrificed their lives. It is also full of unserving bureaucrats and dozens of security organizations who waste the majority of their time fighting amongst themselves, perhaps trying to secure a bigger budget for themselves or increase the boundaries of their power.

The police do their best to confiscate kilos of drugs, which go into tediously calculated statistics. All this takes place as if they did not know that the person whom they just arrested with the drugs is unimportant, that if he were important, then he would not have been there with the drugs in the first place. He is a driver or a triggerman.

Is the *Mafiazation* of society inevitable?

When José Oberholzer was vice president of the Union Bank of Switzerland, he advised many Latin American clients, among them Raúl Salinas de Gortari. In the shady game of moving money, he helped create fronts in order to conceal the real origin of the funds. Now Oberholzer finds himself charged with laundering $150 million of the Medellin cartel's money.

He was arrested by police in Canton de Vaud, Switzerland in February, 1994, together with Sheila Arana de Nasser, wife of Julio Cesar Nasser David, an operative of Pablo Escobar, the late leader of the Medellin cartel. Two months after his arrest, upon the request of the United States under the Legal Mutual

Assistance Treaty, Swiss Authorities confiscated the $150 million.[1]

A judge of Canton de Vaud, Jackes Antenen said that "this is the biggest confiscation of drug money in Swiss history." According to the DEA, David Nasser smuggled more than 25 tons of cocaine into the United States. Consequently, the police continued to look for another $755 million.

Dieter Jann Cerrodi, the Swiss detective who continued with the investigation, accused Oberholzer of laundering money which originated in Latin America. The Swiss attorney general confirmed this accusation. Oberholzer after spending 48 hours in jail, remained under house arrest. However, the judge, considering the Swiss Penal Code of 1990, predicted that "maybe they'll give him a few months in jail."

BETWEEN OPERATION CASABLANCA AND THE BANK OF BOSTON

It looked like a meeting of more than a dozen rich and well-dressed business executives, who had traveled on their private jets to discuss some important agreement over dinner at a casino. After dinner, a convoy of limousines arrived from across 80 miles of desert to take the "executives" from the Casablanca Casino Resort, in Mesquite, Nevada, to Las Vegas, where they were to spend the night. But the vehicles crossed the brightly lit streets at high speed and returned to the highway, where police in patrol cars signaled them to pull over.

Víctor Manuel Alcalá Navarro's chauffeur lowered the window that separated him from the passengers and offered this excuse: "I'm sorry. I'm afraid I was speeding." Alcalá

---

[1] Charles Intrago, *Money Laundering Alert*. This is a specialized monthly bulletin published out of Miami.

Navarro, presumably the most important money launderer of the most powerful drug cartel of Mexico, looked through his window at the group of civilian dressed agents that was coming toward the car and said, "I believe that this is something more than a speeding ticket."

The haul of limousines brought in on that Saturday night in the suburbs of Las Vegas—as it was described on Tuesday by U.S. Customs agents familiar with the operation—was part of what prosecutors describe as the biggest case of money laundering in the history of the U.S., which for the first time tied the Mexican banking system to the laundering of drug smuggling profits.

The three year operation, directed by the U.S. Customs Service, implicated some of the largest and most prestigious banks in Mexico and penetrated the drug cartel in Juarez. Details of the operation, in which more arrests were made on Tuesday, surprised Mexican prosecutors, politicians, and financiers, none of whom were informed about the operation until the formal announcement was made from Washington on Monday.

While Mexican and U.S. authorities had tried in the past to bring people involved in specific cases of money laundering to justice, and had documented the extensive corruption existing within political and justice circles in Mexico, never before had any government put together an investigative team that tried to document systematic corruption based on drug trafficking in Mexican financial institutions.   American authorities indicated that the investigation could involve up to $152 million, in no fewer than one hundred bank accounts in the U.S., Europe, and the Caribbean. This is nothing, of course, compared to the $1.2 billion that the Bank of Boston laundered, but this money had come from outside the U.S., so was considered to be much more serious.

Operation Casablanca started three years ago as a small-scale investigation that attempted to "locate and infiltrate those who were invisible to us." That is to say, entrepreneurs who moved millions of dollars in profits through complex financial paths that converted the cash into earnings from apparently legitimate businesses, as explained by an important supervisor from the Customs Service who led the operation.

The operation really got under way when undercover agents set up a front, a business they called Emerald Empire Corporation, with offices in the Los Angeles suburb of Santa Fe Springs, according to the indictment presented in the federal court of that city on Monday. Agents who passed for executives of the company had gone looking for Mexican banks willing to accept their "dirty money." The fact that the money was always clearly identified as drug profits was never a reason for Mexican bankers to refuse it; the only matter discussed involved the commission to be paid to the banks for handling the money. The figure most often cited was around four per cent of the amount of the transaction.

The supposed drug money was deposited later in Mexican bank accounts under false company and individual names. After the deposit was made, a corrupt bank official, sometimes a branch vice president or a division head, would call an unsuspecting colleague in an American branch of the same bank to say that he had approved a transfer of money involving the false individual or company.

Alcalá Navarro, who quickly realized that he had been caught there at the side of the highway on that Saturday night in Las Vegas, was one of the best contacts for the undercover agents, as the indictment points out: "Alcalá Navarro was able to locate bankers who worked for banks headquartered in Mexico and ask for their help in laundering money representing profits from the ilicit sale of narcotics" and played a key role in recruiting other bankers, according to the indictment.

The indictment describes a series of meetings between Alcalá Navaro and Justice Department informants and undercover agents in which they presumably arranged for the laundering of tens of millions of dollars on behalf of the Juarez cartel and the cocaine and heroine Mafia of Cali.

The indictment recounts a series of six money transfers that totaled six million dollars that were initiated by Alcalá Navarro and which were deposited by money order in the Mexican bank Banorte between November 11 and December 16, 1997. Morover, the indictment lists dozens of deposits that exceeded $10,000, which by law should have been reported as suspicious, but which were not. The side of the deposits varied between $32,000 and $3.9 million.

The indictment further states that on August 29, 1997, Alcalá Navarro, in a meeting with drug traffickers and an undercover agent, sketched out the close ties between people from the Juarez cartel—including its one-time boss Amado Carrillo Fuentes—with "high-level Mexican authorities." At the same time that U.S. prosecutors were looking into the involvement of Mexican banks, they were carrying out a parallel investigation of the biggest and most influential drug Mafia of Mexico, the Juarez cartel, which had been led by Carrillo Fuentes up until his mysterious death during a plastic surgery operation last July.

These were not people dressed in brightly colored tee shirts with their hair greased back. They looked like well-dressed businessmen with diplomas from top-notch schools. They traveled throughout the United States, Europe, and South American, dressed well and eating and staying in the finest hotels—a whole enterprise.

These were the same men who were invited by undercover agents to spend a business weekend discussing and closing deals, while having a good time at the Casablanca Casino Resort. The customs agents chose their Mexican contacts very carefully, so that they would mix easily in a meeting of this type. Some of them arrived at the private airstrip near the casilno in jets belonging to the Customs Service, thinking they were the property of Emerald Empire.

The men were later arrested and taken by limousines supplied by the U.S. government.

Immediately following the arrest in Las Vegas of Victor Alcalá Navarro, the "right hand man" of the financial director of the Juarez cartel, José Alvarez Tostado, the U.S. urged Mexico to arrest Tostado as being involved in the scandal made public on Monday.

The acting U.S. prosecutor in Los Angeles, Julie Shemitz, told the New York Times that American authorities had never "shared any information with Mexico during the investigation for fear of risk to the safety of their undercover agents." Shemitz said, "It is not that we don't believe the Mexicans. In reality we did not speak with anybody. These kinds of operations are so dangerous that we can end up playing with the lives of the agents.

Those first arrested were kept in jail until Tuesday, the twenty-sixth, when they were formally indicted. They were accused of laundering amounts of money between $212,000 and $19 million from drug trafficking. Judge Rosalyn Champan decided that they should remain in custody because they had few financial or family ties in Southern California that might reduce their risk of flight. She added that she would consider later on the possibility of bond.

More than one hundred people are included in the indictment presented on that Monday concerning money laundering in six countries. Operation Casablanca pointed to employees of twelve of the largest nineteen Mexican banks. The case will produce a number of trials that may go on for months.

In the first stage, $35 million were captured, but it is hoped that another $122 million can be seized in bank accounts in the U.S. and other countries. The first eight people indicted, all Mexican nationals, are facing money laundering and conspiracy charges, and if convicted, could be subject to life imprisonment.

Only one of those indicted denied the charges immediately.   José Ángel Cazares' attorney requested dropping of charges against his client, claiming that authorities lacked probable cause to arrest him. The Magistrate dismissed his request "without prejudice," which means that it may be brought up again later.

In spite of supposedly having received juicy commissions for helping to hide the origin of drug money, the eight people appeared before the Los Angeles federal court and made sworn statements that they did not have the economic resources to pay for their own defense; thus, they were assigned public defenders.

The U.N. Office of Drug Inspection and Crime Prevention held a seminar under the auspices of Bolivian organization, the United Nations, and the governments of the United States, Great Britain, and *Citibank. (This was the same bank which supposedly is being investigated for laundering the money of Salinas de Gortari and the Juarez Cartel, an investigation rarely mentioned.)*

The Panamanian Association of Banks (Apabancos) jumped the gun and announced that it would come out clean from any association with the Mexican "scandal," although there had been no indication that Panama was involved.

The U.S. government announced that Operation Casablanca reached Venezuela with the bringing of charges against five employees of four banks of that country. Those five were accused of laundering $9.5 million through the Banco del Caribe, Banco Industrial de Venezuela, International Finance Bank and Banco Consolidado.

Three of the five who were arrested were identified as Carmen Salima Irigoyen, Esperanza de Saad and Carlos Izurieta Valery. The other two are Roberto Vivas and Marco Tulio Henríquez, who were in Venezuela, according the Justice Department. Would it not be cheaper just to investigate the banks that did *not* launder money?   These days we are witnessing an international spectacle of institutionalized cynicism.

Undercover agents of the U.S. Border Police were able to infiltrate drug traffickers and money launderers from Mexico and Venezuela. Everything was carefully filmed and recorded, and in all recordings it was made clear that the money came from drugs; however, the bankers at no point expressed the least concern at that fact, preferring to limit discussions to their commissions.

A U.S. government agency, working surreptitiously in other countries, and using a subterfuge, was able to bring the bankers to the U.S. and put them in jail. Power is what matters. Only the United States can do something like that. Not because the U.S. is better, but because it has greater power.

The Bank of Boston laundered $1.2 billion for the drug trafficker Angiulo, but his drugs came from outside the country. Following this criteria, it would have been possible to invite the president of the Bank of Boston to Mexico and put him in jail there. But no one could imagine that scenario; such a procedure would open up mechanisms of reprisal that are available only to those in power.

How did the investigation of Citibank, Raúl Salinas, and Confidas end up?

IBM

In 1995, it was discovered in Argentina that IBM, in order to sell a computer system to the Banco Nación, had paid $34 million in bribes to various officials of the bank. The Minister of Economy at that time, Domingo Cavallo, provided information to the Argentine judge that made it possible to detect the funds in distant accounts in Swiss banks and in Luxemburg, where the corrupt officials had sacked away their money. After the investigation, several ex-employees of the bank and the local branch of IBM were imprisoned. The problem became apparent when it was discovered, during the same investigation, that there were four employees of the main office of IBM in the United States that had the same responsibility: two Brazilians, Robeli Libero and Marcio Kaiser, an Australian, Peter Rowley, and the American Steve Lew. The Argentine judge asked Interpol to arrest them.

The home office of IBM came to the defense of its corrupt executives. It is strange that the Department of State, which so often complains about corruption, repeated the same tired speech given by the corrupt company. In the United States, they make a sport of talking about corruption in Latin America, but just wait until it appears among top executives of the U.S. Even before the judge requested it, the Department of State spoke out against any order for international capture.

IBM had been in first place internationally in terms of trustworthiness. Now, with the support of the U.S. government, it was determined to sabotage justice in a country where it had made a lot of money, using strategies against the laws of Argentine and the U.S. It was also posed to ignore an international legal order, with the support of its own government.

In other words, IBM was acting just like the Bank of Boston, only a little smaller. The message given to South Americans would be: If you want to bribe, don't do it among yourselves, hurting our interests; if you want to launder money, don't you do it in detriment to our banks, but let us do it, because we have a *special patent*.

Since 1977, the United States has had a law against Foreign Corrupt Practices. An executive of an (American) multinational who bribes a foreigner will be tried *in the United States*.

Argentine Senator Leopoldo Moreau stated that "The speed with which the North American Department of Justice reacted to the request from Argentine prosecutors contrasts with the slowness with which the organization acted on the matter of providing information to Judge Banasco concerning bribe money deposited in American bank accounts."

I

Colombia: The Culture of Death

T he origin of the Antioquians goes back to the era of the Conquest, when the Catholic Kings of Spain expelled the Moors and demanded that any Jews wishing to remain in Spain convert to Catholicism. Many Jews preferred to flee the Old World and arrived in this region in central Colombia, changing their surnames. Therefore, they were called "transplanted Jews." The Antioquians have particular characteristics that differentiate them from other Colombians. One such trait is their great affinity for activities related to trade. Another is their devotion to the breeding of pure-bred horses.

Because of its geographical position, Colombia is a bridge between large consumer markets and drug-producing regions. This "privileged" position for drug trafficking, as well as its social environment of dispossession and poverty, made Colombia a sitting duck for the flourishing of organized crime. And so, Colombia played host to these organizations, where their bases of power were established.

The drug-trafficking organizations, seeking to preserve their illicit wealth, developed what are known as *sicariatos*. Rooted in the cities of Medellin and Envigado, a *sicariato* is an organization composed of youths from the poor areas who are dedicated to the service of the drug traffic. The *sicariato*, sustained by the economic power of the Mafia, is basically a standing army, trained to execute homicides and terrorist attacks of any nature, in exchange for enormous quantities of money and the opportunity for rapid enrichment.

There are schools in Medellin to educate children to enter the business of crime. The children complete their preparation by the time they are twelve to fifteen years old. As opposed to nearly all other criminals, the *sicario,* or assassin, is concerned with making sure everyone knows of his particular areas of "prowess." According to this scale of values, weapons and terror are the instruments of power that permit him to earn respect and admiration in his neighborhood. Each kid aspires to improve his position within the hierarchic structure of the organization. To reach this goal, he must undergo absurd tests of criminal value, which often involve murdering his best friend or his girlfriend as a cold-blooded demonstration of his loyalty to his superior. Recently, ceremonies have been introduced to initiate new recruits into the *sicarios*. One of them consists of trapping a black cat, cutting its head off and drinking its blood mixed with red wine. Through this rite, according to their beliefs, they acquire feline agility in their movements and also the ability to see in the dark.

Each assassin is known solely by his alias. With each order or mission, the assassin assumes a new identity by means of false documentation. Such was the case of "Quica," a *sicariato* chief, who was captured by the army and remained under examination for six days without revealing his real identity. Finally, an anonymous telephone call revealed that Quica was Francis Muñoz Mosquera, who had been involved in more than 50 assassinations and had made a spectacular escape from the jail in Bellavista two years earlier. After his escape, he paid a considerable amount of money to the State Registrar and was able to assume a new identity.

To characterize this social scenario, the press coined expressions such as "the generation with no future" and "the culture of death."[2] This terminology was made common through discussions and forums organized to study the phenomenon of the *sicarios*. The first of these above-noted phrases gave rise to the movie "Rodrigo D. No Futuro," directed by Víctor Gaviria, which met with great success at the Cannes Film Festival. The protagonists were kids of the neighborhood where the movie was filmed. Three of them were murdered during the filming, and the others were killed before the movie was released. Only the principal protagonist, who was a professional actor, survived.

"If one thinks that he can build a better future out of honest work, he's crazy! One must join the cartels and hope for a good hit in order to fill your pockets with cash and die comfortably."[3] These statements synthesize the feelings of absolute loss and doom prevalent in the slums over the last generation, where life expectancy does not exceed thirty years, and each day is lived as if it were the last.

Death is, for them, the possible and dreaded end to each task they undertake. However, it also represents relief from the hardship of their lives; therefore, instead of being events for weeping, funerals are huge feasts with elaborate dinners and abundant drinking. Also central are music and dance, which continue until the deceased himself participates. When, in the early morning hours, his friends pull the body from the coffin and take photographs of one another dancing with him,

---

[2] The first to use these phrases to identify this social phenomenon was General Harold Bedoya, Commander of the Fourth Brigade, in Medellín.

[3] *Los Sicarios en Medellín* (Caracas: Ed. Capriles, 1992).

pictures which the survivors will keep as a last testimony of his existence.

The *sicarios* occupy the bottom rung of the operative levels of the drug cartels. A few of them, in recognition of their skill, become *capos*, or leaders. Otherwise, as a rule, *sicarios* are considered *disposable*, since when one is eliminated, there are ten or twelve other kids waiting for the opportunity to take his place. In fact, the Medellin cartel contracted groups to "clean" the assassins who executed the assassinations; this was to safeguard the contractors of the murder attempts. One of the leaders of such a group declared: "They tell you that the fewer people who have knowledge of a killing, the better. Our clients are quite taken care of. And they should be, since they put much at stake. Therefore, one must make a sweep of all the assassins after each job. It must be done for the safety of all."[4]

The sicarios profess a deep devotion to their mothers, as well as a devotion to Virgin Mary the Patron, in whom is glorified the kindness of their own mothers. Their violation of the sacred commandment not to kill does not, in their eyes, make contradictory their requests that the Virgin protect them and guide them to success in their criminal activities. This view can be appreciated in the following testimony:

"He who kills and does not commend one's soul to the Virgin is sure to be sent to hell. I pray to her nearly every day, and even more so when I'm without money. I say to her: 'My beautiful Virgin, take me from this well so deep, bring me good hits (assignments to kill someone) and permit me to do them well, so that I may give the money to my mother who then will not have to struggle so much to find food. If you should deem my death necessary, then I will go with pleasure because you will be waiting for me. But please, for the sake of lovely Jesus, don't let me land in jail. Kill me before the law gets me' (Manuel F. "Caney," age 22)."[5]

---

4 Idem. Ob. Cit. 3.
5 Idem. Ob. Cit. 3.

THE MILITARY

In 1984, the army had no responsibility in anti-drug operations as there was no political will to combat the drug trade. As the smuggling of drugs to the United States increased, so too increased the flow of money to Colombian governmental organizations. This was proven, for example, when "Chirusa," head of Pablo Escobar's *sicariato*, was detained. He asked the official who had seized him if, by chance, the official knew that he was paying for the maintenance of the Fourth Brigade Intelligence Section's vehicles. When this fact had been established, Chirusa was let go, but by that time he had become so annoyed with the army that, from then on, not a penny was provided for the maintenance of the cars.

There were two periods in which the Colombian State went to war against the drug trade. The first era began in Bogota on April 30, 1984, when Minister of Justice Rodrigo Lara Bonilla was assassinated. The second began in response to the assassination of presidential candidate Luis Carlos Galán Sarmiento, who died in Soacha on September 19, 1989. Both crimes were ordered by the Medellin Cartel.

Of the two periods, 1989 was the crudest. In Medellin the price of two kilos of coca paste was $1,000. After the refinement process, it is reduced to one kilo of cocaine hydrochloride, valued at $3,000, and finally sold by the gram for a total price of $35,000. In this large-scale business, shipments of 1,000 to 2,000 kilos were made weekly.

At that time, Pablo Escobar promised to pay 2 million pesos for each policeman killed in Medellin. The *sicarios* took advantage of the situation by unleashing their vengeance upon the uniformed men of Medellin, killing 150 policemen in the first three months of 1989.

This juicy, illicit trade, which puts money into the pockets of thousands of persons day and night, has begotten a new culture; not a culture based on the value of work, but, for a large part of the population, one based on enrichment through unconditional dedication to one's *capo*. Pablo Escobar, the *capo* of the cartel, is viewed with admiration by many of these individuals because he showed them how to obtain large fortunes with little effort, and in this manner, make themselves into public figures who control the politics of the poor neighborhoods.

In 1990, in the Aranjuez neighborhood, two soldiers were murdered while conducting intelligence operations to capture "Pana," also known as "Panadero," chief of a *sicariato* gang. This neighborhood housed more than 3,000 assassins on the payroll of the Medellin cartel. The "law of silence," observed throughout the neighborhood, was impervious to military intelligence. After the murder of the two soldiers, a procedure known as "the *raqueteo*," or round-up, began. This consisted of cordoning off a neighborhood and carrying out a meticulous, house-by-house interrogation of its residents. The resulting suspects were brought to a nearby school named "Simona Duque." All these procedures were executed without a judicial order, since no judge would dare to sign it. As reprisal, the director of the school, Fabiola del Rocío Loaiza Alzate, was murdered by a *sicario* after she had declined leadership in a protest calling for the army's withdrawal from the school.

At the conclusion of the neighborhood occupation, the Office of Criminal Investigation was asked to file an official report on the status of the 970 delinquents who were placed by the army under the under the jurisdiction of subordinate judges of that office. Though this report was never filed, it was verified through other means that of the 970 detained, a mere 86 remained in jail, 68 had died, and the rest were again at large.[6]

---

[6] *Mi Guerra en Medillín* (Bogotá: Intermedio Editores, 1992).

THE FOURTH BRIGADE

When Dr. Julio Matis, an inspector of the Security and Control Department of the Municipality of Envigado, a civil police force at the service of the *capos*, announced his plans to leave his post, several agents that worked with him thought it best "to silence him" since he knew too many things about their operations. Consequently, Matis sought refuge in the Fourth Brigade, considered a relatively safe haven by those in danger of being killed by the cartels. Upon being interrogated regarding these "things," he began to provide details on the actions of his pursuers:

The agents would leave at night to round up suspects. Just having a Cali license plate would be sufficient motive to stop and investigate the occupants. They were detained at once, without being given opportunity to explain, and were brought in to be interrogated. Those who aroused suspicion of a relationship to the Cali cartel were thrown in jail.

The jail cells at the back were reserved for the next victims who would disappear. They tied up the detainee, then put plaster in his mouth. In the early hours of the morning, he would be taken to some deserted area in the mountains that surrounded Envigado. There, they murdered him with an ax.

The following day, they returned to the same place with an inspector. They inspected the cadaver, and, if it was claimed, would deliver it to the family, informing them that those responsible for the crime were unknown.[7]

Days later, another employee of the Security and Control Department, Marta, sought refuge within the Fourth Brigade. She had received 35 blows with an ax in an attempt on her life,

---

[7] Idem. Ob. Cit. 6.

but she miraculously survived because to her jacket. Another case was that of Security and Control Department informant Eleázar López. Agents of that department fired at him several times, hitting him five times. Nevertheless, he managed to escape with his life and was received into the brigade with his wife and children. General Harold Bedoya, with the brigade under his command, tried to organize a program similar to the Witness Protection Program in the United States. He requested that several justices of the peace be brought to Medellin to begin an investigation of the cases. At the program's peak, the brigade housed 20 justices of the peace, 40 administrative assistants and experts sent from Bogota, and more than 30 witnesses.

Among the first to participate in this program, arriving months before the others, were Roldán Betancur (killed under tragic circumstances), the ex-Mayor William Jaramillo Gómez, and the liberal candidate César Gaviria Trujillo.[8] Twelve of those responsible for the crimes were captured and transported to the Picota National Penitentiary in Bogota, since none of the jails in Medellin would be able to guarantee their safety. This improvised witness protection program was, at its base, an effort to establish peace in Medellin. No security organization in the State wanted to pick up the expenses of the witnesses. In a press conference, General Bedoya delineated the serious accusations against the agents.

In February, 1990, a new *raqueteo* operation began in Envigado which was to be the final offensive. If Medellin is the world capital of drug traffic, then Envigado it is the headquarters of the drug traffickers. It was chosen as an operations center because of its favorable business climate. That is, the mayor is an unconditional agent of Pablo Escobar Gaviria and of the Ochoa family --the Ochoa family created the Security and Control Department.

---

[8] Now the Secretary General of the Organization of American States.

The Municipal Council, in fulfilling orders of the drug lords, published a statement accusing the military of violating human rights. This declaration resonated through-out not only the press, but also human rights commissions that were operating in Colombia.

In large part, the plans and operations of the Colombian Mafia had the approval of the military. Even though the Colombian underworld began as a force run by the Escobars, the Ochoas, and other such families, many ex-officials of the army and police have joined the sicario armies of the drug-traffickers, providing the necessary resources to create a well-run military machine. These men, as they became key pieces in the workings of these organizations, guaranteed the safety of the capo's movements and operations.

In some cases, such as that of General Villegas, this collaboration did not arise spontaneously, but as the natural conclusion to turns in his life. Villegas, upon having difficulties with his marriage, began relations with an intimate "friend" who had been paid by the Mafia to convert him into an informant. This situation, as well as his addiction to alcohol, which he had acquired during this time, cost him his military career. Upon leaving the army, he accepted the position of security chief of the Medellin cartel, working particularly with Pablo Escobar Gaviria, and later, Jorge Luis Ochoa. However, the cartel received some information indicating that Villegas was operating as a double agent, and Gaviria ordered an interrogation. Soon after, his corpse was found on the Palms Highway.

Another case was that of intelligence official Lino Correa. A noted equestrian, Correa had successfully participated in several international contests with his son, who had inherited an interest in horses from his father. Shortly after their move to Medellin, the local equestrian clubs recognized his son's talent for riding. The club that sponsored him also procured horse for him and took care of its maintenance. The success of his son filled Correa with happiness and he was thankful for the athletic spirit of the Antioqians who had made this possible, as riding was too costly a sport for their means. Nevertheless, Colonel Correa felt uncomfortable when he noticed that his son's sponsors were asking him many strange questions; however, he decided not to worry about it, attributing their curiosity to a healthy interest in the militia. For the drug traffickers, any response Correa gave, however vague, was valuable to them as they learned that there was not a single army operation of which Correa did not know. In this way, within a short period, this intelligence officer had become an informant for the Mafia.

The surprising failure of all operations to capture Pablo Escobar caught the attention of the then commander of the brigade, Ruiz Barrier. Barrier ordered that the telephones of certain officials be tapped, since the only explanation for the continuing failure to capture Escobar was disloyalty within the ranks.   Subsequently, Correa was recorded passing on confidential information to one of Escobar's congressmen. Correa was then brought before a disciplinary tribunal and removed from service.   It is said that Correa, enjoying better luck than his companion Villegas, continues to work for the Medellin cartel, and has not fallen from grace with them.

In the course of this struggle, individual soldiers have sometimes   acquired   important,   potentially   lucrative information regarding drug traffickers.   For example, Major Pacheco and Captain Uscátegui profited substantially.   In August, 1990, these officials found out where Gonzalo Rodríguez Gacha, before dying, had buried a large sum of money.   Without telling anyone, they recovered the money and brought it to Bogota. Upon being discovered, they were able to flee the country with their families and today live as millionaires.

Henry de Jesus Pérez, commander of the State Militia of the Middle Magdalena, a staunch enemy of Pablo Escobar, estimated that 50% of the security organizations of the state were combating Escobar and the other 50% were protecting him; therefore, it was impossible to know his true whereabouts. This sentiment was shared by a group of retired officers that made up the "3M," or "Moral Military Movement," who had declared war against officials aiding Pablo Escobar.

On April 9, 1984, at 1:05 p.m., Gaitán, the liberal party leader who was to take power after an overwhelming electoral victory, was assassinated. His political profile was that of a social democrat whose populist style was comparable to Juan Perón's in Argentina. This comparison is based on the new evolutionary course proposed by Gaitán which was rooted in popular socio-political trends and a call for a change in Colombia's ruling classes.

With his death, violence created a martyr of the struggle for political change and shed doubt on the legitimacy of the democratic process. This pessimism was especially prevalent within the political left, within the urban popular sectors and in the countryside. With legal channels apparently closed, the power of weapons was progressively replacing the electoral system.

The game of double circumstances, one domestic and the other international, gave rise to guerrilla violence, which had at its foundation the goal of replacing the democratic order with a Marxist-inspired model. The guerrilla groups FARC, ELN, MPL, and M-19, emerged in response to the political and social oppression exercised by the National Front (el Frente Nacional). Patronage is another factor for the deterioration of the Colombian status quo, the economic model proposed by CEPAL lessened dynamism and opportunity in the private sector while favoring the growth of the public sector. Meanwhile, the development of state monopolies --public services, customs, communications, and ports-- with strong patronage-related interference from the elite political class, generates bureaucracy and corruption.

This false concept of national sovereignty espousing inward development has led to insufficient growth and at the same time has prevented a real opening of the economy. Thus, the state cannot guarantee public safety and order, or execute justice. Moreover, the state intervenes in areas that the private sector would handle more efficiently if it had the space and the freedom to do so. The absence of reformative alternatives, clientelism, attrition within the political parties, and the state's hegemony in economy management have all been detrimental factors of a serious national crisis. This crisis led to an insurgence of subversion and prepared the fertile field for the seeds of drugs.

SHORT STORIES

At the beginning of the 1970's, various groups emerged that were devoted mainly to the traffic of marijuana to the United States. As result of this traffic, a new group of wealthy barons arose. These new players gave rise to incidences such as that involving ex-Supreme Court Justice, Julio Salgado Vázquez. Salgado Vásquez, who ultimately became an advisor to drug-traffickers, was approached by one such mafioso to buy to his house for $2 million, despite its value being no more than $500,000. He requested that the documents of sale show the smaller amount so that the drug trafficker could avoid tax problems. But, once the documents were drawn up and signed, the trafficker refused to pay the ex-Justice the difference, resulting in a public scandal.

Another typical figure was Julio Calderón, who, in partnership with his brothers Alfonso and Lucky Cotes, bought the aviation company Aerocóndor. They filed for bankruptcy of the company, but not before using it to launder money and to finance the construction of an elegant house in Miami that came to be known as *"The Blue Palace."* Calderón also bought the Florida mansion of former President Richard Nixon with cash. In addition, he owned a series of luxury hotels in Barranquilla. However, his squandering lifestyle eventually ruined him, and today he works as an Atlantic Coast deputy for the Ochoa clan.

FIOCCONI AND THE FRENCH CONNECTION

At that time, the kind of marijuana most coveted in the American market was the "red point" or *"punto rojo"* variety; however, the popularity of this strain began to decay for two reasons: a decline in its quality, and the appearance of a new product more easily transported and with a higher profit margin: cocaine. A kilo of this valuable alkaloid was worth almost the same as an entire ship laden with marijuana. There was also another factor in the decline of *punto rojo*: a new strain of marijuana from California, known as *seedless,* or more commonly, *sin semilla,* had begun to flood the market. *Sin semilla* could even be cultivated on an apartment balcony.

Nevertheless, the prosperous period for marijuana generated large sums of dollars for the Colombian black market. It is calculated that in 1978, $1.6 million was illegally brought into Colombia; this compares with $1.734 million which entered through legal goods and services. This illustrates the economic power of drug trafficking and drug-trafficking organizations. When the Julio César Turbay Ayala Administration was inaugurated (1978), the order was given to combat all those involved in immoral or illegal activities, with special emphasis placed on the drug traffickers; however, their vague slogan appeared to protect these criminals: "I will reduce immorality to tight proportions." Many believed that the country was headed toward a period of tranquillity and legality, but in reality what occurred was very different.

One of the cases that alerted the Colombians to the unbridled pursuits of the drug traffickers was that of Frenchman Laurent Charles Fiocconi, a fugitive of the French and American justice systems. Fiocconi was an important link to the *"French Connection,"* a European organization devoted to the trafficking of heroin. Fiocconi was captured in 1970 in Marseilles while delivering 100 kilos of heroin to his boss, Marcel Boucan. A French judge subsequently condemned him to 15 years in prison. At the same time, a New York court sentenced him in his absence to 25 years; however, this did not prevent him from surreptitiously entering Colombia with a fake passport four years later.

In exchange for a small sum of money, Fiocconi became the adopted son of a humble old man of Bogota, whom he later murdered. In 1975, he married a Colombian woman with the surname "Bedoya," and had four children with her. The Colombian Chancellory certified in 1977 that "Mr. Laurent Fiocconi is a Colombian national since he is the son of a Colombian; he was born abroad and is now domiciled in the Republic of Colombia."[9]

Despite his unfettered life in Colombia, Fiocconi had pending against him three extradition requests and eight condemnatory judgments in foreign countries for drug trafficking. However, because he had bounced a check, Colombian authorities arrested him in August, 1977. In the process of detaining him, the authorities found among his possessions equipment for the processing of cocaine.

When they became aware of his past, the case went before the Colombian Supreme Court in order to resolve the issue of his extradition. It proved to be a prolonged legal battle, as the defense had contracted one of the most prestigious law firms in the country, whose attorneys included an ex-minister of the Supreme Court. However, while the Penal Annulment Court

---

[9] Fabio Castillo, *Los Jinetes de la Cocaína* (Colombia: Editorial Documentos Periodísticos, 1988).

was considering if there was sufficient reason to deliver Fiocconi to foreign authorities, Fiocconi decided to finance an escape operation with a group of M19 guerrillas who, like him, were incarcerated in the Picota Penitentiary in Bogota. They managed to collapse a wall using a small bomb and fled to an unknown destination. To date, nothing is known of the whereabouts of Fiocconi.

During the mid-1970's, Pablo Escobar Gaviria was known simply as *Gatillero*, or "Triggerman" of the Colombian mafioso groups. He was especially associated with the notorious, poor slums of Antioquia; nevertheless, his ambitions for power were soon demonstrated.

The appearance of Pablo Escobar Gaviria in the police world first registered in 1976, when he was 26 years old: he was the subject of an inquest regarding car theft. There, he declared that he was a professional car dealer and was also devoted to cattle-raising and agriculture. He also made money selling marble gravestones. He said he possessed from $180,000 to $200,000.[10]

However, the first real problem that Escobar had with the authorities dates to September 5, 1974. A man named Guillermo García Salazar reported that his recently purchased Renault had been stolen. When the police located and intercepted the car, they found Pablo Escobar at the wheel, who claimed that the car had been lent to him by a friend named Francisco Jiménez.

The police apprehended Jiménez and another individual, José Cadavid, whom they suspected as the perpetrators of the robbery. Months later, the three men were brought together – Jiménez, Cadavid and García Salazar – and their testimonies implicated Escobar in running an organization devoted to auto theft.

---

[10] Idem. Ob. Cit. 9.

However, the trial was inexplicably delayed; and two years later, when the trial against Escobar finally began, Francisco Jiménez, José Cadavid and the claimant García Salazar were all found shot dead. This paralyzed the case against Escobar since all the material witnesses were no longer available. Escobar was granted a provisional stay of proceedings.

Pablo Escobar was arrested again in June, 1976 after being apprehended near Medellin with his cousin Gustavo Gaviria Rivero, James Espinoza, Hernando Bolivar, his brother-in-law Mario Vallejo, and Marco Hurtado Jaramillo. Found in their possession were 18 polyethylene bags containing 39 kilograms of cocaine of the highest purity.

This operation had begun two months before, when the Administrative Security Department (DAS) received reports that Escobar and his cousin Gustavo Gaviria were leading an organization of drug traffickers in Medellin. According to the reports, the dealers were receiving Ecuadorian cocaine in trucks posing as commercial transport vehicles carrying car tires. From Colombia, the cocaine was smuggled to the United States by plane.

Monroy Arenas, an army official, decided to send two of his agents in a truck along the same route as that of the dealer's vehicle. Their objective was to make friends with the drivers and collect as much information as possible. Both were discovered as DAS agents but claimed that they had turned to crime since their salaries were not enough to maintain their families. Having pulled off their charade, the agents were included in a meeting in the Colombian city of Itaquí with the drivers of the truck, Pablo Escobar and Gustavo Gaviria.

When the meeting was to take place, Monroy Arenas and other DAS officers arrived to arrest the drug traffickers on charges of violating Colombian drug laws. Escobar and the others were taken to jail in Medellin, and at that point began the ordeal of the judge commissioned to the case.

The two detectives that participated in the operation, Gildardo Patiño and Luis Basque, were murdered within a few weeks. The judge was threatened on several occasions and a plan to murder her was discovered. Just in time, a plot to kill Monroy Arenas was also discovered.

In addition, a question of judicial competence was raised since a border judge appealed the basis of the case. Tired of the pressures, the judge in Medellin transferred the case to Judge Franco Guido Jurado, who resolved to set Escobar and his cousin free, and returned the impounded vehicles. Three months later, Judge Jurado resigned his position and moved to Bonn, Germany with his family.

Upon learning of these proceedings, the judge of Superior Court number 11 of the capital of Antioquia, Gustavo Zuluaga, pronounced judgment against Escobar and Gustavo Gaviria as the principals of the slayings of the police agents. The following day, however, while Zulaga's wife was driving, her car was intercepted by two armed men. They made her get out and subsequently threw the vehicle into an abyss "Next time we won't let you out," they warned her.[11]

A few months later, Zuluaga was promoted to the Penal Tribunal of the Medellin Superior Court for his tenacity in the struggle against crime. The same day of his appointment he was gunned down while on his way home. The Supreme Court of Colombia ordered an investigation, but it never produced positive results. Pablo Escobar was considered a pillar of the community in Medellin and his civic campaigns were hailed by a large part of the inhabitants. Furthermore, he could count on the benediction of two priests, Elías Cárdenas and Hernán Cuartas, who delivered impassioned sermons in defense of his campaigns.

Neighbors from Escobar's childhood neighborhood, La Paz, where he lived for many years and became councilman,

---

[11] Idem. Ob. Cit. 9.

assure that Escobar accumulated his fortune through real estate ventures. This is supported by the fact that Escobar owns about 200 apartments scattered throughout Florida, an airline and a hotel in Venezuela, another airline in Bogota, and several hotels in Medellin. He also owned an estate, known as "Hacienda Nápoles," that featured its own zoo and boasted a list of 843 personnel.

Another Colombian group that began to make an easy fortune through the sale of drugs was the Ochoa family. This group put together its business structure and organization in rapid fashion under the leadership of Sir Fabio Ochoa Restrepo, who quickly enlisted his six children in the business: Juán, Fabio, Jorge Luis, Cristina, Angela and Martha Nevis.

Mr. Fabio Ochoa was considered to be one of the founders of the city of Medellin, where he had devoted himself to the business of cattle breeding. During the 1930's, his personal wealth skyrocketed. The sale of animals and the acquisition of lands had made him one of the most powerful and prestigious landowners of Colombia. Jorge Luis Ochoa, the most daring and risky of the brothers, assumed the leadership of the family upon the death of his father. His business strategy was to begin to penetrate the drug markets in the United States. Toward this end, in August, 1978, he sent his brother Fabio to study the United States, where Fabio noted a great demand for marijuana. Thus, Fabio returned to Medellin and proposed that his family organize a "business" to export marijuana. His proposal was immediately accepted since cattle profits had been hurt by the decay of the exchange terms for that type of product.

In the late-1970's, the Ochoa family began to smuggle marijuana to the United States and contracted the consultation services of Luis "Kojak" García, an expert drug trafficker that knew the perfect routes. With this guidance, they soon discovered that the real business was not in the sale of marijuana, but in that of cocaine.

The fundamental problem was that coca leaves do not grow naturally in Colombia, which meant they had to buy from various groups in Bolivia and Peru. Consequently, Jorge Luis proposed a network with *Cosa Nostra Criolla* that would supervise operations from the coca plantations to the hydrochloride processing in the United States and Europe. Thus, they installed laboratories, runways, and fractionation and distribution centers. In those days in Medellin, there was an average of five assassinations per day attributed to the Ochoas, who paid about $100 for a simple assassination and $30,000 for murdering a minister. Obviously, the assassins originated from the notorious "Greater Medellin," one of the poorest zones of the city, where the inhabitants would do anything for a little money.

One of the men working for the Ochoa family was a Medellin taxi driver named José Ocampo, who began to frantically buy costly properties in the central zone of the city. One of his procurements was the disco "Kevin's," heralded as one of the best in the country. On opening day, they brought in to sing the international singing stars Raphael from Spain and the Brazilian Roberto Carlos.

Ocampo became proprietor of an estate, restaurants, a mall and several supermarkets, such as the one called "Seppy," which he used as a front to launder money from cocaine sales. Moreover, he was widely known as a man of consummate kindness who would not spare any effort to give work to the neediest or to support the construction of playgrounds for children.

His fame grew to such a point that the parson of Necolí, a town not far from Medellin, nonchalantly expressed to a newspaper: "Our town would be nothing without Mr. Ocampo. The people see this man as a work of God who has arrived to help with our development projects."[12]

---

[12] Idem. Ob. Cit. 9.

A small mishap befell José Ocampo when his wife was arrested in the United States with a shipment of 35 kilograms of cocaine. Her bail of $1 million was posted without any problem.

Pablo, Rigoberto and Arturo Arroyave Correa were associates of Ocampo. Pablo was eventually murdered by Jorge Luis Ochoa himself for going independent. The other two brothers, Rigoberto and Arturo, were betrayed and in August, 1986, were arrested in Pennsylvania for smuggling 7.5 tons of cocaine and for laundering $25 million.

Also associated with the Ochoa family was Alberto Uribe Sierra, whose first son Alvaro was the National Civil Aviation Director who granted pilot's licenses to several drug traffickers. Alvaro would later gain a seat in the Senate of Colombia. At one point, Mr. Uribe was about to be extradited to the United States, but the dealings of his son and his friend Jesus Aristizábal, the then Secretary of the Government of Medellin, managed not only to prevent his extradition, but also to set him free. After his death, Mr. Uribe's funeral was attended by the then President of Colombia, Belisario Betancur, notwithstanding the protesters who showed their disapproval to Uribe's ties to the cocaine trade.

Another powerful Colombian drug trafficker was Severo Escobar Ortega, who specialized in transporting cocaine from Bogota to Miami and New York. He was an inspirited, conservative leader who had quickly become an important businessman. Backed by ex-Senator Bertha Hernández de Ospina, who had readily accepted his contribution of $1 million, he won a seat in the House of Representatives. After his stint in the House, he assumed the post of secretary of agriculture, and with state funds ordered the construction of a luxurious pool in the municipality of Medina. Later it was discovered that the dressing rooms were actually laboratories for cocaine refinement.

Escobar Ortega also financially supported the conservative candidates for the presidency of the Republic, including

Belisario Betancur, who would wind up signing his extradition papers years later. Escobar Ortega's New York organization was discovered when the mother of one of his employees tipped off the DEA. Subsequently, Escobar Ortega was followed and arrested in the United States; however, he was mistakenly let back out on the streets when a careless policeman put the wrong stamp on his process papers.

The most legendary and merciless drug trafficker of the interior is Gonzalo Rodriguez Gacha. Known as "The Mexican," this Medellin cartel member operates in Cundinamarca. No official data exists for "The Mexican" – no driver's license, no passport or other such documents– for the Colombian state, Rodriguez Gacha is an archival non-entity. Nevertheless, the state is well aware of the existence and power of this man.

His empire is controlled from a firm called Rodriguez G. & Company. It is the proprietary of an agro-industrial company, eight apartments, several houses in the interior of Colombia, a farm, and a recreational center near Guaymaral Airport, which serves as a hub for his cocaine shipments.

In 1985, Rodriguez Gacha bought the best parcels of lands in the town of Pocho. The parson of the town organized a public protest against Rodriguez Gacha, which took place in front of one of his luxurious discotheques. To appease the people, Rodriguez Gacha offered to repair the church, an offer the priest openly rejected. Soon after, the church building collapsed and the congregation, wielding stones, chased the parish priest away.

In 1986, Rodriguez Gacha celebrated his birthday with a great party, and thanks to his friendship with Captain Yesid Vera, National Police agents served as guards to the party. The guest list included Pablo Escobar, two of the Ochoa brothers, Francisco Barbosa, Gilberto Molina, and other important drug traffickers.

In an interview conceded to the journalist Germán Castro for a television program, Rodriguez Gacha publicly recognized his activities as a drug trafficker, exhibited photographs of his properties, and launched a violent speech against those opposed to drug trafficking. Despite Rodriguez Gacha's appearance and diatribe, the Betancur Administration did nothing to keep the program off the air.

Rodriguez Gacha also attempted to start his own airline, "Aerolineas Espaciales de Colombia" (Special Airlines of Colombia). The attempt failed, however, because his business liaison with the authorities, Luis Guarnizo, was the owner of two small planes that had crashed in the United States with cargoes of cocaine.

It was in the Colombian city of Armenia –the capital of the Department of Quindio and an important center for coffee production– that another prominent drug trafficker, Carlos Lehder Rivas, got his start. In 1972, Lehder made several trips to the United States with shipments of marijuana. The American authorities were able to arrest him in January, 1974, but by the time the case got to trial, he had already escaped from jail.

Despite his absentee conviction and fugitive status, Lehder bought a huge piece of property on Key Norman in the Bahamas, located 60 kilometers south of Nassau and a forty-minute flight from Miami . He paid $155,000 in cash for the property; in fact, the money was not counted, but weighed, since it was all in one- and five-dollar bills. And, when the seller finally did decide to count the money, he was surprised to find almost $10,000 extra.

Using a hotel and several warehouses on Key Norman, Lehder launched his Dutch International Resources Company, Ltd., which in turn operated as a front for his real business: providing hangars and fuel to Colombians that were transporting marijuana and cocaine to the United States. Furthermore, he rented his fleet of five small aircraft at $10,000 each, and would provide a pilot for an extra $5,000.

Lehder asserted on several occasions that he had paid $800,000 dollars to Lynden Pindling, Prime Minister of the Bahamas, not to be bothered. However, Richard Novak, an American professor who gained the affection of the drug trafficker and was permitted on the island to study the hammer sharks, kept a record of all the aircraft that landed and took off. He also took photographs of Lehder's customary visitors and secretly recorded all their activities.

In September, 1981, the United States District Court of the State of Florida issued accusation number 81-82-CR- J-M, which charged Lehder with 12 counts of drug trafficking. This included the smuggling of 3,800 kilos of cocaine from Key Norman to the United States between January and December, 1980.

The DEA had ample information of his activities, but Lehder was also well-informed. When the DEA, in conjunction with the Bahamas police, organized an effort to arrest Lehder, the superintendent from the Bahamas in charge of the operation, Howard Smith, managed to delay it 15 days. This was sufficient time for the drug trafficker to escape Key Norman and return safely to Armenia, Colombia.

When he arrived back in Armenia, one of Lehder's comrades, Jesus Niñio Diez, convinced the new state governor to sell Lehder his private plane for $700,000 cash. Not only was this deal successfully consummated, but soon Lehder was transporting contraband on three other planes, for which he used the same registration number as the governor's old plane.

At the same time, the dealer's cousin, Eduardo Rivas, was working in the National Council on Narcotics, an organization commissioned to promulgate directives in the struggle against drug trafficking, to grant permission certificates for the purchase of planes, to award pilot's licenses, and to grant permission for airport construction. Thus, with his cousin in place, Lehder began to reconstruct his empire, which, according DEA data, enabled him to smuggle an average of 8,000 kilos of cocaine annually to the United States.

Lehder bought several farms and estates in Armenia. One of them was "Pisamal," acquired for five million dollars cash. This site, located in a valley surrounded by mountains, offered excellent security.

He also formed a society called "Cebú Quindino S.C.A.," which served as his center of operations and as a proprietary entity through which he bought the famous hotel "The German Inn." This hotel was the cornerstone in the construction of an entire resort area. The construction promptly began after the bishop blessed the area. Ultimately, Lehder fled from the mountain resort during a police attempt to capture him, and sold the inn for $900,000.

To launder his money, Lehder created a company called "Lehderautos" that theoretically imported automobiles from the United States. Through this agency, he imported, on paper only, hundreds of BMW and Mercedes Benz automobiles. Ironically, his three white Mercedes Benz automobiles had been brought over illegally, which resulted in a citation.

Lehder was also involved in politics and created the National Latino Movement, (Movimiento Latino Nacional), a proselytizing organization through which he sought to oppose the policy of extradition. The Movement's other platforms included the socialization of Latin American economies, the creation of the Latino peso as a regional currency, the nationalization of the Latin American Bank, the cancellation of the external debt through default, and the elimination of the state's use of police as a tool of oppression.

To lobby against extradition, Lehder published tons of pages in the principal Colombian newspapers and magazines invoking the public's support of the Extraditables' Movement in Defense of the Guerrilla. The name was later reduced to "The Extaditables." Lehder, in these publications, made no attempt to hide his involvement in drug trafficking.

According to DEA agents assigned to investigate him, Lehder had returned to Colombia to enjoy his money, convinced that he would never be arrested nor prosecuted. When Lehder began to take note of the real possibility of his incarceration, he lashed out against his pursuers, leaving a trail of dead men.

Finally, due to the cost of maintaining a clandestine life, Lehder decided to spend his final years as a "cook" – a person who refines the chlorohydrate of cocaine – for the Medellin cartel. In exchange for this service, the cartel offered him protection and a medium salary. Nevertheless, in May, 1985, Colonel Jaime Ramírez Gómez was on the verge of trapping him when he found Lehder resting on a small farm located in Airapúa. However, the operation was thwarted when Lehder received notice before Ramírez Gómez could make his move; but in his haste to flee, Lehder had to abandon $1.6 million in cash. He later claimed the money by means of a public letter.

After many attempts by the DEA as well Colombian security forces to capture him, Lehder was finally arrested and extradited to the United States. He was installed in the federal penitentiary in Marion, Illinois, serving a life sentence on top of another sentence of one hundred thirty-five years; he received this judgment in spite of having requested a reduction in sentence for collaborating permanently with justice officials. In fact, Lehder was called on by U.S. officials to testify in the 1991 narcotics trafficking case against Panamanian leader Antonio Noriega.

THE CARTELS AND THE GUERRILLAS

The kidnapping of Martha Ochoa, member of the Ochoa family, in october 1980, was a watershed in the history of Colombian drug trafficking. A faction of the guerrilla movement "M19" kidnaped Martha because they saw in the drug traffickers a source of easy money with which to finance their struggle. The Colombian drug lords considered this an attack against all their members, a show of total disrespect. The cartels knew how to regain respect and decided to act in a forceful, exemplary manner: they created an armed corps called *"MAS"* (Death to Kidnappers). The assembly of this private brigade required the presence of all the big *capos* of Colombian drug trafficking. Even more important than the goal of forming this militia was the safe rescue of Martha Ochoa.

All the bosses of the medium and large cocaine trafficking organizations of Cali, Medellin, Leticia, Bogota, Cartegena and Barranquilla agreed to hold a summit. They met at a location known as "Las Margaritas," a property of the Ochoa family on the outskirts of Medellin.

According to a 1982 investigation of the Colombia Attorney General, the meeting was very brief. The drug lords agreed that each would contribute one million dollars toward the forming of a 300-man, heavily-armed militia. They also agreed to use all their contacts to determine the elements of M19 responsible for the kidnapping, to open a permanent channel of communication for the exchange of such information, and to delineate accordingly the operations that were to follow. Lastly, the cartels agreed to prepare a list of trustworthy government and law enforcement functionaries.

A waiter who served drinks to the drug traffickers during the meeting revealed that "refuge centers" were immediately constructed, like the one located on the property of Pablo Arroyave Correa, called "The Horizon Cattle Ranch." Such locations featured everything necessary for personal security, including camouflaged cellars stocked with several weeks' worth of food provisions, a heliport, closed circuit television, personal guards, automatic weapons, infrared equipment with which to see at night, and grenades and other explosives.

One of the men assigned to bolster support for the mission was Carlos Lehder. Lehder financed the publication of notices in newspapers and magazines expressing that nobody should pay even a penny for the freedom of those kidnapped, that those men who attempted to victimize Colombia's businessmen should pay with their lives. Using such an argument, Lehder was seeking to harness support from the entire class of Colombian business leaders, as they were all constantly subject to kidnappings by the guerrillas.

As a result of these efforts, members of M19 were found tied with chains, unconscious, with signs on their chests saying: "I am from M19. I am a kidnapper." Ten leaders of M19 were kidnapped and killed in Antioquia. Others were simply pointed out to the Army, who would turn them over to the *Verbal Council on Warfare* to be judged.

MAS also conducted "razings" of houses belonging to leaders of the left. These were carried out with the assistance of an Army Intelligence official who would display his badge in order to gain entrance to the residences. After several such *razings*, the guerrillas relented and freed Martha Ochoa.

After this occurrence, an important member of M19 managed to contact the drug traffickers to discuss a mutually beneficial solution to this war between the two groups. T hey declared a truce and never again conflicted with each other.

With the M19 problem resolved, the drug lords decided to have another meeting at Las Margaritas. This time, the objective was to solidify the union they had established and to develop the foundation for a true "cartel;" that is, an organized association of cocaine traffickers that controls its markets without infighting and fixes the price of the drug.

At the meeting, each drug trafficker was assigned a different color that would distinguish its shipments (the American authorities would "not see" shipments of cocaine that were marked with certain colors). The color blue, for example, was given to the Ochoa family; Escobar was yellow; Rodriguez Orejuela was red. They also divided up the markets: the New York market was that of the Cali cartel;

Florida belonged to the Medellin cartel; and it was agreed upon that California (especially Los Angeles) would go to whomever could first consolidate power there, which was to be Rodriguez Orejuela's organization.   Later, this organizational schema developed into a complex system of colors and letters.

For example, calls from Bogota or Medellin were received on public telephones in Miami, New York, and Los Angeles; a voice would simply say: "Red, FDR." The distributor would answer using a key number and the established password. In a few minutes, the phone would ring again from Colombia to confirm the information; with a simple "O.K.," the transaction was verified.

Because the telephone communications were so quick, it was impossible to trace or detect them. The Ochoa family was the first to understand and fully utilize the power of the organization, and they soon were cooperating with the Italian-American Mafia. This alliance manifested itself through a chain of New York pizza parlors known as *"Pizza Connection,"* which served as a front to distribute the Ochoa's cocaine.

The Ochoa organization very quickly reached a tremendous volume of cocaine traffic to the United States. In fact, on February 9, 1984, Jorge Ochoa confirmed through journalist Max Mermestein that they were able to ship 2,000 kilos of 90% pure cocaine each week.

At that time, Pablo Escobar was also reinforcing his cocaine distribution system in the United States. As a monthly average, Escobar was smuggling 1,500 kilos of alkaloid. Moreover, he was smuggling a similar quantity to European markets through Caracas.

If the price of one kilogram of cocaine fluctuated between $25,000 and $50,000, Escobar's monthly profit, deducting expenses and fees to middlemen, was approximately $4 million. Such monstrous profits afforded him the luxury of buying sport clubs, mansions, and hotels, as well as investing in sufficient social programs necessary to win him the popular respect and sympathy that he obviously enjoyed.

For four years, Gilberto Rodríguez Orejuela and Jorge Luis Ochoa used the First Interamerican Bank, which they controlled, for laundering drug money. They used Colombian banks similarly, such as the Banco Cafetero (Coffee Growers' Bank). In April, 1985, an important money laundering operation of Rodríguez Orejuela was discovered. This operation involved the Continental National Bank of Florida, where they had ordered transfers of $40 million to an account they had in the Panamanian branch of the Banco Cafetero. These orders were placed through a Miami organization called The Irving Trust Co.

The big cartels have remained consolidated ever since. The Medellin cartel, led by Pablo Escobar, the Ochoa family, and Rodriguez Gacha, controls the Atlantic Coast of Colombia. The Cali cartel, led by the Rodríguez Orejuela brothers and Santacruz Londoño, commands the southern part of the country.

Nevertheless, the press began to reveal the names of individuals involved with drug trafficking, and increasingly denounced their operations. This heightened attention produced an increase in investigations and raids by Colombian security forces. Consequently, Pablo Escobar had to flee to Australia for a few months where he owned a ranch. Similarly, Jorge Luis Ochoa and Gilberto Rodríguez Orejuela escaped to Spain, where their contacts from their drug operations were strong. Once in Spain, both men decided to set up shop there, since, as one associate advised them: "If they don't want your dollars in Colombia, invest them on the peninsula, where they'll be well received and appreciated. Moreover, there is a socialist regime there that does not depend on the United States."

The lives of Ochoa and Rodríguez became festivals of consumption. They opened checking accounts with huge sums of money and they bought whichever hotels they encountered in their path. Surrounded by women, throwing parties with hundreds of guests, driving luxurious automobiles, joining exclusive Spanish social clubs, their lifestyle began to draw the suspicions of bankers and other businessmen, who saw thousands of dollars flow into their accounts each week.

Moreover, a DEA office had just opened in Madrid on the persistent rumor that Colombian drug traffickers had extended to Spain their network of cocaine distribution and money laundering. Jorge Luis Ochoa, who went by the alias "Moisés Moreno Miranda," had disguised himself with the help of a Greek plastic surgeon who resided in Brazil. But, Ochoa was exposed by a jealous banker who did not enjoy any of Ochoa's accounts or business.

When the two traffickers were arrested on November 21, 1984, they had in their possession a fleet of six BMW's and ten Mercedes Benz automobiles. They also confiscated accounts worth $1.7 million as well as $6 million in cash found in the house where they were apprehended. They had also just purchased a $1.5 million estate on the outskirts of Madrid. The authorities also discovered that the traffickers' operations were executed with the assistance of the most prestigious attorneys in Madrid. Although they had only served the traffickers a short time, the lawyers were implicated by detailed documents found in a briefcase that described the millions of dollars' worth of cocaine transactions. In addition, the authorities seized a small accounting book from Rodríguez Orejuela showing contraband operations involving more than 4,100 kilos of cocaine smuggled from Colombia to the United States in a period of less than a year and a half.

With all that was confiscated, the workings of their network of cocaine distribution were exposed. The traffickers would hire low-income families in Florida and California, to whom they would distribute quantities of cocaine no larger than two kilos. The families received precise instructions on how to hide the alkaloid in their homes. They were also told how to lead their lives so as not to attract the attention of their neighbors: most importantly, they were not to squander their money on parties or social events, especially when they were in possession of the drug. Every two or three days, a truck would come to their homes under the guise of delivering mineral water. The drivers would pick up the cocaine, check it against a list they carried, and pay the family for their services.

The detained traffickers in Spain realized that the only country in the world where they would be able to continue their lives unfettered was Colombia, and so they developed a plan to bring such a situation to fruition. So, back in Colombia, anyone on the Supreme Court of that nation would be marked for death if they opposed the ruling of unconstitutionality of the extradition agreement with the United States, and of any other country that attempted to extradite Colombian criminals. In sum, the traffickers had decided to buy the country.

Events passed just as the traffickers had hoped. The Colombian Government requested the extradition of Jorge Luis Ochoa and Rodríguez Orejuela, and upon Spain's acceptance, they were brought to Colombia under the tightest of security. Once back in Colombia, a young inexperienced judge convicted Ochoa for illegal importation of bulls, and sentenced him to two years in prison.

Three months later, after an appeal, the same judge released Ochoa on a bail of $11,500, and required him to appear before the tribunal twice a month. Ochoa was never tried for drug trafficking, although authorities continued attempting to do so for many years. After her decision to free Ochoa, the judge disappeared and is believed to be living in Europe. According to DEA reports, after freeing Ochoa, the judge met with Fabio Ochoa and Pablo Escobar, who gave her a payment of about $5 million.

Upon his return to Colombian soil, Rodríguez Orejuela was convicted of multiple homicides and was sentenced to one year in a prison in Cali. Everyone in prison called him "Don

Gilberto," and one day a party was thrown in his honor which was attended by the Governor of Cali. Although Rodríguez Orejuela went to trial for drug trafficking, the prosecution only had one witness – a DEA agent who spoke no Spanish. And since the translator spoke very little English, Rodríguez Orejuela's release was almost immediate. As of July, 1987, he has remained absolved of all his crimes.

MONEY POWER

The Rodríguez Orejuela brothers, Miguel Angel and Gilberto, created an economic and public relations empire which had as its cornerstone the Banco de los Trabajadores (Workers' Bank). The Rodriguez brothers understood that running a bank would not only permit them to launder drug money, but, through the business of savings accounts and lending, would allow them a structure with which to approach and cultivate public relations.

The Banco de los Trabajadores was founded in 1974 with an initial base of $500,000. This initial capital was provided by two institutions, the Interamerican Foundation and the American Institute for the Development of Free Unionism, with the object of strengthening unionism in Latin America.

The bi-laws of the bank's constitution represented the interests of its shareholders, which included unions, employee funds, popular cooperatives, and well-known union leaders; but through the years, the bank had abandoned its social goals and only served as a granting institution that issued irrecoverable credits to union leaders. Gilberto Rodríguez Orejuela began looking for a way to convert this institution into a mechanism complementary to his money laundering network. Specifically, he needed a way to channel money from the United States to another bank he owned, First Interamerican Bank of Panama. Because of its statutes, Banco de los Trabajadores could only have workers' cooperatives or unions as its shareholders. Therefore, the president of the institution, Tulio Cuevas, designated Rodríguez Orejuela as manager of the Cooperativa El Hogar, a dependent institution of the bank.

Rodríguez combined two drugstores in order to have a cooperative, which he called Coodrogas, and through this entity he began to quickly buy up stock of the Bank. Within a year, he had obtained a seat on the bank's board of directors.

As a member of the board, the drug trafficker was able to successfully request an assembly of all those necessary to amend the bank's statutes. In this way, he was able to modify the statutes to exclude the participation of the workers.

Having done this, he took control of the bank by purchasing shares through a series of drugstores and laboratories belonging to the Cali cartel: Laboratorios Kressfor, Drogas La Rebaja (Reduced-Price Drugs), Drogas La Séptima (Seventh Drugs), Coodrogas, and Drogas Unidas y Servicios Sociales Ltd. (United Drugs and Social Services). He also bought a large quantity of shares in his own name, as well as in the names of his brother Miguel Angel, his wife Gladys, his brother-in-law's brother National Representative Dagoberto Rivas, and other family members.

In sum, Rodríguez Orejuela gained the control of 75% of the bank's shares and was appointed president of its board of directors. The workers were effectively displaced from their bank, and could not even exert influence through the Bank Supervisory Board, headed by Francisco Ordoñez. The bank was now controlled by Rodríguez Orejuela, who used it as his own "laundromat."

The Rodríguez brothers also obtained permission to set up a Chrysler dealership in Colombia, which they were to call

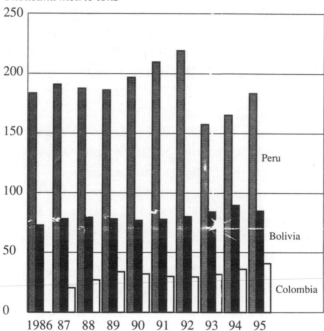

World Coca Leaf Production by Country

Thousand metric tons

Chrysler Discor. However, they had to overcome an initial obstacle. At that time, Chrysler's Colombian subsidiary, Colmotores, managed by Secretary General to the Presidency Germán Montoya Véles, had sole rights to the Colombian market. However, by the time the Rodríguez brothers had finished negotiating with the Americans, the roof of the Colmotores dealership had collapsed. Although the brothers were the official owners of Chrysler Discor Ltd., they placed another man in charge of the operation: Tomás de los Ríos, who is now serving out a prison sentence in the United States for cocaine trafficking.

In February, 1984, Chrysler Discor put in a bid of about $3 million to supply the National Police with vehicles. The contract, however, despite being awarded to the Rodríguez brothers, was canceled because the National Bank of Mexico withdrew its support. The records of the National Police on the Rodríguez brothers must have been amazingly scant since, with the original automobile supply deal thwarted, they then worked out a separate deal by which the Rodríguez brothers sold fiberglass speed boats which the Police would use to catch sea-bound drug smugglers.

The Rodríguez Orejuela brothers went from owning a small group of radio stations to founding the Colombian Radial Group (Grupo de Radio Colombiano) in 1979. The Group is composed of 28 stations operating in Medellin, Barranquilla, Cartagena, Bogota, Paso, Cali, and Palmira.

Consequently, continuing in the recent trend of public denouncements of the traffickers through the media, journalist Ocsar Jiménez and another well-known figure, Alvaro Gutiérrez, went on the offensive against the Rodríguez's radio stations. Their accusations were principally founded in Public Law 129, ennacted in 1976, which stated that no person with a criminal record could own a chain of radio stations.

Nevertheless, the Rodríguez brothers and their radio stations were soon forgotten in the columns of the press. In fact, in 1987 the Colombian minister of communications, Senator Edmundo López Gómez, signed Resolution 675 which officially permitted the existence of the Colombian Radial Group. That same year, López Gómez became minister of justice, and from that position solicited the signature of President Virgilio Barco for a decree he had written that denied extradition to the United States of the drug traffickers Gilberto Rodríguez Orejuela and José Santacruz Londoño.

Immediately after submitting this decree, López Gómez resigned his post as the public pressure on him for having submitted such a proposal was great. He had argued that, as the two traffickers were to be tried in Cali for the same crimes imputed against them in the United States, extradition would run the risk of violating the legal principle *"Non bis in idem,"* that is, that no one can be tried for the same crime twice. President Virgilio Barco, as was expected, signed the decree and neither was extradited.

The regular residence of the Rodríguez Orejuela brothers is in the city of Cali, where they created a company called Security Services, Ltd., which was authorized by the Ministry of Defense to utilize 50 firearms and 100 men. This authorization was granted only after two men signed as guarantors of the good conduct of the brothers: these two men were senators Eduardo Mestre Sarmiento and Germán Hoyos.

The Rodríguez brothers also owned and operated two luxury apartment complexes in Cali, The Founders Mall, a youth recreation company called "Kids' World," the computer companies "Micrometization" and "Five," the discotheques "The Two Happy Godfathers," and "The Godchild's Club," and about 50 bars and restaurants in Cali.

Other drug traffickers did not pale in comparison. Pablo Escobar financed the weekly newspaper, *Medellin Civic*, which publicized all his activities. Its last edition, in January, 1987, was published with enameled paper, and the 72-point headline read: "The People Triumphed. Extradition Falls." Escobar also enjoyed his own private army, called Nitibara Security, authorized by the Ministrer of Defense. Headquartered in Medellin, Nitibara Security had permission for 143 firearms and 215 men.

The Ochoa family controls, by means of its directors, the aviation companies Austral and Executive Pilots, the first of which consists of two jets and a hospital plane that can be utilized anywhere in the world. The second, Executive Pilots, had its operations suspended between August 9, 1984, and July 3, 1985, because of charges of cocaine trafficking. But, on October 28, 1985, Minister of Justice Enrique Parejo González officially negated any history of drug trafficking and the company returned to normal operations.

Austral has a modern headquarters with a private hangar in the Bogotá Airport. This hangar is right next to one registered to Rodríguez Gacha, who also controls various aero-fumigation companies which, in reality, serve as fronts for cocaine traffic.

One of the Ochoa family's men is the ex-representative Hernando Suarez Burgos, a trafficker who runs the furniture factory Modern Metals Ltd., the Hotel Duque, and the factories Luber Confectionaries, The Cicada, and Santa Rita. Suarez Burgos also runs the company Modern Home Appliances Ltd., which has 70 locations throughout Colombia's principal cities.

Some of the ex-legislator's management techniques were discovered by the DEA. One such technique was the selling of defective appliances so that the purchasers would return them for repair. The broken machines were subsequently sent – filled with cocaine– to a repair center located along the border with Ecuador. Later, the appliances were returned to their owners in perfect condition. Despite these practices, the ex-representative was never arrested.

Representative Samuel Escrucería, who did not enjoy the luck Suarez Burgos' did, was arrested on November 5, 1987, while vacationing in North Carolina. He was charged with using his position and immunity to traffic more than four hundred kilograms of cocaine. He was originally sentenced to 240 years in prison, but the good work of his lawyer got him a 30-year reduction in his sentence and a fine of $500,000. The congressman's son, Samuel Escrucería Manzzi, also involved in the same investigation, could not be arrested since he was already back in Colombia, having just been elected deputy by the district of Nariño.

PROCESS MATERIALS

Among the fastest growing businesses in Colombia were laboratories and laboratory supplies, including what are commonly known as precursory substances. In fact, the National Police and the DEA released information regarding the importation of ether during the first half of 1978. The results were surprising: of the immense quantity of ether that was imported by Colombian companies, about 80% was used for the refinement of cocaine. During this six-month period, 3,713,630 kilograms of ether were imported, enough to process 296,876 kilograms of cocaine.

At that time, the largest Colombian importer of ether was Luis Eduardo Orejarena Gómez, member of the board of directors of the oil multinational Shell of Colombia. Orejarena Gómez imported 863,078 kilograms of ether during the above-mentioned six-month period. Along with him, the National Police/DEA report also identified the following firms as the principal importers of ether: Abácidos Ltd., Laboratorios Algubert, Grupo Aldenhoven Group, Grupo Castro Bermejo, Jorge Cueter Lletally Ltd., Dotaciones Universales, Furia Químicos, Productos Químicos Alfa Omega, and Representaciones Continental.

The business of importing such process materials was given a boost by the 1982 decision of President Turbay Ayala, who declared that these substances could be imported free of duties and taxes. However, from 1983 onward, the importation of substances used in the processing of cocaine required a special license granted by a state organization. One of the requirements of this license was a record free of criminal activity.

Despite this requisite, a man connected to the Ochoa family, Francisco Huérfano, was able to legally import 3,000 kilogram barrels of ether in 1983. In addition, his wife imported 400 barrels of ether, 400 boxes of hydrochloric acid, and 100 boxes of sulfuric acid. There were many other people who continued to legally import these substances despite having criminal records, but the majority of the imported chemicals entered the country as contraband.

SPORTS

Another activity that brought the traffickers popular support as well as a means to launder money was sports, especially soccer. However, Coldeportes, the supervisory organization of athletics, has never been vigilant.

The soccer team *Atlético Nacional* (National Athletic) has as its principal shareholder the drug trafficker Hernán Botero Moreno, who is also the proprietor of a chain of hotels. His brother Roberto was convicted in the United States for laundering $70 million. Hernán himself was the object of an arrest warrant in 1981 for laundering $5 million and for being the owner of a 1.762 kilogram shipment of cocaine confiscated in Miami.

Despite dozens of legal maneuvers to avoid his extradition, he was finally turned over to American authorities on November 15, 1984. Consequently, the principal Colombian soccer division suspended games on that day as a sign of protest. Botero Moreno's team was then bought by Ignacio

Aguirre, who also had pending against him a solicitation for extradition by a Peruvian tribunal for cocaine trafficking.

The *Millonarios Sport Club* (Millionaires Sport Club) of Bogota was controlled by the now deceased Edmer Tamayo, who, linked to a 2000-kilo shipment of cocaine, was arrested in Florida in 1982.   After his death in 1983, his estate was represented by the lawyers Germán and Guillermo Gómez. The two attorneys received payment of $15 million for selling all of his shares to Gonzalo Rodríguez Gacha.

In 1984, the Argentine goalkeeper Navarro, who had been contracted to play for a Colombian team, announced publicly that soccer was infiltrated by the drug trafficking Mafia. As the goalkeeper's professional fate was in the hands of an associate of Rodríguez Gacha, Navarro was benched, never to play again.

The *América de Cali*, (Club America of Cali) is owned by the brothers Miguel and Gilberto Rodríguez Orejuela.   The brothers have pending against them a solicitation for extradition by the United States for 15 counts of drug trafficking.

One of the most famous incidents is known as *"Fonseca's briefcase."* Fonseca was a courier for the Orejuela brothers who was supposed to deliver $25,000 to each player of the team if they won the *Copa Libertadores de América* (Liberators of America Cup). On another occasion, the brothers gave an apartment to Roberto Cabañas, a player for the *Conquistadores de Cali*, for scoring the winning goal in a championship game.

The traffickers also invested their money in other sports. After retiring, the former world boxing champion Kid Pambelé formed a sports apparel company with the Orejuela brothers called *Pambelé Productions*. In the sport of cycling, Roberto Escobar (brother of Pablo Escobar Gaviria) personally financed on several occasions the Colombian team in the internationally-known *Tour de France*.

Auto racing also attracted the drug traffickers' money. For example, the Tocanipá International Raceway is owned by

Gilberto Rodríguez Orejuela. The race drivers are supported by all the traffickers. According to reports, when the drivers have to travel across international borders to get to a race, their cars are used to smuggle cocaine. Nevertheless, despite the authorities' efforts, no arrests have been made.

ASSAULT ON THE PALACE OF JUSTICE

An intense period of negotiation with the United States was initiated with the election of Colombian President Turbay Ayala, and culminated with the signing of two agreements on September 14, 1979. The agreements allowed for the extradition of nationals accused of drug trafficking and related offenses, and for the exchange of legal evidence.

Both agreements were adhered to for almost a year before they were officially approved in the Colombian Congress. The text of the agreements was incorporated into Bill number 27, which was approved in absolute secrecy, to be officially enforced in mid-1980.

With this legislation in place, Belisario Betancur (1982-1986) was elected to the Colombian presidency after just having personally received $2.5 million from drug traffickers during the last stage of his campaign. Bernardo Gaitán Mahecha, his first minister of justice, always avoided the issue of extradition. Once, however, when he was about to retire, Gaitán gave orders to capture some small-time traffickers.

Gaitán Mahecha's successor was Rodrigo Lara Bonilla. Within two weeks of taking office, he had already engaged in a political debate with the deputies Jairo Ramírez--a principal operative of Pablo Escobar--and Ernesto Quevedo. The debate was over the applicability of the extradition agreement with the United States.

Within a short time, the daily newspaper *El Espectador* disclosed the criminal histories of Pablo Escobar, Gustavo

Gaviria, Jorge Luis Ochoa, and Jorge Van Griecken. The latter was arrested in a town near Medellin, to be extradited to the United States and tried for cocaine trafficking.

However, President Betancur denied the extradition of Van Griecken, who soon regained his freedom since he was apprehended without a warrant for his arrest. Consequently, an ex-advisor to the Ministry of Justice, Jorge Gonzalez Vidales, contested the decision to deny Van Griecken's extradition before the Council of State. The day Gonzalez Vidales was to present his challenge before the Council, the ex-advisor was killed while driving to his home. The file from the investigation into his death was later burned next to the Palace of Justice.

Rodrigo Lara Bonilla later tried to explain his signature on the decree denying Van Griecken's extradition. He cited the many threats on his life he had received, on top of the request of the President that he sign it. But, Lara Bonilla believed that, if judicial actions continued as they had, the drug traffickers would continue to have their way; he thus made a commitment: to combat drug trafficking, with his very life if necessary, and to fight for the prosecution and extradition of the drug traffickers.

During the first day of 1984, a decree arrived at his office for him to sign. It was from the President. The decree denied the extradition to the United States of Carlos Lehder. Lara Bonilla announced at a press conference that he would never sign it. Various functionaries, including Judicial Secretary to the President Lilian Suárez, tried to dissuade him, but Lara Bonilla threatened to publicly resign.

Soon after, a recording surfaced which featured the private secretary of the Attorney General William Bedoya, offering money to Ministry of Justice functionaries to be given to the minister of justice himself. Representatives of the National Latino Movement, a political arm of Lehder, were trying to appeal to the minister to grant the defense 24 more hours to gather evidence. Bonilla accepted the challenge, knowing full well what they were really expecting from him.

Two Representatives named Lucena and Ortega exhibited before Colombia's legislators a check for one million Colombian pesos ($12,821), signed by the drug trafficker Evaristo Porras Ardila, that had been deposited in Lara Bonilla's account. The check had gone toward Bonilla's senatorial campaign expenses. His brilliant fifteen-year career was under attack, and with it, his struggle against the drug traffickers. "My life is an open book," Bonilla began, answering his accusers. Then Bonilla described, in detail, the patronage that existed within workings of the state. He had embarked on a strategy that must have struck a chord with most of his countrymen: "If you exhibit a check that they supposedly paid me, it must correspond to the sale of my silence. To show the country that this is not the case, I will officially denounce them as a group and individually, and will become their principal enemy." Then he directly attacked the kingpins of drug trafficking: "What do you all think about Pablo Escobar? Do you think it's true that he has amassed this great fortune from his bicycle factory, a few investments, and some lucky business ventures?"

The next day, Lara held a press conference where he publicly exhibited notebooks of Pablo Escobar, Carlos Lehder, the Rodríguez Orejuela brothers, Jorge Luis Ochoa, and those of another two hundred thirty-two drug traffickers. These books contained the names of legislators who had dealt with these men.

Lara Bonilla had indeed become an inconvenience for the drug traffickers. In the next six months, Lara ordered the grounding of 250 aircraft belonging to drug traffickers, signed the extradition papers of 45 traffickers to the United States, and continued to reveal the traffickers ties to politics, business and sports.

However, on April 30, 1984, a group of persons under orders from Pablo Escobar intercepted on motorcycle the car carrying Minister Lara Bonilla. The minister was found with three bullets in his head, two in his chest, one in the neck, and another in the arm. The drug traffickers had killed a tenacious man and removed a nuisance to their businesses. The ball was now in the court of the Supreme Court of Colombia.

Criminal Appellate Judge of Bogota, Tulio Manuel Castro Gil called on Pablo Escobar to respond to charges that he and twelve others were responsible for Lara Bonilla's murder. Castro Gil also ordered an investigation of the roles of Gonzalo Rodrígues Gacha and the Ochoa family in the murder. Three months later, Judge Castro Gil was killed while getting into a taxi bound for his home. The second attorney of penal affairs brilliantly outlined charges against Escobar as the author of the crime, but was forced to flee the country after making this accusation. After a four-month process, Escobar's case was finally thrown out for lack of merit. The only person convicted for the crime was the man who actually pulled the trigger on the minister, a gunman named Byron Velasquez.

The drug traffickers turned their attention to the Supreme Court, and attempted to contract a guerrilla group known as the *Frente Ricardo Franco* (Ricardo Franco Front) to assault the Palace of Justice. The group did not accept the offer since they were still forming their ranks and would not have sufficient organization for this operation. However, the leaders of the group M-19 did accept the challenge, in exchange for $5 million and the necessary arms.

November, 1985 found the French leader Francois Miterrand visiting Colombia. Out of fear of a guerrilla attack during this visit, President Betancur ordered the security in government buildings tightened. Then, surprisingly, on November 6, Betancur postponed a long-planned trip to Europe on which he was to accompany the French leader. He then lifted the extra security measures which he had ordered. On that day, a group of men from M19 forced their way into the Palace of Justice, where the Supreme Court and the Council of State met.

The guerrillas entered the Palace with one clear objective: to take control of the fourth floor, which housed the Constitutional and Penal Annulment Offices. Both offices were responsible for reviewing extradition cases.

The M19 guerrillas, under the command of Andrés Amarales, decided on the spot to prosecute the magistrates for treason. They wanted, moreover, the government to authorize such an action. President Betancur found this unacceptable and responded by sending an elite anti-terrorist squadron to re-take the building. Meanwhile, judges Manuel Gaona Cruz, Ricardo Medina Moyano, Carlos Medellín Forero and Alfonso Roselli, all who had taken positions in favor of the constitutionality of the extradition agreement, were the first to be assassinated. In all, more than 100 persons were killed, including 12 of the 25 members of the Supreme Court; and many of those who escaped with their lives from this incident encountered death a short time later.

Two weeks after the judicial massacre, the new magistrates were sworn in. During this session, various members of the new judicial corps admitted to having received threats, pressuring them to come out against extradition.

Another magistrate from the Penal Office, Luis Aldana, died on October 7, 1986. He had participated in the drafting of the extradition agreement in Washington, and was obviously immovable in his position. Minister Aldana was at home when a coffin was delivered with his name inscribed in it. Already of poor health, Aldana had a heart attack and was flown to Houston for surgery. After he came out of surgery, his oxygen tubes were mysteriously cut and he died immediately.

On December 13, 1986, the Colombian Supreme Court annulled the extradition agreement for its faulty drafting (the drug traffickers were very persuasive in their exposition of judicial reasoning): the agreement had been signed, after its ratification in Congress, by Germán Hernandez, the Minister assigned to the duties of the presidency while the President was away. This type of agreement, the Tribunal pointed out, must be signed by the President himself, and not by any other functionary. They came to this ruling despite the fact that the new Minister of Justice, Enrique Parejo, had already allowed many extraditions.

Parejo had signed fifteen extraditions, including that of Carlos Lehder, and had denied passage of Mafia aircraft as well as issuing various arrest orders. Within a short time, he abandoned his position and was assigned the Colombian ambassadorship to Hungary. On January 13, 1987, a Latin American man approached his house in Budapest and shot Parejo several times, but was not able to kill him. Interpol was able to apprehend those responsible for the assassination attempt. The suspects were of Argentine nationality, with residence in Italy, and were collaborating with the Sicilian Mafia. However, Hungary dropped the investigation and denied the Argentine request to extradite the accused, Carlos Alberto Chiachiareli, Carlos Gómez and Susana Lazati, to Italy.

But, the drug traffickers did not let the issue of extradition rest. They continued to fight against the measures taken by the Barco Administration. Then, they were given an opportunity to deal a death blow to the practice of extradition. The House of Representatives was conducting a debate on constitutional reform, from which any proposed changes had to be voted upon by the people through a public referendum. Escobar could not let such an opportunity pass by, and moved to ensure that the government include the issue of extradition in the public vote. That is, convinced that the public would vote against extradition, Escobar and the Rodríguez Orejuela brothers began to intimidate and bribe legislators.

Thus, in a plenary session of the House of Representatives on December 5, 1989, the proposal to ban extradition became an officially proposed constitutional amendment; during the same session, the Chamber also approved a pardon. However, the day's session was plagued with insults and accusations which flew amongst the congressmen. In the end, President Barco (1986-1990) promulgated the amendment and expounded upon the autonomy and independence of the legislative process.

Finally, in 1991, under the presidency of César Gaviria (1990-1994), a group of 70 were chosen by the public to decide on the constitutional reforms. The individuals in the group were widely known for their personal and professional prestige. In the new political and judicial changes that resulted, there included an article that expressly prohibited extradition:

Article 30: The extradition of natural-born Colombians is prohibited. Further, extradition will not be conceded to foreigners for political crimes or crimes of opinion. Colombians who have committed crimes abroad, as considered in our national legislation, will be processed and judged in Colombia.

And with this article, the problem of extradition was buried forever.

THE FALL OF THE CARTEL

The assassination of Luis Carlos Galán Sarmiento on August 18, 1989, struck a chord within Colombian society. They were tired of spilt blood. With this assassination, the people demanded that the government eradicate the drug traffickers for the sake of social peace.

Luis Carlos Galán was a passionate politician that had made an impression on the Colombian people by denouncing acts of corruption among government officials. He was the kind of public prosecutor that showed that a government with clean hands might be possible. With this platform, he began campaigning for the presidency.

His homicide was planned by Pablo Escobar and Rodríguez Gacha, who contracted a commando group that made a mockery of the 85 secret agents and the police squadron that were guarding him. The attempt was carried out by a team of men split into six groups. The first was located below the stage where the politician would speak; the second guarded the rear and was to respond with fire when the security men reacted ; the third had the responsibility of watching Galán if he managed to flee; the fourth was to mingle among the spectators of the event and eventually fire into the air to create the necessary confusion for the getaway; the fifth would murder anyone who tried to get in the way; and the sixth manned the getaway vehicles for those who escaped.

The assassination of the man who would be President of Colombia, as reflected in surveys, was a demonstration of powertotheBarco Administration. The drug traffickers were not going to negotiate neither a law of amnesty nor reductions in sentences with the government in the event of their capture.

Three months before the assignation, the drug traffickers had attempted to assassinate the Director of the DAS, General Miguel Alfredo Maza Márquez, who was considered a "tough" man that was committed to destroying the criminal organizations. Maza Marquéz had pushed for the denial of negotiations for pardons or for lighter sentences for any drug dealer.

On May 5, 1989, General Maza Márquez managed to escape, with only seconds to spare, an attempt on his life while he was driving to work. On his route, a car laden with 80 kilos of explosives waited for him to pass. In the end, five persons died and several buildings collapsed, however the officer came away with his life since the man who detonated the explosives via remote control triggered them an instant after Marquéz's armored automobile passed next to the explosives.

Maza Márquez had come to the directorship pointing out the level of infiltration the drug traffickers had achieved in the affairs of the state. The director also exposed that the traffickers had hired Israeli mercenaries to give military training. He accused these same Israelis of collaborating in massacres of peasants who sympathized with leftist guerrillas and with militants of the Patriotic Union, and of collaborating in Rodríguez's declared war against the Armed Forces of Colombia.

President Virgilio Barco had been warned of the crimes ordered by Pablo Escobar, not only through reports produced by Colombian intelligence, but through his brother, who was residing in Spain. His brother had sent him a series of documents –compiled by Spanish intelligence services– which described the activities of the Medellin cartel and the offensive that they were planning.

At 20:40 hours, on August 18, 1989, President Barco was informed of the assassination of the presidential candidate of the liberal party, Luis Carlos Galán. He immediately called a cabinet meeting and decided therein to inform the population of what had occurred, to declare a state of siege, to propose a package of measures to reactivate extradition by means of presidential decrees, and to activate a regimen to confiscate or impound the traffickers' goods. Moreover, security forces arrested five men suspected of participating in the assassination. However, almost four years later they were acquitted and released.

The state of emergency that Galán's assassination produced superseded any budget. The multitudes that attended Galán's wake and burial cried out for one thing – justice. Public opinion had issued a blank check to the government to once and for all confront the traffickers.

Within this political panorama were the developing campaigns of those running for the presidency. The aspirants with decent chances to win were César Gaviria Trujillo, the political heir to Galán and minister of treasury and government during the Virgilio Barco Administration; Rodrigo Lloreda, a candidate of the conservative social party; Alvaro Stolen Gómez, a political leader of the conservative wing; and Carlos Pizarro Leongómez, the last commander of Ml9, who transformed the armed group into a political movement.

Forty-three year old César Gaviria unexpectedly found himself in the running for the presidency. This young politician from the interior of Colombia had decided to support Galán in the primary elections of their party, but two days after the assassination, on August 20, 1989, the oldest son of the deceased proclaimed him as the official candidate. Juan Manuel Galán, in front of his father's grave, expressed: *"Doctor Gaviria, take the flags of my father...."* A few months later, Gaviria received, with almost 50% of the votes, his party's official nomination for the presidency.

Pablo Escobar was alarmed by the fact that the Galán's political heir had risen to such a high position; therefore, Escobar ordered a series of assassinations all over Colombia in order to disturb the political climate and to protest the election. On the morning of April 26, 1990, presidential candidate Carlos Pizarro boarded a plane of the Avianca Company bound for Banranquilla, where he had political commitments. A few minutes after takeoff, in spite of the numerous escorts accompanying him, a man approached his seat and pumped nine shots into Pizarro's head, three into his neck and three into his left hand.

It is presumed that the drug traffickers chose Pizarro as a target because of his previous involvement with the guerrilla group M19. The traffickers had a score to settle with this group since M19 had procured a peace agreement with the government without having had included The Extraditables in their negotiations.

On May 26, 1990, the Colombian democracy survived a test of fire. In an election characterized by a 58% rate of voter abstention due to fear of terrorist acts at the poles, Dr. César

Gaviria Trujillo was elected President of the Republic by 2,800,000 votes; in total there were 14,800,000 votes cast in the election. Thus, on August 7, before the presence of more than a hundred chiefs and representatives of state, Gaviria assumed office. It was an open-air inauguration, protected by armored glass, with armed helicopters overhead, and a heavily-armed security force. The new president expressed:

"Today, drug trafficking is the principal threat against our democracy. We will confront it without concessions. There is no other way in which we can eradicate from Colombian life the assassinations, the car bombs, the fallen children on Mother's Day, the soldiers and the humble victims of all kinds of crimes, the agents murdered in the destroyed floors of the DAS building, the policemen riddled with bullets in the streets of Medellin...."

President Gaviria instigated a categorical change in the policy against the drug-trafficking organizations. His basic idea was to inject an element of submission into the judicial system .

On September 5, he announced the enactment of decree number 2047, which categorically denied extradition and substantially reduced sentences for drug traffickers who turned themselves in, confessed to their offenses, surrendered their possessions and provided information on their associates in the organization. With this decree, Gaviria was copying the prevailing judicial and penal modalities in the United States and Italy in order to dismantle the threat of extradition that so enraged the drug traffickers. In essence, he was trying to regain the role of the Colombian justice system, and to end the internal war that had been unleashed.

However, the adopted measures did not produce any short-term results, and César Gavíria began drafting a new decree to yet further reduce the penalties. Decree number 3030 was announced on December 17. It was based on the policy that remorseful criminals who wished to reintegrate themselves with society would be able to do so after fulfilling a minimal penalty. With this legal instrument, a confessor would only be charged with a single offense, and extradition would apply only in cases of flight or of untruthful confession.

Still, this new decree did not produce results since the possibility of extradition was still present; so the government announced yet another decree, number 303, dated January 25, 1991, which widened still more the offers to the leaders of the cartels. Number 303 established that no criminal would be extradited who submitted himself to the Colombian justice system. This instrument made possible the beginning of negotiations between the government and the drug traffickers.

On May 10, 1991, an estate located in Envigado, called *"The Cathedral,"* owned by a leader in Pablo Escobar's organization, Antonio Bustamente, was given to the municipality. The Ministry of Justice and Pablo Escobar had reached an agreement to construct a penal rehabilitation center. A special commission for its administration was created, headed by the Antioquia State's Attorney, the Mayor of Envigado and the Director of the Jail. It was also agreed that the army and the police would only have access to the site in the event of a riot and in such an event, the director would accede jurisdiction when appropriate.

In this way, the government maintained control of the prison and access to the site by the police was restricted. With this stage set, Pablo Escobar prepared to turn himself over to the authorities. He was in control of the situation since any strange goings-on would be relayed to him immediately by the thousands of people in Envigado who owed him favors, who had worked for him, or who had benefited from the prosperity the drug traffic had brought to the municipality. The prison was located on a small plain 2,600 meters high. Access was difficult as it sat among an enclave of several mountains, and its altitude permitted a panoramic view of the area.

On the afternoon of June 19, 1991, Pablo Escobar was taken into custody. A helicopter picked him up from his estate *"El Quijote,"* and transported him to what seemed more like a weekend house than a prison. It featured several sitting rooms and six bedrooms with private baths.

Escobar had established three important conditions: first, his personal security was paramount since his enemies would know where to find him; second, insofar as the proceedings against him, he would confess only to a smaller offense; and third, he would be able to maintain the control of his organization and of the cocaine traffic just as he had done in years past. Regarding the latter, Escobar established a tax on cocaine transportation, which symbolized that the other traffickers owed him for the elimination of extradition and for the peace that had been reached. Consequently, Escobar received a percentage of all cocaine trafficked through the routes that he had established.

As time went by, Escobar gained more and more control of his illicit activities from within jail and even from outside it. For example, he was often seen at parties and sporting events. And his exits were not inconvenient for those responsible for him: the security men that guarded him day and night earned $400 per month, while a soldier only earned $150. As money was no obstacle, Escobar enjoyed a personal, mobile security force that assured his safety everywhere he went.

On January 23, 1992, officials from the Attorney General's Office visited Escobar in "jail" and found that he and his men enjoyed luxuries such as televisions, audio equipment, carpets, sculptures, books, and bathtubs. Of even more concern, the officials saw that Escobar and his men had weapons, communication equipment, telescopes and small quantities of drugs; and what was most unusual was that the authorities had to request permission from the prisoners to enter the jail.

With the report filed by the officials from the Attorney General's Office and another report filed by the DEA, which both described Escobar's excursions and the businesses that he was continuing to handle, President Gaviria decided to retake control of the penitentiary and to move Escobar.   After analyzing the possible legal reasons that he could give for moving Escobar, he was convinced that it would not be a problem since there existed no clause that obligated the government to keep him in that prison. However, it could not be perceived that army or the police were carrying out this eviction as a unilateral act. It had to be clear that the decision was made without pressure from the top of Colombia's political ladder.   For this reason, he designated the Vice Minister of Justice to handle the operation.

As the number of security forces began to increase around the jail, Escobar and his people observed what was happening, dimming the trafficker's hopes for a favorable resolution. Furthermore, the drug traffickers were permanently informed of not only the number of guards posted, but also the exact number of men that were being relocated to *The Cathedral*.

Escobar was concerned regarding a recent resolution of the Supreme Court of the United States, dated June 21, 1992, which stated that American authorities could apprehend criminals in any nation of the world, provided that the criminal had pending crimes within the United States. This policy had justified the kidnapping of Alvarez Machaín, held in Mexico and brought by force to the United States, to be tried for his participation in the assassination of DEA agent Enrique Camarena. The Colombian dealer knew perfectly well that in the courts of Florida there were several pending cases against him.   Thus, he knew that this practice of the American government, to drag people to its court rooms before giving them chance to respond, could become a reality for him.

The United States had also captured the drug trafficker José Matta in Tegucigalpa in April, 1988.   Matta was then brought to Santo Domingo by the DEA, and from there, on a commercial flight, was flown to Illinois were he was to serve a life sentence. Similarly, in 1989 the United States invaded

Panama with the justification of seizing General Manuel Noriega, another of Escobar's old allies. Moreover, he considered the possibility that the DEA was planning to kidnap him and bring him to the United States so that President Bush could capitalize the action during his presidential campaign against democrat Bill Clinton.

Escobar could also not forget the hatred that the police and soldiers had towards him, after decades of his determination to annihilate them. Therefore, a fear of being murdered during the occupation of the prison loomed latently.

Pablo Escobar decided to take the matter into his own hands. On July 22, 1992, just past two in the morning, he escaped from the prison, knowing that his disappearance would put the Gaviria Administration behind the eight ball. He would begin a new stealthy life which would guarantee him greater personal safety; and he would unleash a new wave of violence since the people had forgotten about his power.

In his new life, Escobar reorganized his military structure and sowed terror in the principal Colombian cities. Despite his show of force, a group of men who had to pay him drug trafficking taxes, tired of the way he was commanding his organization, decided to give him a taste of his own medicine. They named their group *The Pepes* (Persecuted by Pablo Escobar), and began to kill his men, burn his properties and rob his drug shipments. *The Pepes* also wanted to capture Escobar, as the government had offered 500 million pesos for the capture of this public enemy.

On December 1, 1993, a DAS commando group shot a nephew of Escobar on the streets of Medellin. When the drug trafficker found out, he called wife and children by telephone.

The communication was delayed and tracked through a system of radiogoniometric triangulation that permits one to determine the origin and destination of a call. It was established within a perimeter of 800 square meters where the trafficker could be found. In a few hours, Escobar called back and the equipment was able to pinpoint the exact location of the call.

The operation was planned. His house was surrounded, and Escobar could be seen inside through binoculars. Special agents found Escobar in their gun sights. At three o'clock, in the afternoon of December 2, 1993, the most sought after drug trafficker in the world fell lifeless after receiving three shots from one of the officers outside.

VIOLENCE AND JUSTICE

To analyze the violence in Colombia, it is necessary to take as points of reference the circumstances, the social requirements and the response. The latter, it must be noted, is inefficient for certain when the state must issue a manifesto to settle differences between the two social spheres. That is, when a state ceases to be the mediator between private interest and the collective interest, and its decisions lean to the benefit of select kernels of the population, it reflects in the community a substantial change that upsets the relationships between the two social components.

In fact, if a state does not respond satisfactorily to the majority's pressing questions, it loses the necessary legitimacy to be respected and obeyed by its citizens. The vast segment that remains eclipsed of official attention, by the same token, loses its value to those political institutions and will seek other roads to administer, by their own means, the functions that originally should be fulfilled by the institutions.

These scenarios foster the success of emerging forces, which are based on wealth, but devoid of morality and of culture. The great majority, overwhelmed by their own needs, are seduced by the mirage of the money. Thus begins the ascent of the emerging classes into the political, social and economic theaters. The rise of private justice, monopolies of the economy, and personal demonstrations, made possible through definitive openings in the socio-governmental fabric, dilute the true notion of the state.

Anomalies and irregularities that at the beginning awaken an attitude of protest, which gradually metamorphosizes in the mental schema of the population. That is, their mentalities go from permissive, to cooperative, to finally incursive.

The negotiation of moral principles in search of economic prebends and material welfare, caused the state to lose its imperium to punish. That is, excluded from the state's punitive orbit are those to whom were accredited economic capacity.

The notion that the political offense and the common offense should be clearly differentiated has been undermined, leaving both offenses to be assessed by the same behavioral standards. On one hand, organized crime emerges with aspirations of raising its status and obtaining special political treatment from the state, but in some cases, the ideological projects fade, leaving their common offenses as *modus vivendi*, or ends in themselves.

This phenomenon should not be attributed entirely to the economic capacity of the drug traffickers or to their devastating intimidation. Rather, this phenomenon coincides with the progressive loss of structural values, parallel to the incursion of forces interested in gaining power by any means necessary, which, in turn, undermines the hierarchy of the democratic system. The results of this scourge, among other effects, feed the flames of guerrilla activity and breathe air into political power vacuums.

A PRESIDENT BEHIND THE EIGHT BALL

In August, 1995, the Colombian government of Ernesto Samper arrived at a critical moment in the execution of its political plan. In spite of apprehending Miguel Rodríguez Orejuela, who had assumed the second-in-command position of the Cali cartel after Escobar's death, they have not been able to dissipate the public's presumption of drug money's involvement in the 1994 presidential campaign. Indeed, the ex-treasurer of the campaign, Santiago Medina, had asserted the existence of a relationship between the Cali cartel, the candidate, and his closest associates.

The recent arrests are especially notable since they occur at a time when the Colombian traffickers are at the height of their power. That is, they are expanding vigorously their cocaine networks in Europe and the former Soviet Union, and forging partnerships with groups within the Italian Mafia.

Miguel Rodríguez Orejuela was characterized as being the most cautious and aristocratic member of the organization. Pending against him were seven warrants for his arrest for drug trafficking and illicit enrichment. He was born in the city of Cali on August 15, 1943. Nicknamed *"El Señor,"* he began his illicit activities in the 1960's with his brother Gilberto, who, like his brother, is also behind bars.

Miguel Rodríguez Orejuela was captured on August 6, 1995, in the city of Cali – capital of the Valley Department, some 250 kilometers to the southwest of Bogota – when he was found in a building located near Three Crosses Hill. After his apprehension, the multimillionaire criminal was housed in an isolated cell in *Picota Prison*, a punishment that the late Pablo Escobar enjoyed, which featured books, a radio, and a 14-inch television with which he could satisfy his passion for professional soccer. He also enjoyed thermal baths, a personal gymnasium and a soccer field.

The operations for the cartel leaders' arrests had begun earlier that year. On June 9, 1995, Gilberto Rodriguez Orejuela, alias *"The Chessman,"* had already taken the helm of the criminal organization when he was captured by an elite unit of policeman in the city of Cali. On June 19, they were able to seize Henry Loiza Ceballos, alias *"The Scorpion,"* who had decided to surrender himself voluntarily to the Colombian authorities. On June 24, Victor Julio Patiño, alias *"The Papa,"* who occupied the fifth place of importance within the organization's hierarchy, was captured. Also, on July 4, the third in command, José Santacruz Londoño, was captured by the Bogota police while dining in a restaurant. And on July 8, another important man in the cartel, Phanor Arizabaleta, turned himself in to the chief of Secret Police, Ramiro Bejarano.

With these arrests began the decline of the greatest drug-trafficking empire of the world, which, at its peak, controlled 80% of the world's cocaine traffic and boasted more than 3000 personnel. Since the end of 1995, the only cartel leader that that remains at large as a fugitive is Elmer Herrera Buitrago, the chief of security for the cartel. The government has offered a $1 million reward to anyone who supplies information as to his whereabouts.

But, these arrests were not sufficient to stop the wave of accusations that have been directed against President Samper. He now finds himself in the middle of a scandal over presumed campaign contributions of the drug traffickers; indeed, the donations in question exceed $6 million. With the arrest of ex-Minister of Defense Fernando Botero, the right-hand man of the president and the keeper of his finances during the 1994 campaign, the political crisis was aggravated to the point of putting Samper's presidency in jeopardy. Botero confessed that the traffickers had infiltrated the upper echelons of political power.

But this was not all. With the arrest of Santiago Medina, a merchant who ran Samper's campaign treasury with Botero, it was proven that, at the very least, Samper's men had received a $50,000 check from the drug traffickers as a contribution to the campaign. Moreover, this is a small sum compared to the $6 million in campaign contributions from the Cali cartel that Botero claims were authorized by Samper.

These developments have led Colombians to distrust their government and above all, President Samper, who has maintained that these contributions were received without his knowledge. According to a major media poll, 77% of Colombians believe that the drug traffickers have financed past presidential campaigns. Samper's position is further compromised if one believes the statements of drug trafficker Nelson Urrego to the daily newspaper *The Times*. Urrego claims to have contributed $100,000 to the campaign of the current president.

In part, the arrest of the Rodríguez Orejuela brothers and the rest of the upper hierarchy of the cartel helped the defensive position taken by the President. In addition, he has been helped by the announcement of internal investigations and other measures designed to alleviate public danger, to protect innocent children, to expedite the administration of justice, to promote citizen participation in the struggle against violence, to punish participants in criminal organizations with prison terms of up to 60 years, and to modify the Constitution to establish penalties of life imprisonment for the heinous offenses of murder and kidnapping. But in the end, the Congressional Accusations Commission –the only entity that can try the President– together with the District Attorney's Office have responsibility for the investigation, and in these bodies and individuals, the Colombian people have placed the credibility of their government.

On February 1, 1996, *The Times* reported that the Supreme Court had ordered the apprehension of four congress members linked to the drug cartels. Among them was Representative Rodrigo Garavito, arrested October 18, 1995, and then released from jail despite the charges against him of illicit enrichment and the falsification of documents.

Another congressman listed by the Court was Senator Alberto Santofino Botero, accused of having links with the Cali cartel since his name appeared in the confiscated accounting records of Miguel Rodríguez Orejuela. Furthermore, Santofino was implicated by Guillermo Pallomari, the ex-accountant of the Cali cartel, as one of 21 congress members who received money from the organization. Also arrested was Senator María Izquierdo, who had to account for two checks to her that appeared in the accounting books of Rodríguez Orejuela. Finally, on February 14, 1996, Senator Gustavo Espinosa was the last of the four arrested, accused of illicit enrichment from his supposed links to the Cali cartel.

But in spite of the announcements and arrests executed by President Samper, on March 1, 1996, United States President Bill Clinton resolved to decertify Colombia as a collaborative nation in the struggle against drug trafficking. This action appears not be directed at the Colombian people, but rather at their president, who, as time goes by, attracts increasingly more accusations of having maintained contacts with the Cali cartel in order to finance his campaign.

Samper responded to the Clinton Administration with a phrase laden with political ink: *"The only certification I need is the one which the Colombian people gave me when they chose me as their president."* Nevertheless, the measure adopted by the Americans put Colombia on a list with Nigeria, Syria, Burma and Afghanistan. The consequences of this rating are more than uncomfortable since, though it does not mean the suspension of economic aid to combat drug trafficking, it does mean a freeze on loans and credits that the South American country may need to improve its economy. Furthermore, it may affect investment of American corporations in Colombia. Moreover, to add salt to President Samper's wound, in the same act that decertified his country, Mexico received certification as a country that cooperates and makes advances in the struggle against traffickers. Meanwhile, ironically, 70%

of the drugs that enter the United States pass through the Mexican-American border.

But within so much scandal, Colombia did receive a consolation prize. On Monday, May 6, 1996, the Samper Administration hailed as a success the decision of the Economic and Social Council of the UN to include Colombia as member of the International Board of Drug Inspection (JIFE). The object of this entity is to promote and supervise the drug-control provisions to which member countries of the United Nations have subscribed.

THE 20 POINTS OF THE (COLOMBIAN) AGENDA[13]

The Agenda of the United States Embassy in Colombia is topped by anti-drug measures, followed by commercial topics, diplomatic complaints and other issues.

➢ Re-establish the extradition of Colombians to the United States.
➢ Achieve the approval of a package of anti-drug laws which would allow for the expropriation of goods that the drug traffickers had acquired in the past – that is, goods not discovered before the vigilance of the new laws.
➢ Permit U.S. vessels to intercept ships carrying drugs within Colombian coastal waters (12 miles), and to seize the boats, the drugs, and the culprits.
➢ Apply a non-liquid, granular herbicide (instead of glyphosphate) that does not become diluted when it rains, and that can be spread from a higher altitude so that the crop-dusting planes cannot be attacked so easily from the ground.

---

[13] *La Semana*, July 12, 1996.

> Illicit drug eradication programs. Such verification will be based on precepts established by both countries, so that Washington's request is satisfied that "Colombia stops saying that a fumigated hectare is equal to an eradicated hectare."

> Increase the amplitude of homicide investigations so that drug traffickers are not only charged with illicit enrichment and drug trafficking, but also with homicide for the killings for which they were responsible.

> Stop the campaign to dismantle a recently created anti-money laundering department. According to Washington, this campaign is being waged by the Banking Superintendency.

> Do not dismiss officials and functionaries of the different state security/police agencies that have demonstrated a commitment to the fight against drugs. According to the United States, it had been (Colombia's) intention to demote some of these men to the reserves.

> Do not debilitate state prosecutors by means of the legal and constitutional reform package proposed by Samper after the preclusion of his case in Congress. The United States has made it clear that it would oppose the Public Prosecutors Office entering into the political orbit of the President.

> Act on the recommendations of the U.S. Marshal, the prison authority in the United States, regarding the high-security "pavilions" in Colombia. According to these recommendations, detained leaders of drug-trafficking organizations should be isolated and unable to communicate with the outside world – that is, they should not be able to continue with their illicit businesses from prison.

➢ Prohibit the Administrative Security Department (DAS) from, instead of cooperating in the war against drugs, becoming a Colombian intelligence and espionage agency which spies on political adversaries and on functionaries of the U.S. Embassy.

➢ Reach an agreement between Washington and Bogota that un-links Colombia from the banana quota agreement with the European Union.

➢ Sign an agreement with Washington for the protection of private and intellectual property.

➢ Suspend what Washington views to be an escalating trend of protectionist measures promoted by (Colombian) Minister of Commerce Morris Harf.

➢ Stop Minister Harf's practice of "systematic lying" (words of U.S. diplomats to high Colombian officials). Washington says it is upset because "each time (Harf) meets with a U.S. official, he claims to have obtained an agreement for the elimination of all commercial sanctions, when this was never the case."

➢ Name a (Colombian) ambassador to Washington who does not have presidential aspirations and who does not spout anti-American rhetoric just to help his ratings in Colombian polls.

➢ Name an advisor to the Presidency of the Republic who would be a permanent interlocutor with the United States.

➢ Stop the Colombian Representative to the United Nations from, according to Washington, "instigating" the 'non-aligned' group of countries against the United States.

➢ Develop effective policy to protect human rights and the environment.

➢ Overcome airport security problems in the principal Colombian cities.

II

Drug Trafficking in the Andes

A United Nations document reflects:

The history of mankind has also been a history of the undue use of drugs. From time immemorial, herbs, roots, barks, plants and leaves have been used to relieve pain and to combat illnesses.

The consumption of drugs in and of itself is not wrong, but unfortunately, there are drugs that initially have a pleasant side effect. What seems to have begun as a recreational activity, eventually became illicit and addictive in use.[14]

Drug addiction has perhaps become the greatest scourge of the modern world. In spite of efforts, controlling drug trafficking remains, at best, uncertain. The impact of drug money destabilizes governments, distorts economies and puts large sectors of society at risk. Narcotics are not only responsible for the degradation and delinquency of some of the youth in developed countries, but also comes to represent a multi-million dollar business founded on violence and corruption.

---

[14] *The United Nations and the Undue Use of Drugs* (New York: 1990).

The United States has resorted to pressuring governments to use military force against drug traffickers and producers. Nevertheless, the use of force alone has not had the success anticipated by those who are in favor of using it. On the contrary, the immense fortunes amassed by the traffickers has enabled them to fortify their armies in order to defend their interests.   These fortunes have further served to bribe multitudes of judges as well as police, military and other high officials of government.   As a consequence, the spread of institutionalized corruption has come to affect the very foundations of the present political system.

The social impact of trafficking illegal narcotics produces insecurity at all levels – personal, proprietary, and institutional – and becomes evident as a grave morally deteriorative element in all aspects of society. The economic impact is even more insidious in that it can not easily be measured, even though drug trafficking feigns too bring relief to some Andean countries. The influx of income derived from coca, marijuana and more recently of poppy plants is at best marginally predictable, which impedes any structured planning of national economies.   Certainly all economic indicators are affected by drug money (narco-dollars), particularly those indexes of inflation, foreign currency reserves, as well as interest rates, property values, salaries, the prices of services, etc..

The cultivation of plants for the manufacturing of narcotics affects the agricultural production of foodstuffs. Areas that are able to produce food are instead sown for the cultivation of the coca plant, which necessarily affects the value and price of food.

This misuse of the land also causes dangerous ecological effects, given the botanical characteristics of the coca plant and the nature of the chemical products used in its processing. The same can be said of the use of phosphates in the eradication of marijuana and poppy plants.

When we speak of Latin America and the drug problem, it is necessary to view each country individually as a separate entity and environment. If, for example, we look at Bolivia, we can observe that a considerable number of its citizens are involved in one form or another in the so called "coca culture;" that is, they either grow coca, chew it, drink it, smoke it, grind it or sell it. In Bolivia, close to 60,000 hectares are presently being used in the cultivation of the coca plant, which will result in the production of 100,000 to 120,000 tons of coca leaf annually. Under Bolivian law it is legal to grow coca plants but illegal to manufacture its refined products. Nevertheless, 80% of this production will be processed into cocaine.

Peru is the largest producer of coca plants in the world. Just as in Bolivia, its indigenous population is plant physically, socially and spiritually involved with coca. For a long time, the county of Cuzco was the heart of traditional production of the coca plant until, as a response to foreign demand, production of coca leaf dramatically increased throughout the country.

The eradication campaign initiated by the Alan García Administration caused the displacement of guerrilla groups such as The Shining Path, which moved to the Ayacucho region, particularly in upper Huallaga. There, using the pretext that there existed a conspiracy between the government and an imperialist power (the United States) to deprive indigenous people of their way of earning a living, guerrillas found fertile ground for their recruitment of troops.

No other country is as besieged with the multiple ramifications of the illicit trafficking of drugs as is Colombia. Presently, drug trafficking affects the political process on all levels: international, national, regional and local. At the same time, there has been a major effort to control the narcotics traffic. Repressive state measures have been put in place to reduce the activities related to drug trafficking. This strategy has been coined "submission to justice." However, although this approach has met with good results, statistics show an increase in the consumption of *buzco*, a paste of cocaine mixed with tobacco and marijuana.

With regard to Ecuador, this country is a marginal producer of coca leaf and cocaine. But sharing a border with Colombia has turned it into a haven for the stockpiling of chemicals used in the manufacture of cocaine as well as for money laundering.

Lastly, Venezuela has made the transition from being an alternative route for Colombian drug traffickers to becoming not only a vital point of departure for U.S. and Europe bound drugs, but also a producer of narcotics. The vastness and complexity of its border, and the continual retreat of Colombian traffickers across these borders due to the pursuit of the Colombian authorities, has contributed to the involvement of this country in the illegal commerce of drugs. Venezuela has become a major money laundering center and also serves as a bridge for the vastly increasing air and sea connections to the consumer countries.

Venezuela was once considered a marginal market, just as Ecuador and Chile were. Alan Riding states in the *New York Times*, July 18, 1987, that, "in 1985 it was evident that the same rivers, paths and landing strips being used to bring chemical products into Colombia were also being used to smuggle cocaine into Venezuela."

Between 1984 and 1987, an estimated 25 to 37 tons of drugs annually came into the country, according to Venezuelan Congressman Vladimir Gessel. In his speech given on May 14, 1988, President Jaime Lusinchi made public his profound concern by expressing: "The nation rejects drug trafficking and the use of drugs. I want to emphasize that this fight should unite us instead of separating us. The problem is serious and the danger is real, powerful, persistent."

At a function of the ninth Andean Parliament in September, 1989, hosted by President Carlos Andrés Pérez at the Miraflores Palace, this head of state was categorical before the Colombian delegation in stressing that his government was committed to going to any and all lengths necessary to fight drug trafficking on all levels.

To speak of drugs in the Andean region is to speak of marijuana, coca leaf, and more recently, poppy plants. These products are seen as elements of aggression against their society. However, not taking into consideration certain cultural traits of the regions that cultivate these products, particularly coca leaf, can lead to misunderstandings that would distort the study of drugs. For some indigenous groups, the coca leaf represents their biological, social, economic and magical values. The use of coca activates the process of social integration. Aside from having intrinsic value in economic exchange, it also serves a fundamental role in social ceremonies and collective myths; it equates to values still nourished by the idea of a magical world.

In the 19th century, due to the general interest in alkaloids and other remedial substances, the German pharmacist Albert Neiman was motivated to synthesize cocaine in his laboratory. The powerful alkaloid quickly generated enormous attraction among scientific circles in the Old World. Sigmund Freud thus became acquainted with this type of alkaloid. As a young professor, Freud was attempting to find a cure for morphine addiction.

COCA AND COCA-COLA

In 1863, Angelo Mariani, a doctor from Corsica, erected a shrine to "Mama coca." This doctor produced a very special wine to which he had added a secret white powder. The highly euphoric properties of the wine won the favor of the followers of the Czar of Russia, the princess of Wales, and T. Edison, all of whom advocated drinking the wine. Pope Leon XIII, who was in the habit of taking a jar of coca leaves with him, sent Mariani a medal of gold for his discoveries and for the wine that he had sent him.

In 1880, the American pharmacist J. Peperton registered the French coca wine, dubbed as the ideal tonic, in the United States. Peperton had modified the formula by diminishing the alcohol content and adding certain ingredients such as caffeine and cola nuts.

The global Coca-Cola empire had been born. The nineteenth century witnessed the end of the legal reign of cocaine and the beginning of the widespread legal use of alkaloids in the Western World. Suddenly, cocaine was denounced as a dangerous seducer. Coca-Cola eliminated it from its formula in 1914.

By way of federal legislation, the United States in 1909 restricted opium. In 1912, the De la Haya Convention was signed, restricting internationally the use of opium. In 1914, a law was enacted which identified all drug users as offenders. In 1924, the United States Supreme Court took the medical profession's viewpoint that drug use was an illness.

On May 2, 1949, the United Nations Commission on Narcotics commissioned a study on the effects of the coca leaf. This study was first solicited by Peru, and then by Bolivia. The conclusions reached in the study exposed that the drug problem was not a phenomenon exclusive to Peru and Bolivia, nor was it solely a result of economic and social factors in those countries. Furthermore, it was determined that cocaine dangerously reduces the appetite in consumers, which leads to a vicious circle of malnutrition.

During Richard Nixon's administration, there was an increase in the number of narcotics users and the use of heroin became widespread. During that period, the World Health Organization recognized that the dependency on pharmaceuticals posed a problem beyond their scope and other organizations within the United Nations. They began to study and discard solutions that were purely repressive or health oriented for lack of a greater understanding. At the same time, there began a massive amount of trafficking and consumption of marijuana in Latin America.

A great invasion of cocaine controlled by international organizations occurred in the 1980's. Cocaine became exploited en masse in Peru, Bolivia and Colombia, thus producing in these countries immense socio-economic problems.

The drugs which pose the greatest threat to the United States are heroin and cocaine. A report entitled National Strategy for the Control of Drugs, published by the White House (United States Government) in September, 1989, indicates: "Virtually all the cocaine that comes to the United States is cultivated in Peru (60%), Bolivia (30%) and Colombia (10%). 80% of the cocaine that enters the U S. is refined in and sent from Colombia."

The report states that Colombia is the principal source of marijuana for the U.S., representing 40% of the market. Mexico represents 25%; 10% is smuggled from other sources; and the remaining 25% is domestically produced.

The other aspect important to the United States is that drug trafficking has been connected to subversive guerrilla activity . As a result, the fight against drugs has taken on an ideological tint, an element of *narco-subversion,* and has become a priority on national and international levels.

In 1985, a White House report indicated that:

Cocaine trafficking is only one of the problems in the Andean region. Economic instability and political insurgency creates challenges to democratic institutions and to the stability of the region. The problems are intertwined. It is impossible to reduce the supply of cocaine simply by attending to one aspect and not the others.

The goal is to motivate the governments of the cocaine producing countries to cooperate with us in significantly attacking the cocaine industry while carrying out their own programs against drugs. To accomplish these objectives, a large-scale and well-maintained campaign will be launched over several years, which will involve the economic, military, and law enforcement agencies. The objectives of this campaign should be:

1) The isolation of the principal areas of cultivation in Peru and Bolivia.

2) The interception of chemical substance shipments needed to manufacture cocaine.

3) The destruction of facilities used in the processing of chlorohydration of cocaine.

4) The dismantling of the trafficking organizations and the eradication of coca leaf cultivation where this may be possible.

We can and must accomplish this with minimum participation by the United States. This is the crucial point. The countries of the region should assume the principal burden.

The pressure the United States is exerting on the Andean governments is precipitating crises in their political regimes, particularly in the coca leaf-producing countries. This pressure has placed this problem on the shoulders of the state. All agree, nevertheless, that the trafficking and consumption of drugs are factors which contribute to violence and corruption, and which weaken the development of emerging democracies. They block the development of legal activities while wasting national resources.

Latin American countries have concluded that the gains obtained through drug trafficking do not compensate for the social, economic and political costs. However, due to weak rural economies, thousands of small farmers and their families depend on the cultivation of coca leaf in Bolivia and Peru for their sustenance, which poses an important political dilemma.

On February 1, 1990, at a meeting in Cartagena de Indias, the presidents of Bolivia, Colombia, the United States, and Peru arrived at a consensus to establish an anti-drug pact. It was the first consorted effort in renewing the attack against drug trafficking, and the consumption of cocaine in particular. At this presidential summit, United States President George Bush recognized that repressive measures alone were not enough to reduce drug production and that the problem required socio-economic strategies with financial backing.

President Alan García at the same meeting, demonstrated that to combat the growing European consumption of cocaine, an economic program was needed that would involve the United States and the cooperation promised by Europe. Paz Zamora, President of Bolivia, put forth the idea of providing financial support for Bolivian farmers who cultivated coca leaf, in order that they might plant alternative crops, with the possibility of distributing these alternative crops in the United States and Europe.

The Cartagena Declaration was neither a sudden nor isolated act. Rather, it represented a strategic effort by the United States toward a more definitive post cold war national security concept. Because of these circumstances, the war on drugs became a central political theme for the United States in Latin America. The Cartagena document divides countries into producers and non-producers, framing Bolivia, Colombia and Peru as being responsible for the production and trafficking of cocaine, and describes the United States as a consumer country and victim.

Two years after the Cartagena Summit (April, 1992), the heads of state of Colombia, Bolivia, Mexico, Peru and the United States, and the Minister of Foreign Relations of Venezuela met in San Antonio, Texas, to express their desire to go far beyond that already accorded in Cartagena. They also vowed "to improve international cooperation in meeting the challenges that arise from global changes in drug trafficking and consumption." The conclusions arrived at during this meeting were summarized in a declaration:

The global problem of illegal drugs and their accompanying crimes represent a direct threat to the health and well being of our countries, economies, societies, and of the harmony of our international relations. Drugs are inducing violence and pharmacological dependency. They present a threat to our democratic institutions and represent a waste of human resources that could otherwise benefit our societies. Alternative crop development programs have proven to be efficient in substituting for coca leaf cultivation in the producer nations. But the cooperative measures must be amplified and strengthened in all areas. The measures against drugs must be undertaken in such a way as to share responsibilities in a well-balanced fashion. The mutual effort can take place observing national legislation and in complete observance of national sovereignty and territorial integrity of our countries, and in strict observance of international law. Therefore it is fundamental that we count on strong economies and innovative economic initiatives to achieve success in the fight against drugs.

However, these meetings did not have the luster or success that was hoped. From the outset a distinction was made between Colombia (a processor nation of cocaine) and Bolivia and Peru, countries that produced coca leaf. Colombia has assumed the strongest position in favor of repression at all costs in the war on drugs. This is a result of the United States' pressure to do so, while Peru and Bolivia have indicated their discontent with the accords reached bilaterally with the United States on the eradication of crops. Bolivian Senator L. Escobar, who was part of the committee that accompanied President Paz Zamora, expressed:

Because of what has been eradicated in the last few years, Bolivian farmers have lost $150 million in income. This is a major sacrifice the United States does not want to recognize. Bolivia has eradicated 20,000 hectares cultivated with coca leaf between 1985 and 1992. Sales of this coca leaf would have benefited 300,000 farmers, who, with the added drop in the price of coca leaf, have witnessed their families' incomes be reduced to an absolutely miserable level.

A similar situation affects 250,000 Peruvian farmers. Because of the repression against those cultivating coca leaf, President Alberto Fujimori maintains that if the armed forces were to enter the region known as Alto Huallaga, *The Shining Path* would certainly recruit new followers and the violence in that region would surely escalate.

THE DRUG CIRCUITS

According to Alain Labrousse, Director of the Geopolitical Drug Observatory, it is now clear that the drug problem has become more international. In fact, the main centers of production and distribution are no longer centered in the Andean countries, but are now spread throughout Latin America.

Other countries like Brazil have emerged that smuggle the coca leaf from Bolivia, refine it and sell it. Money laundering networks similarly have widened in this country. Venezuela, according to Labrouse, finds itself in the same situation and is now a center for trafficking and money laundering.

Argentina has not been able to escape either: laboratories have been found in Salta. Moreover, Chile has become involved in exporting cocaine through Puerto de Antofagasta, and in Uruguay there are large companies that launder money.

Besides these Latin American centers, there are other important focal points for drug trafficking, such as Lebanon and Morocco. Lebanon, prior to the war, produced cannabis and poppy. Today, it also transports cocaine to Spain and the Middle East. Morocco, another key country in the network of drug trafficking, elected not to be a large exporter of hashish to France and Spain in order to become a center of transportation for cocaine and heroin, and in order to cultivate poppy plants. In this author's opinion, there are two threats: first, Africa and the countries of the East, where there are centers for money laundering, could become the new Latin America. There is also evidence of marijuana plantations, and some coca leaf and poppy plantations in this region. Second, countries in the East pose a new problem because Kazakhstan and Uzbekistan are producing hashish and heroin for exportation.

All routes crisscross each other. It seems that the heroin cartels and the cocaine cartels have considerable arrangements to further their commercial ends. Consequently, Colombia has begun to see widespread cultivation of poppy plants. There is hardly a region above two thousand meters in elevation that cannot be threatened with the cultivation of this plant. The visible result of the integration of the cartels is the increase in markets and the diversification of distribution centers.

A recent report by the Spanish Civil Guard considers its country to be the principal center of distribution of Colombian cocaine for the European market. The distribution is carried out through four main routes:

1) The Colombian route: Bogota to Madrid;

2) The Venezuelan route: Caracas to Madrid or to Tenerife and Santiago de Compostela;

3) The Brazilian route: Rio de Janeiro to Madrid or Barcelona;

4) The Argentine route: Buenos Aires to Madrid or Palmas.

The process involved in the production of cocaine is relatively simple. It does not require a great deal of sophisticated technology. The raw substance, coca leaf, is grown in large areas of Bolivia, Peru, Brazil and Ecuador. The steps in the process can be synthesized in this manner: the coca leaves are first mixed with sodium carbonate to precipitate the alkaloid. Afterwards, gasoline and sulfuric acid are added and it sits for twelve hours, after which the mixture is passed through a press in order to mold it into coca paste.

The paste is then mixed with ammonia and potassium permanganate and is filtered to purify it and to produce the coca base. This, then, is treated with hydrochloric acid, ether, and acetone to obtain the hydrochloride cocaine.

It is evident that the process of producing cocaine does not require especially large plots of land, highly skilled labor force, nor a great deal of capital investment. It is also evident that the large profits of the cocaine industry do not arise from the production process itself, but rather from the natural illegal processes that accompany the production, trafficking and consumption of cocaine. These are the factors that make it one of the highest yielding industries in the world. The cocaine business as an illegal undertaking is a high-risk business. It is this very risk that generates profit.

Within the global market for cocaine, the Andean region, and especially Peru, Colombia and Bolivia, have comparative advantages:

1) The absence of state authorities in large areas of these national territories almost guarantee impunity with regard to any illegal activity.

2) The presence of the state authorities has been substituted by social forces such as The Shining Path in Peru, or the Armed Revolutionary Forces in Colombia.

3) There is a high potential for the corruption of competent authorities in these countries. Once the cocaine leaves the state of origin, the possibilities of capture and punishment increase. Nevertheless, the capacity for bribery by the traffickers renders the institutional structures less than airtight.

4) These countries have quite a historical tradition of contraband. Its inception can be traced to the time when our economies became absorbed into the global economy. Having been integrated into global commerce as territorial economies, this region's financial base is supported by tributes from the exterior. This, in turn, has generated the tendency and ability

in some sectors of the population to ignore official controls on production, commerce and a wide array of merchandise.

The laws in these countries have become inoperative due to their continual violation. To this must be added the lack of coercive or severely punitive mechanisms.

Drug trafficking can be classified into three basic categories in terms of its business hierarchy. On the lower level, you have the "mules" or "camels" who transport drugs in small quantities in their belongings and on their persons. These individuals carry out low-level activities and can easily be replaced. Their arrest does not cause alarm or upset the operations of the cartels.

On the intermediate level, one finds pilots, treasurers, and field administrators who direct and carry out the criminal operations. They perform essential smuggling and business functions. Moreover, they frequently have knowledge of the overall operations and members belonging to the organization.

At the top of the pyramid are the heads of the trafficking network. Since they rarely take part in the actual transportation of drugs, they have little to fear in terms of being held accountable. Moreover, these individuals are often able to protect themselves thanks to political cooperation, bribery and intimidation. The main trafficking leaders never touch the drugs or the money. It is always the persons on the intermediate level that carry out these duties. The laundering of money, also a responsibility of the intermediate level operatives, is not only done through banks, financial entities and car dealerships, for example, but through any type of business that has been funded by drug money.

PERU

For hundreds of years, indigenous peoples of the Peruvian Andes have cultivated, chewed and performed ceremonies using the coca leaf. Until the 1970's, the cultivation of coca was constant and was basically used to supply the traditional indigenous use and the state's legal sales to the pharmaceutical industry. Coinciding with the advent of greater consumption in the United States, there also began a structural change in the Peruvian rural sectors that would form the basis for what was to become the largest cultivated crop in the country. High yielding cocaine soon violently displaced traditionally cultivated crops. In addition, due to the limited land available for cocaine cultivation, the agricultural frontier was extended toward the Amazon to the eastern regions of the Andes.

The practice of burning the land and the use of artificial fertilizers soon produced erosion and environmental imbalance and created a need to further expand the area of cultivation. Another contributing factor to the expansion of illegal coca-growing lands was the increasing demand of the international market.

In recent years, Peru has contributed 60% to 70% of the global production of coca leaf, cultivating 120,000 hectares. The central point of production of coca is to be found in the valley of Alto Huallaga, the largest coca-growing area in the world, containing 80,000 cultivated hectares.

The settlers of that region were originally taken there at the onset of the Peruvian government's settlement program during the 1960's. When promises of credit and technical assistance for agriculture were not fulfilled, the farmers were forced to find an alternative that would yield enough to make a living. The cultivation of coca fit these needs.

Statistical Tables

Tables for CY COCA/a		1995	1994	1993	1992	1991	1990
Harvestable Cultivation	[ha]	115,300	108,600	108,800	129,100	120,800	121,300
Eradication*	[ha]	0	0	0	0	0	0
Cultivation	[ha]	115,300	108,600	108,800	129,100	120,800	121,300
Potentially harvestable leaf	[mt]	183,600	165,300	155,500	223,900	222,700	196,900
Seizures							
Coca Leaf	[mt]	40.1	25.2	-	25.0	5.95	38.52
Paste	[mt]		**	7.7	0.75	1.07	-
Cocaine HCL	[mt]	7.70	0.10	0.47	0.23	0.76	-
Cocaine Base	[mt]	15.00	10.60	5.3	6.7	4.41	-
Total Cocaine HCL/Base/Paste**	[mt]	22.70	10.70	5.77	6.93	5.17	8.50
Aircraft	items		4	13	7	10	-
Arrests			6,586	4,824	3,707	2,055	-
Labs Destroyed							
Base: 17		21	21	38	88	89	151
HCL 2		0	0	0	0	0	
Total 19		21	21	38	88	89	
Domestic Consumption							
Coca leaf [mt]		10,000	10,000	10,000	10,000	10,000	10,000
User (thousands)							
Coca		3,000	3,000	3,000	3,000	3,000	3,000
Cocaine		-	-	-	-	-	-
Other Coca		-	-	-	-	-	-

The migration of farmers to the valley was further accelerated by two factors during the 1980's: the enormous demand for cocaine in the United States and the economic crisis in Peru which translated into the absence of legal alternatives for large sectors of the population. 300,000 colonists have come to the region due to the demand for coca. Approximately 120,000 hectares of land are illegally cultivated in Peru and 100,000 tons of coca paste are produced, which are chiefly destined for Colombian laboratories.

These transactions represent an income of close to $1,000 million annually for the Peruvian economy. This is equivalent to 30% of Peru's legal exports and 5% of the nation's gross national product. The profits from coca leaf have also served to lesson the effects of the Peruvian economic crisis. Toward the end of the 1980's, inflation had climbed to 2,775% annually. Real incomes fell to less than $205. The possibilities of getting loans from the international banking community diminished as the country was unable to make payments on the debt that now has reached $20,000,000,000. In this manner, money derived from coca has not only helped to offset the economic situation of a large part of the population, but has also assisted the *Central Bank* with its money exchange needs and has similarly helped meet import requirements. Without the profits from coca, there would have been a need for gross devaluations of their currency in recent years.

The most important banks of the country, including the Central Bank, have branches in the areas where coca is cultivated. Thanks to the growing attitude of tolerance, a large amount of money from the drug industry is laundered through these branches. Minister of Economy Cezar Vasquez Bazan has recognized that the elimination of the coca industry would usher in the total collapse of the Peruvian economy. The great majority of people in Peru do not hold the war on drugs as a high priority. This sentiment is especially true for the Altos de Huallaga region, one of the world's largest producers of coca.

A survey taken in 1990 in Lima put the economic crisis of the country at the top of Peru's priority list, followed closely by the guerrilla situation. Only 4% of those surveyed mentioned drug trafficking as a major problem.   The disinterest demonstrated toward the fight against the cocaine industry can be explained by the relief this segment provides from the economic crisis – relief on all levels of the society, from the state level to the individual.

No solution put forth to eradicate illegal coca cultivation can ignore this reality. Without a program of substitution of crops that would render a yield comparable to that of coca, farmers will not have a clear incentive for cooperating with the programs of eradication.

BOLIVIA

The use of coca in Bolivia predates this millennium.   The Aymara Indians used it before the conquest of the Incas, during the 10th century.   Its use by indigenous peoples has physiological, social and ritual purposes.   The chewing of coca leaf provided resistance to hunger and drowsiness during long journeys and hard work.   Moreover, coca leaf symbolized wealth.   The cultivation of coca leaf was monopolized by the Incas, and members of their upper class were covered with leaf in their tombs.   In the Indigenous tradition, coca leaf was an integral part of rituals performed by priests and visionaries.   It is also noteworthy that, for the Indians, this traditional use of coca leaf has never constituted a problem of any sort, neither physiological, nor social, nor sociological.

At present, the coca remains central to the indigenous culture. Besides its use as a stimulant and in rituals, coca also has medicinal value.   While the legal production of coca is centered in the Yungas region, the Chapare area is the main

Boundary representation is not necessarily authoritative.

Panama

Venezuela

Barrancabermeja

Medellin

Colombia

Puerto Carreno

Pacific Ocean

★ BOGOTA

Cali

San Jose del Guaviare

Florencia

Mitu

Ecuador

Amazon

Tumbes

Iquitos

Brazil

Rio Huallaga

Rio Marañon

Rio Ucayali

Santa Lucia

Upper Huallaga

Trujillo

Tingo Maria

Aguaytia

Peru

Apurimac

Pacific Ocean

LIMA ★

Ayacucho

Cusco

Bolivia

Puno

Tacna

★ LA PAZ

Cochabamba

Santa Cruz

Chile

Sucre

Density of coca growing areas

High   Medium   Low

0   200   400 Kilometers

0   200   400 Miles

center of illegal cultivation. During the 1960's and at the beginning of the 1970's, the government of Bolivia encouraged its Indigenous peoples to migrate to the Chapare area, with the intention of extending the agricultural frontier.

The Unites States Government was an active participant in these programs, financing the construction of a highway in 1971. This road facilitated the penetration of the area by the settlers and provided them easy access to the market place.

By 1981, the Chapare population had tripled since the 1960's. The government strategy for agricultural development, begun a decade before, had collapsed. This left a high-yielding and illegal alternative. Due to the lack of technical assistance, limited credit, and the aridness of the soil, and the increasing U.S. demand for cocaine, the farmers in that area began cultivating coca.

The military regimes of the 1970's and early 1980's consisted of firm allies for the producers of coca. The producers soon became financial supporters in order to help maintain the regimes in power, and therefore increase their profits. During the 1980's, amidst the collapse of the legal/formal economy, the cultivation of coca became the highest yielding and most dynamic product of the nation. Toward the middle of the decade, Bolivia's foreign debt payments had increased significantly. This, of course, made drug money all the more welcome.

For many years, Bolivia has been second only to Peru as the world's leading supplier of coca. Presently, it is producing 80,000 tons of coca leaf, or a third of the total supply. Most of the coca becomes processed into cocaine in Colombian laboratories. Nevertheless, in recent years there has been a growing amount processed in Bolivia, which causes conflict with the Colombian traffickers.

According to an advisor to President Paz Zamora, Bolivia is the Andean country whose economy is most dependent on the production and processing of coca leaf and cocaine. The illegal profits for 1987 rose to $1.5 billion. This is equivalent to 30% of the gross national product.

According to the same advisor, $600 million remain in the country. This equals the total of all legal exportation. It is no coincidence that the importance of this illegal industry has flourished in the midst of a desolate economic crisis. Bolivia is one of the poorest nations in South America, with the lowest life expectancy and the highest infant mortality rate. Moreover, at the beginning of the 1980's, its gross national product shrunk by 20%, while per capita consumption fell by a third. Unemployment had doubled, and the inflation rate was rising at levels without precedent in Latin America. The importance of tainted money became evident in the management of this macroeconomic crisis. The administration of President Paz Estensoro, upon assuming power, put in place an orthodox plan of austerity in 1985. The currency was devalued by 95%. Gas taxes went up by 1000%. All restrictions on imports and exports were lifted and all government subsidies ceased. By the same token, the plan facilitated the entry of illegal capital into the economy. Moreover, it was prohibited by law to investigate the source of any fortune amassed within the country, and there was a general amnesty declared for repatriated capital. At the same time, the requirements for selling foreign currency to the Central Bank were deregulated.

In this manner, the economic adjustment was weathered through the economies of cocaine and coca. International reserves began to increase, due in part to the drug money. This permitted the stability of the national currency and diminished inflationary pressure. In addition, this illegal industry absorbed the economy's displaced labor force. This lessened the social pressures, for as the official unemployment rate went up, the labor force employed at Chapare also grew.

According to estimates, some 300,000 people in Bolivia are directly dependent on the commerce of cocaine. This number constitutes one fifth of the economically active population. The president himself has used this statistic in attracting international funding for eradication programs for illegal cultivation.

The Bolivian government instituted a volunteer program of eradication by compensating the farmer for each hector in which coca leaf was eliminated. The government understood that the illegal crop was necessary for the survival of these farmers. The plan met with success as prices fell during the first half of 1990. However, his success was due to the fight against Colombian traffickers following Luis Carlos Galán's assassination. Therefore, as the drug traffic was renewed, and in turn, the price of coca leaf rose, the farmers reverted once again to planting coca in the absence of competitive economic options. This plan again demonstrates that no strategy will meet with success unless there is an alternative option of comparable yield for the farmers.

ECUADOR

Which is the Andean country with the smallest role in producing coca and cocaine? The first Ecuadorian cultivation of coca did not appear until 1984. This occurred not far from the Colombian town of Utumayo, in the Ecuadorian province of Nato. Of course, this proximity to Colombian territory is no coincidence. The emergence of the first harvested crops are a result of an offensive taken by then governor of Colombia, immediately after the assassination of Minister Rodrigo Lara Bonilla in 1984.

Due to this event, the Colombian traffickers sought sanctuary in light of the government's offensive. They then relocated some of their activities to the south. This hypothesis infers that Ecuadorian nationals were not the ones who had surrendered Ecuadorian territory to this high-yielding business. However, it is clear that if the growth of these cultivated areas in subsequent years is observed, Ecuadorian participation will clearly be present, along with that of their Colombian counterparts.

Ecuador first appears in international coca production statistics in 1986, with 2% of the total production. In years since then, it has never surpassed 1%. With coca production being such a high yielding business, it is difficult to understand why the Ecuadorians have not increased their production, especially if they were in fact in control of the cultivation in their country. The only sensible explanation that can be given is that the Ecuadorian cultivation is controlled by foreign traffickers (probably Colombian) who revert to production in those areas only when they are reaching serious limits in their own areas of cultivation. In one way or another, it is certain that the role Ecuador plays in the global coca production is a minor one. Nevertheless, the country is located at a strategic point between the origin of the raw material and the refined product; that is, Ecuador is directly between Peru, the largest grower of coca, and Colombia, the largest producer of cocaine. This scenario – Ecuador's geo-logistical importance – has transformed this nation into a provider of chemicals used in the processing of cocaine and into a facilitator of money laundering. The expansion of the chemical-producing industry in Ecuador has been notable. In the first half of 1989, the chemical and plastic sectors increased by 30%. This clearly represented a divergent tendency when compared to the gross national product or any other economic sector. Moreover, the importation of legal chemicals has significantly increased beyond the needs of the country. In addition, through intelligence surveillance, constant shipments of ether and acetone have been detected. These are essential elements in the transformation of the cocaine base into chlorohydrated cocaine.

Andean Region
Coca Cultivation and Leaf Production

	1991	1992	1993	1994	1995
Net cultivation	**206,200**	**211,700**	**195,700**	**201,700**	**214,800**
(hectares)					
Peru	120,800	129,100	108,800	108,600	115,300
Bolivia	47,900	45,500	47,200	48,100	48,600
Colombia	37,500	37,100	39,700	45,000	50,900
Potential leaf production	**317,700**	**329,100**	**273,700**	**291,200**	**309,400**
(metric tons)					
Peru	209,700	219,200	157,600	165,400	183,600
Bolivia	78,000	80,300	84,400	89,800	85,000
Colombia	30,000	29,600	31,700	36,000	40,800
Potential cocaine	**805**	**835**	**715**	**760**	**780**
(metric tons)					
Peru	525	550	410	435	460
Bolivia	220	225	240	255	240
Colombia	60	60	65	70	80

Production in **Peru** jumped in 1995 because the extensive new fields planted in 1993 reached maturity. Farmers continued to plant new fields in the Upper Huallaga Valley, Aguaytia, and Apurimac growing areas while further cultivation abandonment was detected in the northern Huallaga Valley. In 1995, **Bolivia's** eradication program held cultivation near 1994 levels, and the destruction of mature coca resulted in a significant drop in potential leaf production. **Colombia's** farmers continued to expand cultivation, particularly in southern Guaviare, Putumayo and Caqueta growing areas resulting in an overall increase even with an active eradication program. Bolivia and Peru production estimates reflect new yields and cocaine processing efficiencies resulting from USG research over the last few years.

In terms of money laundering, taking into account various sources, it is estimated that profits from this enterprise probably reached $400 million to $1,000 million in 1989. With regard to the reliability of these figures, it is worth noting that the higher figure was mentioned by the president of the fiscal council and former Minister of Finance, Alberto Tahik.

Other sources from the U.S. have estimated that the amount of money laundered annually between 1980 and 1985 is between $200 million to $500 million. Using the conservative number of $400 million, it can be concluded that the impact of the illegal economy on Ecuador is impressive. This conservative number would correspond to 20% of all exports, including petroleum. This would indicate a high potential for increased aggregate demand and incentive for production (of cocaine). What is not known, however, is what fraction of the resources remain in the country. Since Ecuador plays a different role than that of Peru, Bolivia or Colombia, as a center for money laundering, it is assumed that a good portion of the funds are funneled back into the international finance system once they are laundered.

Taking this factor into consideration, some analysts have lowered their estimates of resources from drug trafficking to between 100 million and 150 million dollars (5-8% of total exports). Nonetheless, this is quite a considerable amount for a country that scarcely participates in the world production of cocaine. Most of the laundered money seems to come from Colombia.

A notable increase in tourists to this country during the second half of the 1980's is a reason for supporting this hypothesis. That is, these tourists injected dollars into the economy, not pesos as they did before. In addition, the dollar can be purchased most cheaply within Ecuador in the town of Tuncán, which sits along the border with Colombia.

The productive sectors that lend themselves to money laundering are agriculture, and to a lesser extent, the mining industry. The acquisition of land by Colombians has been particularly noticeable in the areas of Santo Domingo de los Colorados, the province of Pichincha, and the province of Los Ríos. The magnitude of this phenomenon is so great in the Santo Domingo de los Colorados area that this region is sarcastically called "Santo Domingo de los Colombianos" (The Colombians' Santo Domingo). Indeed, Colombians have purchased, and at exorbitant prices, more than one third of the land in this region.

In the midst of this situation, the attitude which the government has taken is basically one of repression toward small traffickers and some consumers, without considering the economic and social complexities of the problem. Perhaps the reason is that an income of 200 to 400 million dollars per year translates into a considerable base for the Ecuadorian economy.

III

THE CUBAN CONNECTION

Since 1931, the Republic of Cuba has been a signatory of the Convention on Narcotics, signed during the Second International Conference on Opium. For over half a century, Cuba has subscribed to the conventions elaborated therein with the goal of limiting the use, the production and the illegal trafficking of drugs. In 1973, Cuba adhered to the Convention to limit the production of psychotropic substances, as it did in the Protocol of Paris, which updated this Convention. Cuba had signed similar agreements at the 1961 Convention on Narcotics, and at the 1971 United Nations Convention on Narcotics and Psychotropic Substances.

Nevertheless, at the beginning of the 1960's, the phenomenon of drug trafficking took root on the island and was met by the indifference of high government officials that had arisen from the Castro Revolution of 1959. Seemingly forgotten was Disposition Number 6, dated October 7, 1958, wherein the head of the Revolution, Dr. Fidel Castro Ruiz, prior to his triumphant entrance to Havana, expressed:

It is the responsibility and objective of the Revolutionary Movement and this Administration to eliminate totally the illicit use of drugs which in reality, makes impossible any true physical, mental and economic development of the Cuban people. In view of this, the Rebel Tribunals of Judges and Auditors, as well as the police and military authorities, because of the great responsibilities of their positions, are called upon to give special attention to this Disposition, and to act severely in all cases that come to their attention and fall under their jurisdiction in order to totally eradicate such a dangerous public threat.

From October 1970 to March 1981, the forces of the Border Guard of the Republic of Cuba registered 83 violations to Cuban air space and coastal waters. They captured 328 drug traffickers. The amount of drugs seized in this period totaled 250 tons of marijuana, 1 ton of cocaine, 735,000 pills of Quaalude and 147,000 pills of Dialudid.

In spite of the revolutionary slogans and subscribed agreements, various high members of the Cuban government had become involved in drug trafficking and had suffered no consequential effects. In November, 1982, the District Attorney of Miami accused Cuban officials of smuggling cocaine into the U.S. from Cuba. According to the District Attorney's Office, a Colombian drug trafficker named Jaime Guillot-Lara had sent drugs from Colombia to Cuba and had them retrieved by boats south of Florida in order to transport them to North American territory. Included among the documents obtained in order to prove the illegality of Guillot-Lara's activities was a record documenting that 1.2 million kilos of marijuana and 40 kilos of cocaine had been smuggled by way of Cuba.

Witnesses brought forth to testify against Guillot-Lara in Miami declared that Fernando Ravelo, the Cuban ambassador to Colombia at the time, had petitioned for an official green light from Havana for all the drug shipments to Cuba. The smugglers used the code pass "Viviana" to alert the Cuban Navy when the drug-ladened vessels were approaching.

Accusations fell on the Cuban Vice Admiral Aldo Santamaria, who was in charge of supervising, protecting and refueling the Colombian drug boats. Nevertheless, this vice admiral was never charged in Cuba; in fact, Fidel Castro alleged that these types of judgments and imputations were part of a new imperialist slander campaign.

Fidel Castro and the Colombian drug traffickers had maintained close contact for quite a long time for political convenience. In fact, in the late 1970's, the Cuban leader had instructed his intelligence services to penetrate the drug cartels in order to obtain up-to-date information on what was fast becoming one of the most powerful political and economic forces in Latin America.

During the early 1980's, Castro used his contacts with the Medellin Cartel to send arms via plane to the M19 guerrilla group in Colombia. The airplanes flew over Cuban air space without anyone asking questions and picked up arms on makeshift landing strips on various islands throughout the Caribbean and at times in Cuba itself.

NORIEGA

The ties between the Cuban government and the Colombian drug traffickers became evident in 1984, when Fidel Castro stepped in to resolve a 4.6 million dollar dispute between General Noriega and the Medellin Cartel. The Cartel threatened to kill Noriega if he didn't return the money that they had paid to protect an enormous cocaine laboratory in Panama that the DEA had destroyed. Castro convinced his Panamanian counterpart to reach a compromise.

One morning in June, 1986, an exiled Cuban named Reinaldo Ruiz entered an office of the Cuban government in Panama City to ask for an exit permission for his niece to leave

Cuba. This modest event set in motion the biggest political scandal involving drug trafficking in the history of the Cuban Revolution.

Reinaldo Ruiz had fled Cuba in 1962, three years after the revolution, to settle in the city of Miami. He began working in food retail stores until 1974 when he was arrested at the Los Angeles airport for attempting to smuggle 15,411 Puerto Rican lottery tickets into the U.S. He had bought the tickets with $90,000 and planned to double his money since the lottery was illegal in California at that time. He was found guilty and after two years in prision, was freed on a bond of $500. At that point, Ruiz relocated to a Los Angeles suburb where he accumulated a small fortune selling real estate. With this capital, Ruiz started a travel agency in Panama and began taking advantage of the rich profits of drug trafficking that his new Colombian wife carried out. Moreover, Ruiz found yet another way of rapidly increasing his profits: the sale of Panamanian visas to Cubans who wanted to flee Fidel Castro's island.

One morning in June, 1986, Ruiz encountered a problem with respect to a Cuban visa that his travel agency could not solve. In this case his objective was to get his niece out of Cuba, but there was an obstacle that seemed almost insurmountable. Cuba denied exit visas to persons under the age of 21, maintaining that they should pay back with their work the free education they had received from the communist system. Reinaldo Ruiz needed special authorization and he knew he could obtain it. The only question was how much they would charge him. Feeling confident, Ruiz went to a building near central Panama City where *Interconsult*, a Cuban government enterprise was headquartered. Interconsult's business was to solve problems involving immigration. Ruiz entered and asked to speak with the manager. Minutes later, Reinaldo Ruiz was surprised to find that the manager of the enterprise was none other than his cousin Miguel Ruiz Poo.

THE MC DEPARTMENT

Reinaldo and Miguel celebrated their unexpected reunion and immediately solved the small problem of the visa, beginning to discuss matters of greater importance to both of them. Miguel Ruiz Poo began telling in great detail the true purpose of his business. It was, actually, an organization operating under the auspices of the Ministry of the Interior of Cuba, whose true objective was to procure foreign currency and articles which could not be obtained due to the American embargo. The organization was known as the MC Department, its initials standing for "convertible money."

One of the propositions first suggested by Ruiz Poo to his cousin Reinaldo Ruiz consisted of Reinaldo buying computers in the U.S. and bringing them to the island by way of Panama. They would begin with a test run of a shipment of IBM computers and some cable television decoder boxes.

In a few weeks, both cousins had created a lucrative business in contraband. To transport the electronics, they had been able, with the MC Department's assistance, to contract captains of vessels willing to defy the U.S. embargo.

These navigators, known as *lancheros,* who for the most part were exiled Cubans, were able to come and go undetected by the U. S. Coast Guard. The only kind of lancheros capable of accomplishing these missions, were the drug smugglers, since no one else knew the Florida Straits as well as they did.

Everything was working perfectly well, and soon they realized there was a new and highly lucrative enterprise they could exploit: the trafficking of cocaine. So, when Reinaldo Ruiz proposed this kind of business, his cousin was not the least bit offended. They knew this was the chance of a lifetime to make some serious money. However, Ruiz Poo had to arrange a meeting and confer with his superiors at the Ministry of the Interior.

Ruiz Poo's superior at the Ministry of the Interior in Cuba was Major Padrón Trujillo, who went to visit Panama in August, 1986. The three men met for lunch and Reinaldo Ruiz explained the details of the plan. Ruiz's wife had a contact with the brother of Pablo Escobar, the head of the Medellin Cartel, and he would supply the cocaine.

Two of Ruiz's planes, a Cesna 401 and a twin engine Piper, would transport the cocaine from Colombian territory to Cuba. Once there, the cocaine would be deposited on speed boats that would take it to the Florida coast. The most important aspect for Ruiz, was that the Cubans authorize the landing of the planes on the island and that the merchandise remained there only a few hours before it was picked up by the boats.

Major Padrón was visibly in favor of the operation, but he knew that he did not have the rank to guarantee drug flights over Cuban air space. Although Fidel Castro himself authorized flights over Cuban air space carrying Colombian cocaine in exchange for the drug smugglers taking arms on their return for the M19 guerrillas, for Major Padrón to authorize the arrivals and the storing of narcotics on Cuban territory exceeded his power. He would have to consult with the highest in command in Havana.

In November, 1986, the Ruiz cousins left Panama for Cuba on a regular flight on Compañía Aérea Cubana de Aviación. They were to meet with one of the highest officials of the Ministry of the Interior to discuss the plan. Upon their arrival, they were escorted to an office on 66th Street and were met there by Colonel Antonio "Tony" De La Guardia, who was the top official of the MC Department. Tony immediately embraced the business of drugs, and Reinaldo Ruiz didn't bother to ask if the operation had to be approved by a higher command; after all, De La Guardia was a colonel and they were speaking in his office of the Ministry of the Interior.

PANAMANIAN ENTERPRISES

De La Guardia was no ordinary official. He was a member of the elite of the Ministry of the Interior, a man who had acquired an enormous amount of economic and political power during the 1980s. At the helm of MC, the colonel had *carte blanche* to travel wherever he wanted when he wanted, and to organize clandestine companies throughout the globe.

He was a kind of super secret agent who spent a good part of his time abroad. He would establish business firms in Panama, or orchestrate agreements in Mexico to sell Cuban cigars in the U.S.; or he would travel throughout eastern Europe in order to acquire arms whose destinations would be the various pro-Cuban guerrillas in Latin America. This colonel, besides being one of the elite of the secret agents, was one of the few under Fidel Castro's protection.

CONTACTS

The Cuban leader had discovered De La Guardia in 1961, two years after the Revolution, during a canoe regatta that took place annually at Varadero Beach. Castro was there to inaugurate the regatta and to award prizes. The winners turned out to be the De La Guardia twin brothers, and so they were invited to a party to celebrate their triumph.

At the celebration, Fidel learned that both brothers had attended the University of Havana, although when the Revolution erupted, both of them had left the Island, to live in the U.S. No sooner had Castro's men begun their victorious entrance to Havana in January, 1959, than the brothers left Florida and returned to Cuba.

During the social and sporting events of 1961, the brothers Tony and Patricio De La Guardia gained Castro's favor. The revolutionary incorporated them into the troops of the Ministry of the Interior to combat the counter-revolutionaries that remained. In a few months they became captains and earned a reputation for their audacity on the battlefield.

In 1962, during the Soviet missile crisis, Castro sent Tony De La Guardia on a special mission to New York. The young official traveled as part of the delegation that accompanied the Minister of Foreign Affairs at that time, Raúl Roa, to the United Nations.[15]

In 1971, after the election of the Chilean leftist President Salvador Allende,[16] Tony De La Guardia headed the first contingency of special Cuban troops sent to provide military advice and support to the United Popular Government of Chile.

In 1975, Tony De La Guardia traveled to Switzerland carrying $60 million, ransom money that the Argentine guerrillas "Montoneros" had pocketed for the kidnapping of the industrial impresarios Jorge and Juan Born.[17]   In 1978, already the top officer of the Special Forces of the Ministry of the Interior, De La Guardia commanded the group of military advisers that participated in the war in Nicaragua. De La Guardia also joined the Sandinistas in the taking of the presidential palace of President Anastasio Somoza.

In January, 1985, Fidel Castro honored De La Guardia with the rank of Colonel and put him in charge of the MC Department under the Ministry of the Interior. Those were difficult times in Cuba. The Reagan Administration had

---

[15] It is speculated that Tony De La Guardia had the mission of planting a bomb in the United Nations. Rafael del Pino, *Proa a la Libertad* (Ed. Planeta).

[16] Salvador Allende assumed the presidency of the Republic of Chile in 1970, and was ousted in 1973.

[17] Mario Firmenich, leader of the Montoneros guerrillas in Argentina, stated that the rescue money was later deposited in the National Bank of Cuba in Havana. Guy Gugliotta, "The Curious Case of the Guerrilla Gold" in *The Miami Herald*, November 11, 1989.

stiffened the trade embargo and had blocked all political contacts with the island. Cuba desperately needed to increase its exports and to import technology from the West. For that reason De La Guardia's mission was to create a network abroad, of well-disguised business entities that would carry out transactions without anyone suspecting Castro's behind-the-scenes involvement.

After a few months on his mission, the colonel established excellent contacts with the banking and business underworld in Panama. Moreover, a great many of his business associates were well connected to drug trafficking.

This is why, when he met with Reinaldo Ruiz and Major Padrón, De La Guardia was so quick to accept and personally guarantee the proposed transportation of cocaine.

On April 10, 1987, Reinaldo Ruiz launched his first smuggling operation through Cuba. But things did not go well. From a conceptual point of view, the plan was almost perfect. Two pilots were to fly from Fort Lauderdale (U.S.) to Colombia, and from there transport 300 kilos of cocaine, landing them at the beach at Varadero. The cargo, hidden in cartons of Marlboro cigarettes, would be picked up by Ruiz's speed boats and taken quickly to the coastline of Miami. The Cesna would then return, empty and "clean," to Fort Lauderdale International Airport on the Florida peninsula.

The operation started off fine. As the smugglers entered Cuban air space they used the pre-established codes. Then they heard strong radio interference coming from a Cuban MIG that had come out to meet them. The military plane escorted the Cesna to Varadero where they landed without incident; after all, agents of the Ministry of the Interior were there awaiting their arrival. They unloaded the cartons and hid them in sheds belonging to the Cuban Border Guard. A few hours later, the speedboat "Flérida" arrived and they began loading the drugs. But after that, everything went wrong.

The crew of the Flérida were to set for the high seas and load the cargo onto another boat. However, due to bad weather the other boat never showed up. The crew of the Flérida then decided to continue the journey until they reached the southern coastline of Florida. But a U.S. Coast Guard vessel sighted the drug smugglers navigating along the southern Florida keys. The Coast Guard vessel immediately gave the order to board and inspect the Flérida. Since the boat under suspicion did not heed the order, the Coast Guard chased it at full speed. The smugglers frantically began to throw the cartons of cocaine overboard, leaving in their wake a trail of white foam. By the time the patrol had overtaken them, the smugglers had dumped 206 kilos of cocaine. All were arrested, with 94 kilos of cocaine still on board.

Meanwhile, a foolish mistake ruined the pilots' safe landing in the U.S. After sending a radio dispatch to the U.S. air traffic controllers, stating that they had experienced technical difficulties and had had to touch down in Cuba, the pilots tried to land at Fort Lauderdale International Airport, their point of origin. The U.S. Customs officials immediately suspected something was wrong: pilots flying out of the U.S. are aware, or are so notified in Cuba, that upon leaving Cuba and returning to the U.S. they can only land at Miami International Airport, where upon arrival, they will be subjected to security procedures. These pilots, who only used to fly from Colombia to Panama, were not familiar with these special regulations.

The Customs officials were waiting for the plane on the runway and examined it in detail. Nothing was to be found but the names of the pilots and the plane's registration in Reinaldo Ruiz's name. These individuals were all registered with the DEA and were tracked from that point on.

Rienaldo Ruiz and Antonio De La Guardia did not become intimidated by their initial failure at trafficking cocaine, nor did they lose much time in planning a new operation. Their team had committed several errors but they could learn from them. The most important thing was that the Ministry of the Interior had adhered to the plan and would keep on cooperating.

FROM SOUTHEAST ASIA TO FLORIDA

Planning the second operation was a bit more complicated. The Colombian sources did not want to supply a new cargo of cocaine to a group they considered amateurs. After several weeks of negotiating, on May 1, 1987, Reinaldo Ruiz was able to get an important shipment of cocaine supplied by a group of Colombians from within the lower ranks of the cartels. For this operation, Ruiz contracted a new pilot named Hu Chang. Chang was an ex-combat pilot from the Nationalist China's Air Force, and owner of a small aviation company called Chang International which operated out of the Miami Airport. What Ruiz did not know was that Chang was a regular informer for the DEA.

Hu Chang was legendary for those who knew of his past. He had been a mercenary in every war that had erupted in Southeast Asia. For instance, he had been contracted as a pilot by the CIA during the Vietnam War. Chang sought political asylum in 1981 because he had already been tried in Taiwan for espionage on behalf of Mainland China. Chang opted to become an informant for the DEA after a long, drawn out series of negotiations with the Immigration and Naturalization Service.

The DEA plan was to have Chang continue with the preparations up to the day of the flight. At that time, Ruiz and his accomplices would be arrested on the runway before they departed the Miami Airport, to be charged with conspiracy to traffic cocaine.

May 9, 1987, was to be the grand day. Chang and Ruiz started the motors and took the plane to the runway, but upon discovering a mechanical problem, they decided to postpone the flight. At one side of the runway was a heavily armed team of DEA men who were stunned to see the plane return to hangar. After waiting for almost three hours, the DEA agents canceled the operation, being convinced that the smugglers had postponed the flight at least until the following day.

Ruiz, however, insisted on repairing the plane immediately and after a few hours they were once again on the runway. Chang was expecting the agents to arrest them when they attempted to take off, but no one was there. A few moments later they were in the air heading toward Colombia to pick up a shipment of cocaine. Chang did not know if the DEA had changed plans or if the agents had failed in executing the operation.

Both men loaded the 400 kilos of cocaine and flew to Cuba without incident. They landed at Varadero and just as before, the cocaine was stored in a shed belonging to the Cuban Border Guard, to be taken later to two fast speed boats that would leave for Florida. The cocaine arrived in Miami two days later, just as they had planned.

Reinaldo Ruiz owed Chang payment of $10,000 for his services, and on July 3, 1987, Ruiz went to the pilot's offices to make good on his debt. Ruiz was very pleased and wanted Chang to get ready to make weekly flights in the future. Upon learning of the payment, several agents concurred on confiscating the money, but Chang protested: "I risked my life on this flight and you did nothing. You have to let me keep part of it."

As Ruiz began meeting with the Chinese pilot on a regular basis to organize the shipments, the DEA installed hidden video cameras behind Chang's desk. Chang could activate the cameras and tape recorders by pressing a button on his telephone, the one next to the one used to page his secretary. Further visits were kept on file. At last there was solid evidence that linked Reinaldo Ruiz, Antonio De La Guardia, the Ministry of the Interior of Cuba, senior Cuban generals, important Panamanian officials and Colombian smugglers to the business of drug trafficking.

The recordings revealed Reinaldo Ruiz boasting of his exploits, while Chang pretended to be astonished in the presence of a man who became more and more boastful:

"If you have a solid agreement, they won't detain you. I have an agreement with the top flight commander of the fighter pilots in the Cuban Air Force over there . . ."

"When we flew, they were there. I swear it. They asked me if I needed an escort. Can you imagine? Forget it man! Over there you can feel safe, because we are protected."

"You know what? You know what we have? Are you going to believe me if I tell you? You know those big military ships, the ones that are equipped with radar and all that? We have two torpedo boats! . . .And they can run up and down the entire American coast, and they can tell us 'go over here' or 'go over there!'. . ."

"I'm going to let you know something and I'm not lying. I have flown to places in Cuba that nobody knows about. I'm talking about military airports. I'm talking about camouflaged MIG 20 jets. Do you understand ? . . . They'll always help us."

"We have to keep inside Cuban waters and air space because there we are protected. There, one can work freely . . ."

"Fidel doesn't see the drugs, but he knows everything. And if somebody accuses him of drug trafficking, who can prove it? They can't produce one damn bit of evidence! Look, you can accuse Cuba of anything you want, but if he doesn't admit it, what's the point? What can they prove? Not a thing, my friend, not one thing!"

"We're all making millions and nobody can complain. Fidel is making more than ever. Castro knows how to take care of business! He's not messing around . . . If the money is right,

*why fuck around with dumb stuff?   He must be doing
something right to be living like a Duke . . ."*

*"We do our part and put ourselves on the line.   Everything
turns out all right, but we don't forget Fidel's money.   You
mustn't forget to make a deposit to Fidel's desk drawer..."*

On February 28, 1988, Reinaldo Ruiz arrived from Mexico
City at the Omar Trujillo Airport in Panama.   After getting
through immigration and customs controls, Ruiz's plane was
boarded by a lieutenant of the Panamanian Defense Force.   The
officer informed him that he had a warrant for his arrest for
drug trafficking.   But Ruiz was not worried and decided not to
resist.   He went with the officer to the headquarters of the
secret police of the Noriega regime.   When they arrived, he was
surprised that his photograph and fingerprints were taken like
a   common   criminal.   He   was   furious,   and   despite   the
consequences, asked to call Havana and speak to Colonel Tony
De La Guardia in order to clear things up.   From the Ministry
of the Interior came the response that the Colonel could not
help him, that he had other more important matters to attend.

Early the next day, he was taken to the airport where DEA
agents were waiting to take him to Miami.   Just a few weeks
had passed since a U.S. court had accused General Noriega of
drug trafficking.   The Panamanian government, desiring to
clean up its image, decided to sacrifice Ruiz since he was not a
part of the inner circle of Panamanian drug traffickers and he
posed no threat to Noriega.

On March 1, 1988, The Panamanians and DEA agents
arrested 15 persons that were taken to the U.S. and accused of
smuggling cocaine into the U.S., Haiti, and the islands of Turks
and Caicos.   On March 3, Fidel Castro was informed of these
events and advised his officials that, for a while, Colombian
cocaine was not to be allowed to touch Cuban soil.

A few days later, the entire world would begin learning of
the ties between Castro and his revolutionaries with drug
trafficking.   *The Miami Herald*'s editorial on March 10, 1988,

revealed part of the recorded conversations between Ruiz and Chang, stating that the earnings from drug trafficking had gone to "Fidel's desk drawer." Meanwhile, Tony De La Guardia received information that Ruiz, along with the others that were arrested, were ready to plead guilty and cooperate with the U.S. authorities in order to have their sentences reduced. Ruiz in particular would testify of the Cuban Minister of the Interior's role in the trafficking of cocaine. Ruiz knew that Tony De La Guardia represented a valuable prize for the U.S., and if he confessed all that he knew and had seen, he would be compensated with a major reduction in his sentence.

Fidel Castro became aware of the impending crisis, and for that reason put his own brother Raúl Castro, Minister of the FAR (Revolutionary Army) in charge of initiating a vigorous investigation. The objective was none other than to "clean the house" and to prove the innocence of not only Fidel, but of the entire Revolution.

Toward the end of 1988, tension was extremely high between the military and the Ministry of the Interior. The military contingent of the FAR, complained openly that the officials of the Ministry of the Interior were brazen in showing off their privileges. Both sides accused the other of corruption and inefficiency.[18]

Quite differently from their more austere military colleagues, who did not travel abroad, nor deal in foreign currency, the officials of the Ministry of the Interior had access to most of the products from the West that they desired. Moreover, within the Ministry itself, the MC Department enjoyed a certain autonomy. Due to its secretive nature, the

---

[18] For further information on tension between the military and the Ministry of the Interior, see: Rafael Fermoselle, *Cuban Leadership After Castro: Biographies of Cuba's Top Generals* (Miami: Ediciones Universal, 1988).

MC Department was not subject to any kind of audit. On the books, it operated with a budget of $70,000 annually, but everyone was aware that the budget was nothing more than a symbolic number.

The MC Department had several offices in Panama. It operated with hundreds of companies throughout the globe and generated millions in foreign currency. The operation had converted the Ministry of the Interior into one of the most important powers within the Cuban system.

Raúl Castro ordered his intelligence services to work day and night in their investigation of cocaine trafficking. He needed a weapon against his adversaries, and was determined to prove that the Ministry of the Interior was solely responsible for the clumsy drug operations.

During the investigation, the Cuban leader's brother came upon evidence that linked Antonio De La Guardia to General of Division Arnaldo Ochoa. Although Raúl Castro could verify a friendship and business relationship between the two, and that some of Ochoa's men had collaborated with the Ministry of the Interior in its operations, Raúl Castro did not have anything solid against him. At the same time, Raúl Castro had to decide whether to promote Ochoa to Commander of the powerful Western Army, which included command over the Navy and Air Force of that region as well.

GENERAL OCHOA

Arnaldo Ochoa had joined Fidel Castro's troops at a very early age. He was one of the first rebels to occupy the Cuban city of Santa Clara and he participated in all the important battles that made the Revolutionary Forces victorious on January 1, 1959. Once Castro assumed power, Ochoa became captain in the new Revolutionary Army and fought against the exiled force that was backed by the CIA in the Bay of Pigs

Invasion in 1961. During the following years he continued to fight the contra revolutionary guerrillas.

In 1977, he was promoted to Commander of the troops of Ethiopians, Cubans, Poles, Hungarians and East Germans that made up the forces in Angola. He also organized the Armed Forces of Granada and provided military training for the armies of South Yemen, Syria, Vietnam, Libya, Afghanistan, Iraq, and Laos. In 1983 he was sent to Nicaragua as a military advisor to the Sandinista regime and collaborated with their forces to repel the U.S.-backed Contras.

In recognition of Ochoa's deeds and achievements for the Castro Revolution, in 1984, The Cuban regime bestowed on him one of the highest honorary titles ever given: the Order of Hero of the Republic of Cuba, and the Order of Máximo Gómez of the First Degree. The decrees, numbers 250 and 251 of January, 1984, were published in *Grama*,[19] state: "The life of comrade Ochoa Sánchez is a living example of those qualities and merits in men of humble origin...that cultivate the authentic traits of modesty and sincerity, and who enjoy the respect and admiration of the masses." The statement added that his career served as " a stimulus for all soldiers."

Besides the medals, there was another powerful reason that the rest of the generals in Cuba treated Ochoa with the greatest respect. He was one of a few Cubans who could speak to Fidel casually, so much so that he would kid him and pester him about the way he (Fidel) dressed. That alone stood for more than any rank or office.

Just like other troop commanders, Arnaldo Ochoa would make business deals that would help finance his military campaigns and improve the conditions of his troops. Ochoa's predecessors in Angola had increased their armies' budgets by exporting diamonds, marble, quartz, and other products, and Ochoa followed suit as well. He began using his worldwide

---

[19] The official newspaper of the Communist Party of Cuba.

contacts to make lucrative arms deals. In 1987, he closed a deal with the Nicaraguan Sandinistas to sell 100 German M79 grenade launchers and 12,000 projectiles for $161,000. In 1988, he again took advantage of his contacts in the international arms market to buy 100 military radios for the Angolan Army for the sum of $595,000. He also became involved in organizing various operations in which the Cuban Air Force transported sugar to Angola. Sugar was one of the few products Cuba had in abundance. For a considerable time, Ochoa obtained $17,000 a month from these sugar sales.

At one point, Arnaldo Ochoa, through one of his closest confidants, Captain Martínez Valdéz, approached Colonel Antonio De La Guardia, a person that was in an excellent position to help him sell his products abroad.

Undoubtedly, Ochoa had become a man of great influence, with a command of 300,000 soldiers that would follow and support him. In Raúl Castro's estimation, the general had become too popular a celebrity and needed to be stopped. Moreover, Arnaldo Ochoa was too greatly influenced by the Soviet officers, the *"perestroikos"* whom he had come to know in Angola and the Soviet Union. For that reason, the brother of the Cuban leader understood that in some way or another Ochoa had to be removed from Cuban life, especially considering Ochoa's political skepticism that would undermine the Revolutionary enthusiasm of the Armed Forces of Cuba.

The nail that sealed the coffin presented itself in 1989. The U.S. authorities had so much information on the collaboration between the Cuban government and the Colombian drug traffickers, that they planned a spectacular strike: to arrest the Minister of the Interior of Cuba, Division General José Abrantes.

The U.S. Customs Service, with the help of the Department of Defense Intelligence Agency, the DEA, and the District Attorney's Office of Southern Florida, developed a plan designed to entrap José Abrantes during a meeting with cocaine traffickers. The meeting was to take place at sea somewhere between the Bahamas and Cuba. Once there, he would be detained and brought to the U.S. to face charges of drug trafficking. The plan was dubbed *Operation Greyhound*.[20]

The District Attorney's Office would coordinate the task force. U.S. Customs and the DEA would be in charge of the covert operation. Meanwhile, the Department of Defense Intelligence Agency would provide the intelligence necessary to coordinate the participation of the U.S. Navy and Air Force in case the operation should turn into a pitched battle with the gun boats that would surely escort José Abrantes.

The man who was to lure the Minister of the Interior of Cuba to the meeting at sea was convicted drug trafficker Gustavo Fernández, an ex-CIA collaborator who had been given a sentence of 50 years for smuggling 300 tons of Marijuana. Fernández was an exiled Cuban, who, in spite of being imprisoned, kept strong ties with former partners on the island of Cuba. On May 13, 1989, he was released from the prison at Okeechobee, Florida, in order to carry out Operation Greyhound.

Fernández set himself up in a house in the Florida Keys, south of Miami. He was allowed to wander through the streets from 8 a.m. to 5 p.m., while being watched by Customs agents. As time went on he demanded greater freedom, maintaining that he couldn't be very convincing as a drug smuggler keeping those hours. His demands were agreed upon and gradually he was allowed to be more independent. He was given a brand new Lincoln Continental, a large motor boat, $5,000 a month and a 45 caliber pistol.

According to the plan, Fernández was to offer U.S. military secrets to the Cuban government. One agent had given him classified documents with the Department of

---

[20] See: Carl Hiassen of *The Miami Herald*, who cites Lucy Morgan from *The St. Petersburg Times*, August 23, 1989.

Defense letterhead containing information regarding recognizance satellites over Cuba. These satellites had the capacity to take infrared photographs that penetrated the foliage of the Cuban forests. The information was legitimate and, although not very detailed nor worthy, it was sufficient to entice the Cubans. In exchange, the Cuban government was to authorize Fernández to land a plane loaded with 1,500 kilos of Colombian cocaine. Fernández showed his concern for his safety when demanded that Minister Abrantes himself be present at the meeting to seal the pact.

However, in the end Fernández turned out to be more shrewd than any of his associates in this deal. On the morning of June 2, 1989, he took his boat loaded with his luxurious automobile and headed for the high seas. The ex-convict arrived on the Cuban coast where he remains living a privileged life-style. He had revealed the plan to Castro's men in exchange for a "good life." The U.S. government cloaked Operation Greyhound in a veil of silence. All of the information was immediately classified as confidential.

Fidel Castro and his brother Raúl had enough intelligence information to come up with the appropriate measures. They both understood that the drug problem would attract major problems to the island. The entire situation had to be resolved as soon as possible with a political decision. On June 12, 1989, Fidel and Raúl met for several hours. This was the end for Antonio De La Guardia, Arnaldo Ochoa and the rest of those involved in drug trafficking and other acts of corruption.

THE PROCESS

On June 14, 1989, 14 persons were arrested, accused of committing offenses against the country, abuse of power, and toxic drug trafficking. Those detained in this case, numbered 1/89, were:

Antonio De La Guardia	Patricio De La Guardia
Michael Ruiz Poo	Arnaldo Ochoa
Jorge Valdés	Amado Padrón
Antonio Sánchez Lima	Leonel Estévez
José Luis Pineda	Eduardo Díaz Izquierdo
Alexis Lago	José María Abierno
Gabriel Prendes Gómez	A. Rodríguez Estupiñan

The same day, *La Grama* newspaper published a communiqué of four paragraphs that read: "We find ourselves having the distasteful duty of informing the public that the General of Division Arnaldo Ochoa Sánchez, who had received important responsibilities and honors from the Party and the Revolutionary Armed Forces (FAR), has been arrested and submitted to investigation for the serious charges of corruption and dishonest management of economic resources." It said furthermore that Ochoa had incurred "serious violations of moral and socialist laws." With respect to all the men charged, the paper confirmed that "the inexorable weight of Revolutionary justice will fall upon them."

The first judicial step constituted a summons to an Honor Court of the Revolutionary Forces to decide on the future of General of Division Arnaldo Ochoa and his men. Raúl Castro himself, Minister of the FAR, delivered the accusation report on July 1, 1989, where he stated:

> *The actions of Ochoa were concealed under the apparent devotion of his troops, who enjoyed a fine quality of life, which in reality served as a pretext to Ochoa's out-of-control desire to accumulate wealth and advance his businesses. These actions were carried forth in the face of their illicit criminality, and were performed at the cost of violating all procedures, regulations, and laws, including those of states friendly to us, as was the case*

with the diamonds and ivory contraband, and in so doing, betrayed the confidences of their governments.

Castro continued:

> *As has been revealed, Ochoa reserved his most select time for plotting and advancing, through his assistant Captain Jorge Valdés, his delirious goal of becoming a drug trafficking czar. Moreover, though not excusing from responsibility individuals already involved with drug trafficking – such as Colonel Tony De La Guardia and his men at the Ministry of the Interior of the MC Department, it is logical to assume that the climate of impunity and the ease of Ochoa's unfettered activity meant for these elements that a man of merit and prestige in walked the same road and would provide his cooperation.*

In conclusion, Castro expressed:

> *Dear citizens, we know how to deal in exemplary fashion with Arnaldo Ochoa's affront to the country and to the Revolutionary Armed Forces. On him must fall the rigor of the law. The precedent of his military career, far from being extenuating, will harshen the penalty in proportion to the honor and confidence that was bestowed upon him.*

After listening attentively to the allegations, General Ochoa was given opportunity to respond:

> *Words fail me, because not only are you and the Cuban people the ones which I have undignified, but I have also undignified myself, because today I can see the big picture and the great horror that I have committed . . . And yes, I want to tell the citizens that I betrayed the country and I tell you with all honor, treason is paid with one's life. I believe that today the court of my own conscious is harsher than any.*

In summation, he added:

First, I want to say to the members of the Court that I will maintain an attitude concordant of a General of the Armed Forces until the last consequence of my actions has been carried out. Second, I want to say to them that I do not harbor any reproach for what has been said here, since I share the opinion that all that has been said until this moment is a just and impartial assessment. I believe firmly, consciously in my guilt, and if I can yet be of assistance despite my bad example, the Revolution has me at its service; and if my penalty is execution, which of course it may be, I promise you that my last thought will be for Fidel, for the Revolution that he has given to the people.

On July 3, 1989, the 47 generals and admirals that made up the Military Honor Court met to discuss the case, and sustained:

In an exemplary manner, unparalleled in our history, our Revolution considers that the embarrassing actions of the irresponsible group that, moved by vulgarity and the profiteering end of the sweet life associated with such insane, fantastic projects, have implicated our country in drug trafficking.

The imperialist enemy is rattled. Their principal internal problem, day by day, is drugs – a cancer that erodes their consumptive society and generates each year hundreds of thousands of millions of dollars that feed the international drug traffic.

They do not know yet whether to benefit from the battle that Cuba wages, with her strict reasoning and revolutionary principles, against the same phenomenon, giving them the chance to use this episode to make infamous campaigns against our Revolution . . . The enemy is trying to take advantage of this episode, attacking the cleanest political and judicial process that can be conceived by asserting that the accused are drugged and that their confessions are mechanical. Miraculously, they have not accused us of brutally torturing them. Some hypocritical groups that claim to represent human rights are beginning to shriek, claiming a lack of just judgment, that the accused do not have guarantees for an impartial verdict, et cetera.

It is evident that the organs of United States intelligence knew fully that from 1987 airplanes with cargoes of drugs originating from Colombia were landing at Varadero airport with the complicity of Cuban officers. They knew who those officials were, since we know today that they had agents infiltrated among those which participated in these operations. Nevertheless, they did not inform the Government of Cuba, neither in an official nor confidential manner. They could have stopped the flow of drugs passing through various routes to the United States, but instead they worried much more about obtaining arguments for their campaigns against Cuba.

Arnaldo Ochoa, as well as Antonio de la Guardia and his group, exposed the country and the Revolution to fatal dangers, not only because Cuba would be presented with irrefutable evidence of these acts, but because to undermine the morals and prestige of the Revolution is to sharpen the claws of imperialism against our country and to weaken our defenses. With their irresponsible conduct, they were putting in jeopardy the fruits of the heroism, blood and sweat of so many years of struggle.

Therefore, this *Military Honor Court*, exercising the legal and regulatory powers that are conferred to it, with respect to the conduct of the *Division General Arnaldo Ochoa*, RESOLVES:

1- To propose to the Minister of The FAR and to the State Council:
a) The withdrawal of the honorable title of Hero of the Republic of Cuba and other degrees, medals and conferred decorations.

b) That the President of the State Council and of the Government and the Commander-in-Chief strip him of his rank of division general and expel him from the FAR.

c) That he be placed at the disposition of the Special Military Court to judge his crime of high treason against his country and apply to him the weight of the law in correspondence with the extreme seriousness of his offenses.

2- That political organizations and the National Assembly, given the gravity of his deeds, expel him from the Party and therefore from its Central Committee, and deprive him of his position as Deputy of the National Assembly.

On the July 6, 1989, the Special Military Tribunal began its brief consideration of Ochoa's sentence. To begin, Ochoa himself was called to testify before the Court, fulfilling his responsibility dutifully at all times:

PROSECUTOR: Ochoa, let us speak of your investments. Your idea was to support Pablo Escobar by opening a route through which he could pass drugs to the United States?

OCHOA: Yes.

PROSECUTOR: And you were not going to receive any benefit from this?

OCHOA: No. In what way could I benefit?

PROSECUTOR: That is to say, Cuba would not receive any benefits?

OCHOA: Yes. Cuba would receive all the benefits.

PROSECUTOR: What do you mean *all*?

OCHOA: Yes, he had to invest the money in Cuba.

PROSECUTOR: Then we are talking about a money laundering operation in Cuba.

OCHOA: Yes, but in reality the investments were in buildings.

PROSECUTOR: In buildings?

OCHOA: Yes, in tourism, because we wanted to make investments in the tourism industry.

PROSECUTOR: What guarantees did you have that they were going to invest in Cuba?

OCHOA: Well, the trust that came with my years of dealing with him.

PROSECUTOR: You speak to me regarding your trust in Pablo Escobar?

OCHOA: Yes.

PROSECUTOR: What benefits was Cuba as a country going to receive from all this?

OCHOA: Well, if tourism is developed, Cuba benefits.

PROSECUTOR: Did you ever stop to think what would happen if it was discovered that drug money was being invested in our country, or that we launder drug money?

OCHOA: No, truthfully, I never thought of it.

PROSECUTOR: You never thought for an instant of the discredit it would be to Cuba?

OCHOA: No, but you are right. I acted stupidly, I acted irresponsibly. I sit now in deep consternation.

PROSECUTOR: Ochoa, there is one question that has been churning in my head because of my recent exposure to a series of events in the struggle against drug traffic. We were summoned by the United Nations, where we had the chance to see the consequences of drug consumption, above all in youths, and even in children. Didn't you ever feel repugnance for the consequence of your actions. Did you believe that someday you might be like Pablo Escobar, and feel happy about it, knowing that you were murdering a good part of humanity to enrich yourself and make hotels in Cuba?

OCHOA: In truth, you are right. I never stopped to think; when one's path is twisted, it conforms with nothing.

PROSECUTOR: Do you believe that our Revolution can live subsidized by drug traffic?

OCHOA: No, the blame is mine, though you hate me for it, it is mine.

Then Antonio De la Guardia was called before the court, who likewise did not deny the charges against him.

ANTONIO DE LA GUARDIA: I want to indicate here that I accept all the charges that are levied against me, and would like to emphasize that I am the most responsible for what has happened – I have great responsibility in this matter. Furthermore, none of my superiors had knowledge of this. I want to indicate also that the fundamental motivations behind all my operations were found in my distorted, irresponsible character; in how much a moment of corruption would affect what I would come to possess – all this blinded me, made me unable to look with my conscience at the serious mistakes that I was committing. I am totally conscious of the damage, of the great mistake that I have committed and the harm I have done to Fidel, to the Revolution, to my fellow citizens, to my institution, to my children – damage that it is irreparable. We forget who we are, we betray the image of our martyrs and of our revolutionary heroes. My conscience is very heavy; I have betrayed them despicably. Really, I did not think about this at the time. However, this is not erased in my conscience. We deserve the worst, that you punish us severely. It is impossible to betray the Commander in Chief, the Revolution, and my fellow citizens who were loyal to me for so long. I recommend that this serve as an example for other soldiers or revolutionaries, so that they will not commit the offenses that I have committed. Furthermore, I exhort the rest of the detainees to maintain an honest civic attitude and admit to what they did and why they did it. I hope someday, though the present is too soon, that in the distant future you will be able to forgive me and recall me as the revolutionary that I was and not as what I am now. That is all.

PROSECUTOR: Accused De La Guardia, Mr. Arnaldo Ochoa presented a declaration before this Court. For us it's important to know, in detail, your relationship with Arnaldo, when this all began, and when the trafficking of drugs became involved in your relationship.

DE LA GUARDIA: My relationship with him began in 1988, when I traveled to Angola. I don't recall if we spoke of drugs at that time, nor can I estimate when we did, nor under what circumstances. I do know that when we did speak of this, he told me of the economic possibilities that large drug operations could offer, and of countries that were living off of that – these conversations were very general, and did not go into the specifics of any operations with which I was involved. However, he was aware of my involvement in certain operations, that I was conducting them with planes that were entering Cuba and boats that carried drugs from our territory to the United States. However, I commented to him that my vehicles, the boats, were small and that the crews were very irresponsible, because sometimes when they were being pursued, they cast the drugs overboard. Therefore, I proposed to him the use of a large ship, one of the merchant marine.

PROSECUTOR: A merchant ship laden with drugs?

DE LA GUARDIA: Yes.

PROSECUTOR: How much would such a ship hold? Hundreds of tons?

DE LA GUARDIA: No, I don't think that much. Maybe five or ten tons.

PROSECUTOR: Who would provide you with the drugs?

DE LA GUARDIA: Ochoa told me that it would be Pablo Escobar.

PROSECUTOR: Ochoa told you that there was a link with Pablo Escobar?

DE LA GUARDIA: I learned of the negotiations with Escobar through our associate Jorge Valdés, who told me he had gone to see Escobar.

PROSECUTOR: Jorge Valdés traveled to Colombia to see Escobar?

DE LA GUARDIA: Yes. He was traveling with a Colombian passport, he later told me.

PROSECUTOR: Ochoa also spoke to you of that relationship?

DE LA GUARDIA: Yes, he told me on several occasions of his contact with Pablo Escobar. He even told me that he had had communications with him on a regular basis in order to plan operations.

PROSECUTOR: I ask you: did either of the two of you ever awake from your dream and realize that this country could never live on the money of drug trafficking?

DE LA GUARDIA: No, in truth we never thought about it – you are awfully right.

After that, Amado Padrón was called to testify. Padrón had replaced Reinaldo Ruiz and his cousin Ruiz Poo, and channeled their drug trafficking operations.

PROSECUTOR: Where was your first contact with Ruiz and Ruiz Poo?

PADRON: In Panama, when, I must confess, I began my new role as an entrepreneur.

PROSECUTOR: Entrepreneur?

PADRON: Yes, I am speaking of the drug trade. However, the first serious conversation we had was here in Cuba in the MC Department.

PROSECUTOR: And what did Ruiz Poo propose to you about drugs?

PADRON: He told me that his cousin's wife was Colombian and there was a possibility of channeling drugs through Cuba.

PROSECUTOR: Were you not annoyed that he had made this proposal?

PADRON: Well, at the beginning yes, but later I discussed it with Tony De La Guardia. We proposed it to him and he told us how we would do it.

PROSECUTOR: What story did you tell the border patrol so that they allowed the passage of the planes?

PADRON: That part was coordinated by Tony.

PROSECUTOR: You consulted with Tony about all your operations?

PADRON: Correct, all of them.

PROSECUTOR: And if Tony was abroad, you waited until his return before you proceeded?

PADRON: This is correct.   If Tony was not here, the operations waited.

PROSECUTOR: Can you tell us the quantity of operations that were made?

PADRON: Not, not the total, but for example, in April of last year we did five.

PROSECUTOR: In a month?

PADRON: Yes, in only a month.

PROSECUTOR: You never felt like the authorities were on to you?

PADRON: No, we always thought that everything remained in secrecy. On the occasions when our boats were confiscated in the United States, they never said they were coming from Cuba, they always said they had come from the Bahamas.

PROSECUTOR: You don't think, then, that the DEA had the slightest idea of what was going on?

PADRON: At the beginning, no, but I suppose they found out when Reinaldo Ruiz was captured.

PROSECUTOR: They discovered $294,918 that you were hiding in a refrigerator. Where did that money come from?

PADRON: That money was the payment from the last two drug operations that were made. I am speaking of one month ago.

PROSECUTOR: Mr. Padrón, we found 156 kilograms of cocaine buried in Rosemary Key.   We believe that this shipment was yours, and according to the criminology laboratory, that cocaine was 100% pure. If this was yours, why did you bury it?

PADRON: The drugs belonged to me and an associate, Eduardo Díaz Izquierdo. We buried it because they ordered us to hold off with everything for a while.

PROSECUTOR: Who ordered this?

PADRON: Tony De La Guardia.

On July 9, 1989, the Tribunal completed its debates. The Prosecutor, Brigade General Juan Escalona Reguera, concluded by summarizing the case requesting the death penalty be applied to Arnaldo Ochoa, Tony De La Guardia, Amado Padrón, and Jorge Valdés, and giving penalties of 10 to 30 years imprisonment for the rest of the accused.

> *It is evident beyond any legal technicality, that at the top of the serious and proven charges, for which penalties are clearly outlined in our outstanding laws, Ochoa's greatest crime was having betrayed his people. In the view of the court, it is evident that the delicate situation resulting from Ochoa's treason has gravely injured the prestige of the Revolution and its international credibility. These principals are sometimes the only weapons upon which our country can depend against the aggression of imperialism.*
>
> *Ochoa has betrayed, first and foremost, Fidel, who, it is not enough to say, is technically his Commander in Chief. Ochoa knows, like everyone, that he has betrayed a symbol, a clean history that has never been tarnished with untruth. In attempting to undermine the credibility of Fidel, Ochoa and his companions drove a dagger into the back of our country.*
>
> *Of what did Ochoa tire? It was not of military service, because he is not a career soldier, nor does he come from a family with a tradition of military service. Moreover, there has never been a soldier who has tired of so attractive a service as his. Ochoa was tired of the public service, was bored of living*

consecrated to a cause, was tired of fighting and working for others, was tired of the struggle to liberate the people; and so he decided, with full knowledge of his actions, to live his own life. Ochoa chose other models and other roads: the model of Pablo Escobar, czar of drugs, millionaire without control of anybody, submitted to no discipline, nor contained by any ideological principle. He chose the road of easy money, that of drug trafficking.

These men have committed aberrant acts. By order of responsibility: Antonio De La Guardia, responsible for principally involving Cuba in the traffic of drugs, for sheltering himself in the confidence bestowed upon him to direct a department with the noble goal of breaking the American blockade, and for using and abusing his power for the vile traffic of cocaine. There has never been a drug trafficker with comparable advantages and resources. Tony De La Guardia made Cuba hostage to the international drug traffic. Tony De La Guardia and the others seated with him were capable of paralyzing our most vital services of national defense. De La Guardia inhibited our control over illegal air and maritime navigation. Having the air corridors of the country at his disposal, he counted on his jurisdiction to violate all our migratory regulations, to permit the entry into this country and the concealment of foreign criminals, and to prevent due action of the authorities. Furthermore, as a result, it is very difficult to establish how many of those boats were occupied by agents of the CIA and what operations were carried out by the special services of the enemy. Tony De La Guardia can not claim naiveté; his crime is treason, the most repugnant offense to his country, to his people and to his institution.

The accused have performed hostile offenses against foreign nations, what is a significant provocation since we speak of toxic drugs. These acts potentially put us at risk of war or reprisal, and expose innocent Cubans to possible danger. These assumptions are clearly supported in the incidences that we have examined in this case. But I say to the Court that I do not only *refer to our relationship with the United States, but also to those of Colombia, Mexico, and Panama, who were also injured by their activities.*

This rain of injury, infamy, and lies that falls at this time on our country, principally motivated by imperialistic press agencies, but now with the excuse of the actions of the accused, permits them to confirm with certainty that Cuba is linked to the business of the drug trafficking. More than 10 million Cubans must suffer patiently the vexations, the press campaigns, and the horrors that are spoken of the Cuban Revolution, thanks to the work of these 14 citizens that were born in this country.

On July 10, 1989, the Special Military Tribunal announced its verdict, condemning to death Arnaldo Ochoa, Antonio De La Guardia, Jorge Valdéz and Amado Padrón. Thirty-year prison terms were given to Patricio De La Guardia, Antonio Sánchez, Eduardo Díaz Izqierdo, Alexis Lago, Miguel Ruiz Poo and José María Abierno. Luis Pineda, Gabriel Prendés Gomez and Leonel Estévez received penalties of 25 years in prison. A smaller sentence of ten years was given to Antonio Rodríguez Estupiñan.

On July 11, those sentenced to death filed an appeal, requesting that the State Council reconsider case 1/89. Article 483 of the Law of Military Procedure establishes that in cases where capital punishment is the sentence, the accused cannot be executed without previous approval by the State Council, a body which has the right to issue a pardon.

The Council met on July 12. Present were all 29 members, including the Castro brothers, Raúl and Fidel. They resolved to confirm the court's mandate and to ratify the death penalty for the accused. The last to give his opinion in the meeting was Fidel Castro, who said: "On behalf of those who have died for this worthy and respectable country, for the ideals that they defended, and for the homeland of which they dreamt, we are obligated to be severe."

On July 13, at dawn, the condemned--Ochoa, De La Guardia, Valdéz and Padrón--were executed. The latter three faced the firing squad with complaints and pleas for clemency. Ochoa, before his end, simply turned toward the soldiers that were aiming at him and said: "I only want you to know that I am not a traitor. Boys, fulfill your duty, I have nothing against you. You are only following orders." A few moments later his life was extinguished.

Fidel Castro watched the scene on a videotape that the military physician brought to him hours afterwards. With his eyes fixed on the monitor, he finally commented: "He died like a man." For the Government of Cuba, this marked the turning of one of its most complex pages since the revolution began. The mat of cocaine traffic had been closed.

IV

Mexico

Mexico entered the international narcotics-trafficking market in the beginning of the 1970's. Its principal operations at the time involved smuggling large quantities of heroin to American cities. This traffic came about, in large part, because of the efforts by American and French authorities in 1972 to crack down on the French Connection, a dominant trafficking operation whose central enterprise was Turkish opium production. As a result of this crack down, the traffickers in New York and other cities of the East Coast needed to find another country or region which could supply them with heroin, a drug of high demand during that period.

The smuggling of Turkish opium and heroin to the United States demanded an elaborate, complex, and costly smuggling operation. Meanwhile, as Mexico was "just around the corner," hundreds of kilos could be brought to the big United States cities in cars, small boats, and simply in small hand-carried bags by those who crossed the border each day.[21]

---

[21] *Drug Trafficking in Mexico* (DEA report, 1987).

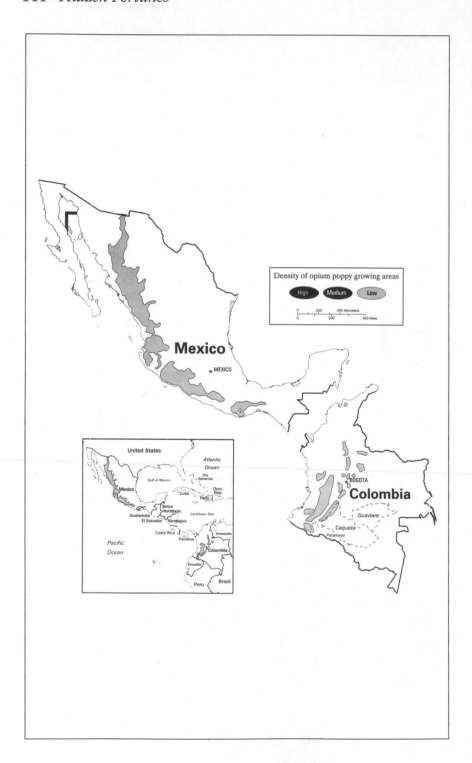

Latin America
Opium Cultivation and Production

	1991	1992	1993	1994	1995
Net cultivation	**4,910**	**3,310**	**3,960**	**5,795**	**11,590**
(hectares)					
Mexico	3,765	3,310	3,960	5,795	5,050
Guatemala	1,145	negl	negl	negl	negl
Colombia					6,540
Potential production	**52**	**40**	**49**	**60**	**118**
(metric tons)					
Mexico	41	40	49	60	53
Guatemala	11	negl	negl	negl	negl
Colombia					65
Potential heroin	**5**	**4**	**5**	**6**	**11**
(metric tons)					
Mexico	4	4	5	6	5
Guatemala	1	negl	negl	negl	negl
Colombia					6

Opium production in **Mexico** declined with an increase in eradication efforts in 1995. Poppy cultivation in **Guatemala** remains at negligible levels, chiefly because of continued US-funded eradication programs. Because of Bogota's eradication program, poppy cultivation in **Colombia** appears to have stabilized at a relatively low level. Eradication operations along both sides of the border between northeastern Colombia and northwestern **Venezuela** have stemmed nascent opium production there.

The region of the Western Sierra Madre mountains receives moderately humid winds of the Pacific Ocean, creating a perfect environment for the cultivation of all types of crops. This region comprises the states of Sinaloa and Durango. The capitals of these states, Culiacán and Victoria, respectively, were considered the main centers for the cultivation, packaging and commercialization of vegetable products such as tomatoes and cucumbers. The poppy cultivation for the production of

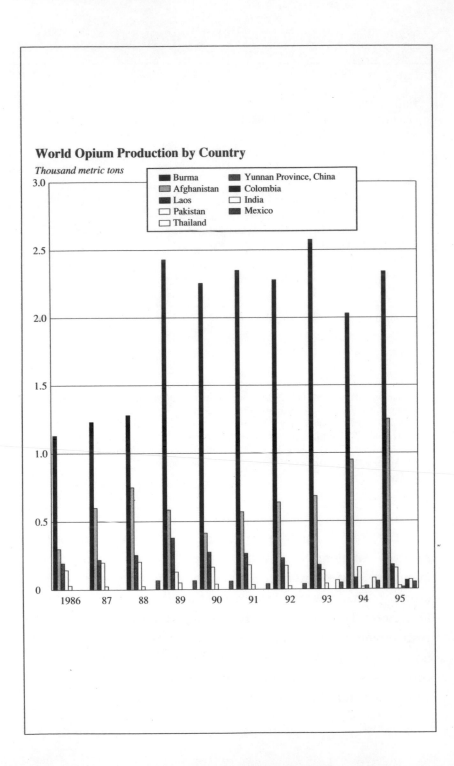

World Opium Production by Country

opium was introduced at the beginning of the century by Chinese railroad workers who were working in the eastern region of Mexico. During World War II, the Mexican government legalized opium production as it was needed in the United States for the production of morphine for American soldiers abroad.

In the 1950's, several farming families had begun to dedicate themselves to heroin production, the product to be shipped to selected American cities, such as Los Angeles, Houston, and Phoenix. Through the early 1970's, this business, although small in scale and without any real organization, yielded quite attractive sums of money which traditional crops had never been able to produce.

Through this commerce, many people had managed to acquire small fortunes, but there was one man, Jaime Herrera Nevares, that stood out as a legend in his time. "Don Jaime," as his friends called him, was born in 1927 in the town of Las Herreras in the state of Durango. He learned quickly the importance that Mexico could have as a heroin-producing country. Together with his large family of eight brothers and four sisters, they decided to put together a real organization devoted to trafficking heroin to the major cities of the United States. Their business would be completely vertically integrated – they would cultivate the poppy, extract the opium, refine the heroin, and transport the drug to the centers of consumption.

The Herrera family had an advantage with respect to other drug traffickers. Their organization was composed entirely of family members: all of Jaime's brothers and sisters were married (including Jaime, who had married twice), and the whole extended family participated in the operation – wives, in-laws, cousins, nephews and nieces. In fact, by 1980, the family had integrated 200 blood relatives into the business. This wreaked havoc on Mexican security forces and the DEA since it was impossible for agents to secretly infiltrate their organization or to co-opt informants. The younger members of the family were sent to the United States to help with distribution, those of intermediate age were in charge of transportation, and the elders remained in important Mexican cities (such as Culiacán, Victoria de Durango, Ciudad Obregón, Chihuahua, Cuidad Juarez or El Paso) to supervise operations. The family smuggled heroin northward through simple methods – in cars with false gas tanks, in trucks, or simply in the clothes of those who crossed over the U.S.-Mexican border. According to DEA analysts, between 1975 and 1978, the Herrera family managed to smuggle an estimated 60 million dollars worth of heroin, dominating the markets of Chicago, Denver, Pittsburgh and Miami.[22]

Owed to heroin profits, Jaime Herrera Nevares' purchases in Durango included two mansions, two hotels, a construction company, a discotheque, a bowling alley, various auto repair garages, and hundreds of hectares of land in the countryside. He also owned a house in Guadalajara. Moreover, Herrera was considered a *humanitarian benefactor* since he had built three public hospitals in Durango and supported neighborhood organizations by paving and lighting roads, building schools, and constructing playgrounds.

In addition, he was able to maintain his immunity from the authorities:

> *He had cultivated tight contacts with the majority of policemen and municipal police chiefs, directors of the security forces of the various Mexican states, and mayors and governors. Furthermore, the trafficker financed the campaigns of young leaders who wanted to make a career out of politics. All of these people were quick to tell Jaime Herrera of any new developments.*[23]

---

[22] *The Socio-economic Impact of Drug Trafficking in the State of Durango* (Mexico: DEA report, August, 1987)

[23] Ob. Cit. 2.

Moreover, the Herrera family never resorted to violence to eliminate competition. Rather, all confrontations with other traffickers and internal family disputes were resolved directly by Jaime, who, with his paternal conversational style, was able to fix the problem with calm stability.

One of the people who tried to compete with the Herrera family in the state of Sinaloa was Pedro Aviles Pérez. Aviles, a Mexican born in 1940, began his illicit activities at an early age by smuggling automobiles, and by the beginning of the 1970's, he was transporting heroin to Southern California. However, due to the conflict with the Herrera family in this enterprise, he abandoned the heroin trade and smuggled marijuana instead. He built a large organization running marijuana to the United States, and had made contacts with other South American traffickers to collaborate in cocaine smuggling and distribution. His operation had headquarters in Tijuana and Mexicali, two border cities in Mexico's Northwest; he resided in a third northwestern city, San Luis Río Colorado, where he owned one of the largest mansions that has ever been built there.

In 1973, Phil Jordan, a young DEA agent working out of Phoenix, convinced Mexican Federal Judicial Police officials of the need to jointly plan and execute an operation to arrest Pedro Aviles Peréz. The Federal Police decided to break into five houses belonging to the trafficker and found, in basements and storage areas, 25 tons of marijuana, 42 kilos of 90%-pure cocaine and a few grams of heroin; unfortunately, Aviles successfully avoided capture as he had fled several hours before the operation began.

Another trafficker who operated in western Mexico was Alberto on the streets of Miami. With the little money he had saved, he decided to become a pimp and began managing a group of prostitutes. Within a few months, he had made a large sum of money, which he reinvested into his operations, and created an expansive ring of prostitution and woman trafficking.   By 1970, Falcón was one of the best-known jet-setters in cities such as Miami, Los Angeles and New York. He got around in these cities in one of his four Rolls Royce automobiles, the only type of car in which he would travel.

Alberto Sicilia Falcón not only offered his women to important businessmen, but also cultivated relationships with many of the principal drug traffickers of South America and Europe. Consequently, he soon became an important trafficker himself, moving cocaine, heroin and marijuana.   With connections in Mexico City, Guadalajara and Tijuana, Falcón smuggled drugs mostly to Los Angeles, and from there distributed the contraband to other United States cities.

Falcón was able to flourish in the drug trade due in part to information he received from several DEA agents.   His relationship with the assistant regional director of the DEA in New Orleans, Joseph Baca, was discovered in 1976 through an internal investigation by his boss, the regional director in New Orleans, William R. Coonce. Coonce's report outlined frequent calls made by Baca to the various residences of Falcón, both in and outside of the United States.   The report also revealed Baca's credit card purchases, which easily amounted to more than his salary, and a $700,000 house in Tijuana under the name of his wife for which Baca paid in cash. Consequently, the administrator of the DEA, Peter Bensinger, called on Baca to explain. At the meeting, Baca denied everything and quit. The report was subsequently put in the hands of various officials who decided not to file a formal accusation. They decided that the evidence was circumstantial and that their jurisdiction to investigate issues outside the perimeters of the U.S. territory was limited.

At the end of 1973, DEA agents in Los Angeles decided to form the Central Tactics Unit for the purposes of complementing intelligence tasks and collecting the necessary evidence in order to bring down Falcón, who had become a 'drug trafficking czar' in all the major cities of the United States and Europe. Having had grown to a team of more than 50 agents, the Central Tactics Unit finally completed their mission in July, 1978 when Falcón was arrested by the Mexican Federal Judicial Police. His apprehension represented one of the most important arrests the Mexican Federal Judicial Police had made in cooperation with the DEA.

Nevertheless, Falcón continued to manage his businesses from jail through one of his most trusted associates, Manuel Salcido Uzeta, who was better known by the nickname *Cochi Loco* (Crazy Pig). Salcido immediately became the new Mexican heroin baron, establishing himself in the city of Mazatlan, on the Central East Coast of Mexico. His partner was a man named Juan Ramón Matta Ballesteros, who also had ties to Falcón. Together they contacted an eager, small-time heroin trafficker, Miguel Angel Félix Gallardo, who operated out of Culiacán. The three traffickers laid the groundwork for what would in a few years be known as the Guadalajara cartel, an organization that would dominate large parts of the heroin and cocaine markets in the United States. Moreover, the Guadalajara cartel operated in cooperation with the Medellin cartel (headed by Pablo Escobar Gaviria) and used their network of contacts.

The years 1974-75 exhibited an explosion of the supply and demand of Mexican heroin in the United States. Although the Guadalajara cartel had not yet formed, there had already developed a region in Mexico devoted to opium cultivation and heroin fabrication. This region was known as the Golden Triangle of Mexico, which referred to the routes that linked the three cities of Chihuahua, Culiacán and Guadalajara. Consequently, a group of DEA agents proposed to their superiors in Washington that one possible solution was the irradiation of the opium fields in this region in Mexico, a suggestion that had already been presented to President Nixon in 1973. As a result of this proposal, President Ford began to pressure his Mexican counterpart, Luis Echeverría,[24] to accept the option of eradication. Various other politicians also did their part to pressure the Mexicans to accept this plan. Among them was Congressman Charles Rangel,[25] who visited the Mexican states of Durango and Sinaloa at the end of 1974 and invoked the necessity to terminate the opium plantations by means of crop dusting.

This action was opposed by the Attorney General of Mexico, Pedro Ojeda Paullada, who claimed that it could endanger the population of the western Sierra Madre region if the Americans dusted with toxic chemicals such as *agent orange*, which was utilized by American troops in Vietnam. However, the United States Government proposed using a herbicide called 2,4-D, a product with very low levels of toxicity to humans. This chemical was also known to Mexican farmers, who had used it to clear sections of land without harming the mineral properties of the soil.

President Echeverría accepted the proposal in early 1975, despite the anti-American sentiment that existed; that is, sentiment that the Americans were meddling in Mexican affairs. Moreover, many felt that President Echeverría was catering to American interests since he wanted to cultivate support among American officials for his candidacy for secretary general of the United Nations, a position he could obviously not obtain without taking a firm position against heroin production in his country.

To bring the plan to fruition, the United States Department of State agreed to lend financial support to the Mexican Government: 39 Bell helicopters and 22 small planes rigged with crop dusting tanks were donated, along with an annual contribution of $10 million. In addition, the United States Government contracted the services of an Oregon crop dusting

---

[24] Luis Echeverría was President of Mexico from 1970 to 1976.
[25] Charles Rangel was a democratic congressman from the State of New York.

company, Evergreen International Aviation Inc. (the majority of whose pilots were Vietnam veterans), to assist in the eradication of the opium plants. The entire operation would be coordinated by the Mexican Attorney General's Office and the DEA.

Thus, Operation Condor, as it was called, began in November, 1975. In a way, for the Mexicans, the operation signified an opening in their air space since the majority of pilots were American, though trained for their mission by Mexicans. The pilots flew over the entire western region of Mexico, observing virtually meter by meter each of the plantations. After the report they subsequently submitted was approved, they returned to the air and discharged hundreds of liters of herbicide.

Operation Condor was touted by both governments as a *model program* that should be imitated by other countries. In addition, tours were organized for reporters for them to film and publicize the successes and advances that had been achieved in the war on drugs. Although the destruction of the opium plantations was evident, neither the owners of the plantations, nor the farmers that cultivated the opium plants, nor those who refined the heroin were ever arrested. The reason was simple: the DEA did not have jurisdiction to do it,[26]

---

[26] At the end of 1975, the provisional president of the United States Senate, Mike Mansfield, drafted a resolution that would directly affect the operations of the DEA. This legislation, which was approved by Congress in June, 1976, stated the following: "In conforming with the law, no official, agent, or employee of the government can participate in any direct police action in a foreign country with respect to the war against drugs." Obviously, this was a blow to the DEA, who were now prohibited from making arrests outside United States soil, even though they were still allowed to continue intelligence operations, joint operations, information exchanges, and consultation in foreign countries. In practice, this legislation obligated DEA agents, after doing all the work, to turn their back while the Mexican Federal Judicial Police made the arrests.

and the Mexican Federal Judicial Police had no intentions of
arresting any important drug traffickers.

Travis Kuykendall, a high-ranking DEA official in Mexico
from 1972 to 1985, described the situation as follows:

> *If you find yourself in a country like Mexico with the duty*
> *of eradicating drugs, and your host country does not recognize*
> *the gravity of the problem, how does one convince five Mexican*
> *policemen to go out and arrest a big drug trafficker who is*
> *protected by thirty armed bodyguards?   Even worse, if we*
> *cannot collaborate in the arrests, my only function is to sit in*
> *my office and sip coffee.   The great motivation that we used to*
> *have was that we patrolled the streets all over Mexico, certainly*
> *at high risk, and stuck our noses into everything.   Now the*
> *Mexicans, when we want to proceed, tell us: 'Hey, boys, don't*
> *take this stuff so seriously!'   They have lost all respect for us.*
> *The Federal Police doesn't do anything, and even smile in our*
> *faces, and some start to show us money that they had collected*
> *for doing nothing.*

The Mexican Government had run out of excuses for the
lack of arrests. The traffickers continued to live in their luxury
mansions, unmolested by the authorities. The government
finally took action in December, 1976 by naming two
prominent officials to head Operation Condor. The first, Jaime
Alcalá García, an official of the Mexico City police, was looked
to by all as a sort of *'James Bond-style'* super agent. The second
was an official from the Public Prosecutor's Office, Carlos
Aguilar Garza, who was nicknamed "The Elliott Ness of
Mexico." Their orders were to terminate the opium plantations
in the states of Sinaloa and Durango, and to crush the heroin
trafficking organizations.

The pressure on the traffickers was intensified. An
average of twenty flights each day were made over the region,
and Aguilar Garza and Jaime Alcalá visited different areas
each day, interrogating the farmers there, and giving orders to

burn or destroy the heroin refinement laboratories that were discovered. Both men traveled by helicopter and were accompanied by heavily armed federal policemen. The DEA agents simply coordinated the operations; however, after a while, they began to realize that dozens of farmers had been incarcerated and forgotten about, and that legal cultivations were often burned and precarious rural shacks destroyed.

In May, 1977, the College of Law of the City of Culiacán denounced Carlos Aguilar Garza and Jaime Alcalá García for violating human rights. Members of the college publicly threatened to go before the United Nations with their story. They accused the government of using torture to obtain information: using electric shock, submerging their heads in water until they were almost asphyxiated, burning various parts of their bodies with lit cigarettes, making them drink gasoline, amputating fingers and ears, and provoking abortions in pregnant women. Nevertheless, in December, 1977, after interpolating Peter Bourne, the Director of the White House Drug Abuse Policy Office, a subcommittee of the United States Senate stated: "The measures that the United States and Mexican governments are taking to control the abuse of drugs constitute the most exemplary demonstration of international cooperation in the world today." The Jimmy Carter Administration, which touted human rights as the foundation of its foreign policy, continued labeling *Operation Condor* as a model program, and the American press never considered or printed anything on what many called the dark side of the war on drugs.[27]

---

[27] If human rights truly were violated, why did DEA agents not intervene? For Travis Kuykendall, the answer was easy:

> *First of all, we have the Mansfield Law, which prevents us from intervening in arrests in a foreign country, and all the agents have very precise orders to abide by this law. Moreover, if one of us was to witness an illegal arrest, what action could we take? None of us is in a position to confront the Federal Police, and moreover, if we*

The American agents in Mexico were worried about their own safety. The Mexican Government, despite the requests of the State Department, repeatedly refused to grant diplomatic status to DEA employees. Since they could not enjoy the immunity or the protection of such status, they were forced to roam the Western Sierra Madre region of Mexico with only a tourist visa, and, just like other tourists, they could not carry arms. However, the issue of carrying a gun was settled verbally in a *gentlemen's agreement* between officials in Washington and Mexico City, but the Mexicans could not guarantee that the gun-carrying DEA agents would not be arrested by local police. In addition, several agents complained of their phones being tapped by the Federal Police. But in the end, nobody wanted to send bad news back to Washington, and all DEA agents understood that their whole attention and focus would be needed to achieve the objective of eradicating the opium plantations from Mexican soil.

THE FIRST DEALS

When all was completed, Operation Condor was not only the first joint effort of the two governments in the war on drugs, but also resulted in the destruction of 22,000 acres of opium plantations, sufficient to produce eight tons of heroin. Needless to say, the United States celebrated this as a victory. However, in January, 1978, Mexican President José Lopez Portillo[28] announced that the Americans would no longer supervise the reconnaissance and crop dusting flights. His intention was to reduce as much as possible the presence of American agents in Mexico; from here on, all the operations

---

did so, it would be considered as an intrusion in a direct police action, a thing that the law obviously prohibits.
[28] President of Mexico from 1976-1982.

would be carried out solely by the Federal Judicial Police of Mexico.

This decision or change in policy had nothing to do with inconveniences in the execution of operations, but rather with the growing anti-American sentiment among Mexicans resulting from a dispute between the two countries over natural gas prices. President Jimmy Carter had decided to reduce United States petroleum dependence on the Middle East, and had intended on negotiating an agreement with President López Portillo for the importation of Mexican gas. An agreement was finally reached when, after turbulent negotiations, Petróleos Mexicanos, the state-owned petroleum company, acquiesced to a low price for the gas. In return, López Portillo solicited a substantial withdrawal of DEA agents from Mexico, leaving the eradication operations to be totally managed by the Mexican Federal Judicial Police.

On March 8, 1978, the American pilots and about ten agents were withdrawn from Mexican territory, and from that moment on, Mexican officials declined to submit reports or other such information to the DEA. Nevertheless, the few Americans that were officially accredited to remain there, tried to discretely evaluate the continuity and progress of the operations. Their conclusions were surprising: the planes only made one flight every two or three days, and the herbicide that was supposed to be dropped had been replaced by water.

By the end of 1978, Carlos Aguilar Garza had been promoted to district attorney of Baja California, and Jaime Alcalá had been named commander of the Mexican Federal Judicial Police in the city of Tijuana. Both men had solicited their transfers for reasons of health, but according to the DEA, the two men had other reasons: informants stated that the men had changed sides and were now working with various drug traffickers. American investigations confirmed these accusations. Aguilar Garza had purchased various properties in San Diego and two hotels in Tijuana; meanwhile, Jaime

Alcalá had bought a luxury hotel in Guadalajara. These men, who had supposedly been hidden in order to renew their battle against the drug traffickers, were actually in business with their old enemies. However, their lives ended suddenly in March, 1985. Alcalá was murdered in plain daylight on a main Guadalajara street, and Aguilar Garza was in a plane that blew up while transporting cocaine to the United States.

SHELTERED BY THE CIA AND FBI

By the beginning of the 1980's, the cartels of South America had caught the attention of the world, as the production, transportation, and commercialization of cocaine and marijuana originating from this continent continued to increase. World political leaders constantly engaged in dialogues in an effort to join forces to battle drugs and the drug trafficking organizations. Meanwhile, the traffickers, on their part, were developing new methods to expand their illicit businesses. In addition, the new traffickers were utilizing modern smuggling techniques, employing airplanes, radars, sophisticated communications equipment, specialized lawyers, accountants, bankers, agricultural engineers to improve their cultivations, chemists and other specialists. Indeed, these organizations were truly international businesses, but they needed the cooperation of police, mayors, governors, army generals, judges, and in some cases, federal government ministers.

The great majority of Europeans placed the blame on the Latin American governments for not taking concrete actions to confront the problem. Their harshest words were aimed at Colombia, Bolivia and Peru, although the rest of the countries of the region were also considered to be involved at various levels in drug trafficking and in the laundering of the drug money.   However, Mexico was different: no one accused this country, nor even mentioned it.

Mexico had become for the United States a country of critical geopolitical importance. The Ministry of the Interior of Mexico housed the Federal Bureau of Security (Dirección Federal de Seguridad or DFS), which performed operations in conjunction with the American CIA and FBI. The DFS was used by the Americans to gather information, take photographs, wiretap suspects, and keep abreast of the intelligence activities related to Cuban and Soviet (KGB) missions in Mexico City. For United States intelligence, this data was of vital importance. The DFS cooperated in full: once they obtained the desired information, it was given to the United States ambassador, who brought it directly to Washington for analysis. This relationship, which began in the early 1970's, had been cultivated by the White House despite having had to look the other way when it came to the alleged methods used in the Mexican effort against leftist urban guerrillas. These practices included torture, murder, and the disappearance of persons.

The tolerant attitude of United States administrations regarding illegal activities of DFS members was brought to light in November, 1980. At that time, the California Highway Patrol began an operation called Operation Cargo, which was designed to catch a gang of car thieves operating in Southern California who stole luxury automobiles and shipped them to various cities in Mexico. According to police records, over the three previous years, the gang had stolen 300 Jaguars, 100 Porches, and a smattering of Jeeps and other costly cars; later, the stolen automobiles were sold at a good price to members of Mexican high society. Through Operation Cargo, the police were able to apprehend one of the car thieves; but the police were perplexed when their catch claimed to be collaborating with the FBI, and exhibited credentials that supported this claim. The police immediately called the chief of the FBI in San

Diego, Norman Zigrossi, who gave precise orders not to arrest him, to bury the case, and to end Operation Cargo.

The FBI knew that the director of the DFS, Miguel Nazar Haro, drove a Dodge van, a yellow Porche, and a blue Ford – all stolen from the Los Angeles area. However, this was not the only case. In fact, a great number of cars stolen from the United States were parked in front of the DFS building in Mexico City. Information on each one of these automobiles was supplied by an informant, Bobby Montoya, who also photographed or filmed those who used the vehicles. Unfortunately, in July, 1981, Montoya was found dead on the outskirts of the Mexican capital with two bullets in his head. This event exceeded the patience of some FBI officials, who, in turn, allowed Operation Cargo to be resumed.

Consequently, four persons of Mexican nationality were arrested in San Diego. The four agreed to cooperate with the American authorities in exchange for reductions in their sentences, but only circumstantial evidence against Nazar Haro could be gathered. Douglas Schwartz, an assistant of the public prosecutor of the case tried to formally charge Nazar Haro with conspiracy to commit a crime; but Gordon McGinley, the FBI legal representative in the Mexican embassy, met with the DFS director, who agreed to stop the car theft. Nevertheless, Schwartz formally charged Nazar Haro before the courts of San Diego, an act that provoked an immediate reaction from McGinley, who, on August 17, 1981, sent a cable to Washington stating the following:

> *The CIA and the FBI have the clear conviction that, in relation to our interests and those of the security of the United States, information on leftist terrorism as well as intelligence and counterintelligence operations that are carried out in Mexico may be jeopardized if the case against Nazar is continued and he is forced to resign from his post.*

Regardless of this, Schwartz and his boss, William Kennedy, continued to push the case, finally requesting that the Department of Justice make a decision on the matter. Lowell Jensen, the Assistant Attorney General for the Criminal Division, advised Schwartz to ease up and let the case be resolved by a preliminary hearing instead of being taken up by the Grand Jury in San Diego. On March 26, 1982, a local newspaper, *The San Diego Union*, published an article describing the case.[29] The article mentioned FBI and CIA operations in Mexican territory and what had happened with Operation Cargo. The scandal was especially embarrassing for the government, who blamed the prosecutor, William Kennedy, for having leaked the information to the press. Kennedy was then dismissed from his post by President Ronald Reagan. In addition, Nazar Haro resigned from his position in Mexico.

In spite of everything, the trial proceeded forward. It began on April 21, 1982, and Douglas Schwartz was able to maintain his job, and act as prosecutor during the event. Despite protests from the CIA and FBI, Nazar Haro had been flown in from Mexico to be judged with the accused. After two days of testimony, the jury found Nazar Haro guilty of conspiracy to steal automobiles. However, the next day, before the judge handed down the prison sentence, Nazar Haro's lawyer Marvin Mitchelson, an ex-legal advisor for the CIA, submitted the $200,000 bail that had been set. Nazar Haro was free after having had spent only fourteen hours in jail. He crossed back into Mexico immediately and to this day, his name appears on a list of fugitives of American justice.

Nazar Haro's successor was José Antonio Zorrilla Pérez, a man who was connected to Nazar, and who would continue cooperating with CIA and FBI operations. Nevertheless, the

---

[29] "CIA Intervenes to Block Charges in Car Theft Case," Jon Standefer, *The San Diego Union*, March 26, 1982.

relationship between the DFS and the DEA, insofar as drugs were concerned, was not very good. In fact, conflicts between the two departments would affect diplomacy between the two countries.

The number of persons accused under Operation Cargo was 38, of which 24 were employees or officials of Mexican security agencies. Within the formal accusation documentation, Douglas Schwartz described the operation in detail, explaining that various agents, officials and commanders of the DFS would impart precise orders regarding the cars they wanted. These cars were then stolen from the streets or from dealerships in north San Francisco, Los Angeles, San Diego, or San Antonio.   Usually, the lower-ranking agents would accompany or drive the stolen vehicles across the border, displaying their credentials to protect them. Sometimes they would have large trucks loaded with stolen cars. The vehicles were permitted into Mexico as a result of their contacts within the Mexican Customs Service. Once in Mexico, the cars were then delivered to those who had requested them, or to other locations where they would be sold at a good price. Various stolen vehicles were seen regularly in the garages of the DFS building in Mexico City.

THE GUADALAJARA CARTEL

At the start of the 1980's the DEA had only twenty-two agents working and living permanently in Mexico. Among them were James Kuykendall, Tony Ayala, Pete Hernandez, Enrique "Kiki" Camarena, and Butch Sears. These men witnessed the relocation of the old drug lords of the Western Sierra Madre region to the city of Guadalajara. Even more importantly, they witnessed the emergence of new leaders and a new generation of drug traffickers who imitated their

Colombian counterparts in terms of their quest for power and their criminal brutality.

The leaders of the Guadalajara cartel were Rafael Caro Quintero, a young man of 29 years, an old outlaw named Ernesto Fonseca, and Miguel Angel Félix Gallardo, born in Culiacan in 1946. None of them had completed primary school, but thanks to their illicit businesses, they were now in control of hundreds of millions of dollars, in cash and investments, in the major banks of the world.

Rafael Caro Quintero was in charge of coordinating general operations and cultivating contacts among police and governmental agencies in Mexico and the United States. Miguel Angel Félix Gallardo oversaw all cocaine traffic to the markets in Southern California. The smuggling was accomplished through a squadron of more than fifty pilots. They would first pick up the cocaine in Colombia, then stop in northern Mexico to refuel, then fly on to a determined clearing, ranch, or hidden runway in Southern California. Félix Gallardo had assembled heroin refinement laboratories in the western region of the United States and in some East Coast cities as well, thanks to his contacts there. The trafficker also had good relations with the Mexican Federal Judicial Police since he had worked for them until 1980, as the Governor of Sinaloa Leopoldo Sánchez Celis' personal bodyguard. Consequently, Félix Gallardo's friendship ran deep with members of both local and federal police.

Although, Félix Gallardo liked the diversity of trafficking heroin, marijuana and cocaine, he preferred cocaine. Cocaine was more lucrative than the other drugs since it arrived in Mexico already refined, with the Colombians already having done most of the work. All the Guadalajara cartel had to do was transport and distribute it – which meant the superior profits of the drug without having to worry about plantations being discovered, or the quality of the soil, or getting the right fertilizers, or refining, or packing it, etc. All that the Mexicans had to do, was pick it up in a small plane, fly at low altitude across the U.S.-Mexican border, and land in the United States. Operation completed.

Ernesto Fonseca was in charge of supervising the opium and marijuana plantations, locating lands for further illegal cultivation, resolving disputes with farmers, and finding and puting to work new irrigation techniques in lands that were too arid. Fonseca, the oldest of the cartel leaders, born in 1931, also participated in other activities of the organization. At times, he would oversee the transport of cocaine and marijuana from Tijuana to Los Angeles, or would involve himself in the heroin distribution in San Diego.

For DEA agents, and especially for Kuykendall and Camarena, the Guadalajara cartel represented in 1982 one of the largest cocaine-, heroin- and marijuana-trafficking organizations in Latin America. It was estimated that the Guadalajara cartel smuggled a ton and a half of cocaine monthly into the United States, a quantity that not even the Colombian cartels had achieved yet. Although the perspectives in Guadalajara were discouraging, under Kuykendall's experienced guidance, Kiki Camarena, Pete Hernandez and Butch Sears began to look for informants and to make contacts with politicians, businessmen and a few federal policemen. Their objective was to develop means to monitor the activities of the traffickers and, if possible, gather concrete evidence against them.

In January, 1982, Butch Sears received information that Miguel Angel Félix Gallardo was using the Banco de Guadalajara (Bank of Guadalajara) to launder money from his businesses. With this information, Sears requested permission from the Mexican Government to gain access to the bank's records in order to determine the financial transactions of the trafficker. The request was rejected due to bank confidentiality regulations. However, a DEA agent in Lima, Peru, obtained copies of checks made out to Félix Gallardo that had been deposited in the Banco de América (Bank of America), the funds of which were to be transferred to another branch of the bank in San Diego. Within one month, the Peruvian branch of Banco de América received $20 million of the trafficker's money, much of which was transferred to the bank's Mexico City branch. Another portion of the money went to the Banco Nacional de México (National Bank of Mexico). The DEA agents watched the cartel move an estimated $200 million annually. The money was deposited into the traffickers' accounts through bills of exchange of $50,000 or $70,000, or through the purchase of bank checks for quantities exceeding $40,000.

One of the principal depositors of Félix Gallardo's money was Tómas Valles Corral, a Bolivian accountant who had dual residence in Bolivia and Colombia (he would later lend his services as a financial advisor to Pablo Escobar, leader of the Medellin cartel). Valles Corral made four deposits of $200,000 each to the Banco de América in Mexico, which were then transferred to the Swiss Credit Bank in Europe.

The DEA also obtained records showing cash transfers to Rafael Caro Quintero from Roberto Suárez Jr., member of one of the best known cocaine-trafficking families of Bolivia. The transfers were for $275,000 each, money subsequently managed by the Swiss Banking Union.[30]

---

[30] The transfers and deposits that were made into the traffickers' accounts at Banco de América and Banco Nacional de Mexico enjoyed total impunity. In the instances where money was transferred to the United States from Mexico, the U.S. Department of the Treasury informed the officials of Banco Central de Mexico (Central Bank of Mexico) of the presumed illegality of the funds, but the Mexican appeared to have no interest in the matter and defended the confidentiality of bank records to the letter. It should be noted that in the United States, any financial or bank transaction over $10,000 is regulated in order to snub money laundering operations. In these cases, the Department of the Treasury makes a record of the clients who carry out the transaction, who are then constantly monitored.

Nevertheless, in 1982, the only Guadalajara cartel leader under serious investigation by American prosecutors in San Diego was Ernesto Fonseca.   The United States Customs Service had begun to investigate him when individuals linked to the trafficker had attempted to bring $2 million into the country without declaring it.   Customs agents knew that various persons had been entering the country with money, and then depositing it in banks or small financial institutions to launder it.   The Americans also knew that Fonseca was living temporarily on a ranch that he owned in Santa Fe, New Mexico.   This ranch was not only visited regularly by Rafael Caro Quintero, but was also used as a storage facility for shipments of marijuana and cocaine.   On April 26, 1982, the U.S. Customs Service requested a warrant to search the property, but it was denied since narcotics and money laundering investigations were not under their jurisdiction; such investigations were performed by the DEA, the local police or the FBI.   Unfortunately, while the DEA was in the process of requesting a search warrant of their own, Ernesto Fonseca escaped back to Mexico.   When DEA agents finally got to the ranch, all that they found were the clothes that the trafficker had left in the closet.   The chance of arresting him had evaporated.

In May, 1982, an informant of Enrique Camarena showed up at the agent's office with an incredible story.   The man said that he had seen approximately 200 acres of marijuana plantations about 200 miles northeast of Guadalajara, in the state of San Luis de Potosí. Camarena did not believe him – the plantation he described could have been almost anywhere *except* in the region he had named, which was in the middle of the dessert where only cactus grew.   But the man insisted on what he had seen.   He said the marijuana plants were watered by special underground irrigation canals which channeled

Although the confidentiality of bank records is incorporated into federal banking law, this surveillance process is considered legal.

water from wells.   Also, he said that two small planes flew over the plantation, spraying water on the plants below. Finally, he claimed to have seen on three occasions Rafael Caro Quintero and Ernesto Fonseca arrive to the area in helicopters piloted by federal policemen.

The DEA agents were not very convinced as to the validity of the story, but they felt obligated to investigate since, if the cartel really had managed to grow marijuana in the arid regions of central Mexico by means of sophisticated irrigation and fertilization techniques, the problem would be more than serious.   That is, if the claims of the informant were true, the marijuana production potential of the cartel would be incalculable.   Therefore, Camarena wanted to confirm the story, but an informant of Pete Hernandez had also claimed to have seen the plantation, and added that it was protected by various commanders of the Federal Police, and that the armed men who guarded the area were local policemen.

Enrique Camarena asked to be put in charge of the investigation, and he would coordinate the efforts with Kuykendall. Camarena would head the operation. For him, the quickest and easiest way to confirm the story was to inspect the area from a small airplane or glider; however, DEA agents were not authorized to fly over Mexican air space unless they had express consent from the Attorney General's Office of Mexico, and such permission could only be officially solicited by the American Embassy.   Therefore, in August, 1982, Kiki made several automobile trips to the vicinity of the supposed plantation. Although he did not find any concrete evidence, he did notice something strange – for such small country towns, there was an unusual amount of ground and air traffic. Trucks, small planes, and all-terrain vehicles came and went in all directions, none of which seemed to belong in that area. In addition, he would receive absolute silence when he discreetly questioned anybody about anything related to marijuana. Camarena took a few photographs, which really showed nothing in particular, and wrote a report in an attempt to persuade the United States ambassador, John Gavin, of the existence of the plantation.   However, as there was not sufficient evidence, Gavin declined to intervene in the matter.

Although it was almost impossible to get any real evidence, Enrique Camarena continued working. Finally, he spoke with Kuykendall and Sears about the possibility of making a flight over the area. Despite being prohibited to do so, one morning in September, 1982, Camarena hired a pilot to take him to the area in a small glider. The suspicions proved true, only to his surprise there was not only one plantation, but many, separated from one another by short distances. Kiki not only took photographs of green fields of marijuana emerging from the rustic earth of central Mexico, but also filmed the entire discovery. He finally had concrete proof. On September 28, without offering any explanations as to the manner in which the photographs and video tape had been obtained, United States Ambassador John Gavin officially requested that the Attorney General's Office of Mexico do an investigation into what had been discovered and that the necessary measures be taken to destroy the plantations.

On September 30, 1982, seven helicopters left the city of Guadalajara at dawn. Aboard were Federal Police officers, army officials and DEA agents Kuykendall and Camarena. When the helicopters arrived at the plantations, all were shocked – the green fields went on for hectares and the technology used to support these fields was on the cutting edge of agriculture: after benefiting from 200 tons of chemical fertilizer, a canal-based irrigation system and a network of sprinklers, some of the plants had reached 1.8 meters in height. Nevertheless, upon arriving at the site, they could find neither a drug trafficker nor a farmer in the area. So although the DEA agents felt victorious as the plantations were burned, those responsible for them were never arrested – a scenario that would repeat itself again and again.[31]

The State's Attorney's Office in San Luis de Potosí behaved evasively to Camarena's demands that they deal with the traffickers, denying him information related to the case. But Kiki persisted and turned over evidence related to a Mexican man named Antonio Pérez Praga, the presumed supervisor of the plantations and an associate of Ernesto Fonseca. Despite Kiki's efforts, Pérez Praga was never arrested.

A few weeks later, another informant showed up at the DEA office in Mexico City and spoke of other plantations belonging to Rafael Caro Quintero. These were presumably located in the State of Sonora. The story was recorded in detail by a new DEA agent who had arrived from the United States, Roger Knapp. Knapp consequently relocated to the city of Culiacán and gathered more precise information regarding the 170-acre marijuana plantation. Knapp tried to convince local police officers to execute a joint operation. He finally traveled to Ciudad Obregon to set up a base of operations and proceed from there. At six in the morning the following day, Knapp was wakened by a commander of the Mexican Federal Judicial Police named Esparragoza, who insisted that Knapp suspend his activities or else he would be arrested for interfering with a federal investigation and meddling in the

---

[31] Years later, James Kuykendall would reflect:

When we were in the air about twenty miles from the indicated place, we began to see huge splotches of dark green, which grew as we approached. When we landed, it was almost unbelievable. There was marijuana all around and we were in the middle of the desert. Their were thousands of improvised fields – it is something I will never forget. But the worst of it was the feeling I shared with Kiki that we were in real trouble. These fields were under commercial airline routes and must have been known about for a long time, and

internal affairs of a foreign nation.   Knapp called James
Kuykendall and explained the problem.   Despite Knapp's
protests, he was ordered to return to Mexico City.

Knapp was not alone in this situation as other DEA agents
had encountered similar inconveniences. Unfortunately, there
was nothing they could do since none of them were in a
position to confront the Federal Police.   Kuykendall sent a
confidential memo to American Ambassador John Gavin in
which he stated that Rafael Caro Quintero enjoyed the
protection of the Federal Judicial Police, and that they were
interfering with DEA agents whenever they tried to
investigate.   Something had to be done, or the traffickers
would continue with their large-scale operations sheltered by
the negligence and corruption of Mexican authorities at
various levels.   Kuykendall demanded not only the
intervention of the Ambassador, but also called for more
drastic measures involving the President of the United States
or the Congress.

Gavin understood the seriousness of the complaint and in
January, 1983 organized a meeting in San Antonio between
Kuykendall and three important State Department officials.
The DEA agent exhibited photographs and related his
experiences in detail, but when he was almost finished with his
monologue, he was interrupted by his State Department
counterparts: "You speak of corruption in the government.
There is no need to continue. Our role in the government is to
preserve our interests in Mexico, and what you propose would
jeopardize these interests."   And that was the end of the
meeting. Not satisfied, the persistent Kuykendall sent a cable
directly to the White House. He never received any answer.[32]

---

*consequently, must have enjoyed enormous protection from the
Federal Police.*
[32] The cable Kuykendall sent on February 3, 1983, ended with the
following thought:
*Guadalajara continues to be the city where Mexico's principal drug
traffickers live. They work in an environment of impunity thanks*

Despite their hampered condition, Kuykendall, Camarena, Sears, Hernandez and Knapp tried to continue with their jobs. To release some of the tension, the five men would frequently gather in a bar called *Camelot*, a few blocks from the American Consulate in Guadalajara, where they would exchange opinions and discuss their work. Their presence in the bar was known by many Mexicans, but at that point, they did not care. One evening in March, 1983, a short man approached them and told them that an ex-employee of Miguel Angel Félix Gallardo was in the Zacatecas prison. This ex-employee, the man told them, would be willing to talk to them in exchange for their protection. The DEA could not guarantee the protection of the presumed informant, but Butch Sears made a trip to the prison anyway, and asked to speak to the inmate named Claudio.[33] The guards would not let Sears inside the prison, as the American DEA agent had no credentials or diplomatic passport. Finally, Sears convinced the guards to let him pass, with the aid of some money as his price of admission. Sears passed through the main cell block to Claudio's cell, where the inmate invited his visitor to enter and take a seat. They talked for almost two hours. The informant had worked as a bodyguard for the trafficker, and was fired when he asked for a raise in pay. He found himself living in the street with a wife and children to support. And then, to top it all off, he was arrested for carrying a gun without a permit. So far, the informant had not told Butch anything novel, but the man was acting out of revenge and said he would testify against Miguel Félix Gallardo, should he ever be caught. This offer constituted a success for Sears – now all he had to do was arrest Félix Gallardo. However, when Sears

---

to the corruption of the police, judicial and political communities.
These institutions constitute real obstacles to the effective execution
of our investigations and to the development of our activities.
[33] "Claudio" is a pseudonym; his real name was never disclosed.

asked to leave the prison, he was taken to another cell and detained there for eleven hours without explanation. When he was finally let out, a guard informed him that Claudio had hung himself and that the presence of an American agent during such an event could place them in a compromising position.

This case proved not to be a unique one, however. A similar event happened a short time later to Kiki Camarena when an informant asked the agent to accompany him to the international airport in Guadalajara, where he was going to buy a kilo of cocaine from Rogelio Guzmán, a trafficker linked to Rafael Caro Quintero. Camarena and Kuykendall related the story to the commander of the Federal Police, Nicolás Flores Almazán, so that he could be present and arrest the trafficker. However, on the day of the operation, neither the informant nor Rogelio Guzmán showed up. The DEA agents looked everywhere for their informant, until finally, three days later, Kiki saw his name in the newspaper obituaries. Butch Sears confirmed his identity at the morgue. The informant had been tortured and murdered.

Kiki Camarena was still not ready to give up the fight, and by mid-1983, was convinced that Rafael Caro Quintero was the leader of the Guadalajara cartel. His informants had told him of an immense quantity of land that the traffickers had dedicated to marijuana and opium cultivation, but so far the leads had not amounted to anything. Kiki Camarena, Roger Knapp and James Kuykendall put together a report describing the situation and submitted it to Ambassador Gavin, hoping he would informally authorize certain undercover operations on Mexican territory. The agents had given a name to their investigations – Operation Miracle – since it would be nothing less than a miracle if the American Ambassador backed and defended their main objectives: to make flights over the suspect areas and, if possible, arrest Rafael Caro Quintero, and execute all these operations without the knowledge of the Federal Police. Officials in Washington were quickly informed of the intentions of the DEA agents in Mexico, and to avoid any potential political conflagrations between the two nations, named Ed Heath as the DEA chief of operations in Mexico. The new field general, who had been assigned his new post on the recommendation of Francis Mullen, Administrator of the DEA in Washington, immediately addressed the complaints of Kuykendall and Camarena. He made it clear to them that under no circumstances were they authorized to board a plane to inspect possible illegal sites. According to Heath, everything had to be done within the limits imposed by the Mexican government, and when possible, with their cooperation. Despite the explicit instructions, Camarena disobeyed orders and continued his incursions, writing up reports and sending them to certain congressmen and other U.S. politicians.

Ed Heath successfully cultivated friendships with a few members of the Attorney General's Office of Mexico and with a few Federal Police officials. In a truly diplomatic fashion, he managed to establish an excellent dialogue with the director of the Federal Police, Manuel Ibarra, and the majority of their meetings were also attended by Ambassador Gavin. The relationship was cordial, and the other DEA agents watched as pleasantries were exchanged, and dinners and meetings came and went, and all the while, nothing was happening with the war against drugs. Even worse, Heath used a good part of their budget to organize social events, which irritated the rest of the agents. In mid-1983, Kuykendall and Camarena went to Heath's office with photographs of the plantations and various reports showing a rise in marijuana and heroin production on the part of the cartel. They demanded a concrete plan followed by direct action. Heath called Manuel Ibarra, Chief of the Federal Police, and offered to share the information in exchange for allowing DEA agents to observe the subsequent operations. Ibarra accepted. Heath then delivered to Ibarra the addresses and telephone numbers of Caro Quintero and

Félix Gallardo, as well as a detailed report showing how they ran their businesses. In early June, 1983, it appeared as though Operation Miracle would bear its first fruit. Dozens of local and federal police and a few DEA agents searched houses in Guadalajara, Mexico City and other cities of the Interior. It was a rake operation that dug its claws in, at all levels of the criminal organization. Drugs of all types were found. In all, two hundred kilos of marijuana and almost one hundred kilos of heroin were confiscated, seven heroin refinement laboratories were destroyed, and seventy persons were arrested. The operation seemed to be a great success, except that neither Caro Quintero nor Félix Gallardo were apprehended. In fact, even though drugs were found in houses belonging to the two men, neither the Federal Police nor the Mexican Attorney General's Office accused either man of wrongdoing. Camarena and Kuykendall knew that those who were arrested were only the little fish. More information would need to be collected before they would be able to challenge the real players of the cartel.

Very few United States officials or congressmen, with the exception of those who received the unofficial and confidential reports of Camarena, were informed of what was really going on in Mexico. As a result, a group of congressmen formed the House Select Committee on Narcotics Abuse and Control. The committee met on June 22, 1983, to draft a statement to Dominick DiCarlo, the Assistant Secretary of State for International Narcotics Matters. DiCarlo admitted in testimony that Mexico was a country involved with international drug trafficking, but minimized the gravity of the problem. He maintained that "the illegal marijuana plantations are really quite small and thus are difficult to find." He also added that the State Department considered that "talk of plantations in the dessert is an aberration, lacking of all logic." DiCarlo explained that the Mexican authorities were aware of opium plantations in the Western Sierra Madre region as well as some refinement laboratories located in small towns along the U.S.-Mexican border, and that plans to eradicate this type of drug activity were well under way. They had been continuing, DiCarlo assured, the eradication campaigns that the two countries had initiated long before. Despite Dicarlo's message, John Thomas, an assistant of DiCarlo who testified just hours later, told the gathered parliamentarians that many American pilots continue to spot from the air opium and marijuana plantations all over the Western Sierra Madre region, and that "the Mexican Government is surely equally aware of the existence of illegal cultivations. It's time for someone, in this case me, to raise the alarm in order for all to understand the problem that we face."[34]

In August, 1983, democratic Congressman Charles Rangel, member of the House Committee on the Judiciary and of the House Select Committee on Narcotics Abuse and Control, decided to travel to Mexico City to assess the situation of the men assigned there. Kuykendall wanted to speak with the legislator, but Ambassador Gavin and Ed Heath did not authorize such a meeting. Rangel's agenda was plagued with protocol receptions and courtesy visits, such as those with the Attorney General of Mexico and with the Mexican Federal Judicial Police. Obviously, the DEA agents in Mexico were never included in these functions. After his trip, the Congressman wrote a report which stated the following:

> *I found the DEA men enthusiastic about the cooperation they are receiving from the Mexican Federal Judicial Police. They have made substantial arrests and progress against drug trafficking along the border and in the interior of the country. The Mexican Government continues to move forward with a successful eradication campaign against drugs, a program which can be praised for its professionalism, competence, performance,*

---

[34] *Hearings of the House Select Committee on Narcotics Abuse and Control* (Washington, D.C.: Government Printing Office, June 22, 1983).

experience and techniques . . . which has become something unique in the world . . . As it has always been between us, Mexico is a good neighbor.[35]

Some members of Congress who normally supported Rangel were quite critical of the report. Representative William J. Hughs, a democrat from New Jersey, member of the House Committee on the Judiciary and chairman of the House Subcommittee on Crime, not only questioned the document, but also distrusted the anti-drug efforts and attitudes of Ambassador Gavin and Ed Heath as much as those of the Mexican Federal Judicial Police. Representative Hughs also questioned the lack of attention given to the DEA agents, and recommended that Mexico be watched closely.[36]

In early 1984, an informant approached Kiki Camarena with information and evidence that the traffickers Rafael Caro Quintero, Ernesto Fonseca and a man named Juan Esparragoza were putting together a fund to finance a marijuana plantation of hundreds of acres in Zacatecas, Durango and Chihuahua. Camarena shared the information with Kuykendall and together they flew to the outskirts of Zacatecas where they confirmed the existence of the cultivations. The flight, piloted by an ex-soldier of Mexico, Captain Alfredo Zavala, was made in the face of their prohibition to do so. Upon returning to the American Consulate in Guadalajara, they drafted a series of reports about the discovery. The reports also noted that

---

[35] "International Narcotics Control Study Missions to Latin America," House Select Committee on Narcotics Abuse and Control, Government Printing Office, Washington, D.C., August 2, 1984.
[36] In a 1983 meeting of the House Select Committee on Narcotics Abuse and Control, Representative William Hughes expressed the following: "The Mexican Government is plagued with acts of corruption tied to drugs. We cannot continue saying that everything is all right when, in reality, the situation of the DEA agents is unsustainable and their lives are in danger." Representative William

Commander of the Federal Security Office Felipe Aparicio Núñez as well as Federal Police Commander Galo Gutierrez not only knew about the plantations, but were receiving approximately $9,000 - $12,000 each month from Rafael Caro Quintero. Enrique Camarena and Roger Knapp drove to Galo Gutierrez's office and, without wavering, questioned him regarding his relationship to the drug traffickers. Just as unwaveringly, the Commander responded: "They come and they make you an offer, the terms of which are very simple: collaborate or die. Of course, everyone prefers health to death."

Later, in April, 1984, Ed Heath harshly reprimanded Camarena and Knapp for having gone to Galo Gutierrez. However, the real reason for his anger was that the two agents had acted without ever consulting him, and had never even told him about the plantations, which he finally heard about through the Federal Police. Heath, together with Ambassador Gavin, made a series of attempts to persuade the Mexican Government to make aerial incursions over the cultivations and use defoliants to eradicate them. Although he offered no concrete reasons, Camarena vigorously opposed the measure, but his pleas were ignored by his supervisor. On May 28, 1984, under the command of First Commander Miguel Aldana, the Federal Police boarded their helicopters and began the operation. One hundred seventeen persons were arrested, 20 tons of packaged marijuana and 200 liters of hashish oil were confiscated, and 150 acres of marijuana plants were defoliated. Heath was pleased with the results, but Camarena and the other DEA agents were furious. For them, the results did not compare with what could have been achieved if they had waited a bit longer. That is, neither Rafael Caro Quintero nor Ernesto Fonseca were among those arrested.

Hughs, congressman from New Jersey, member of the commissions on Justice and Merchant Marine and Fishing Affairs.

On May 30, James Kuykendall drafted a report that was later delivered to his boss in Washington, Francis Mullen. The report stated the following:

> *I think the executed operation serves to demonstrate the existence of illegal plantations and, based on what was found in Zacatecas, the technology that is used in developing them. Also illustrated here is the level of impunity that the traffickers enjoy. You cannot ignore the presumed complicity of various officials of the Mexican Federal Judicial Police with respect to this matter. What we have found is really quite scant compared to what our informants tell us. I strongly suspect that we are caught in the middle of an operation of the Mexican Government which, on one hand, tries to show the world the forces it employees against drug trafficking, while on the other hand, is covering up a great number of other plantations and refinement laboratories. This time, the Federal Police did well and we were able to count on their cooperation. However, it is evident that those truly responsible for the drug operations were alerted beforehand since the majority of those arrested are simple farmers.*

The DEA agents had their reasons for disliking Ed Heath. In part, they did not trust him because they saw him more as an ingenuous diplomat than a man committed to confronting the drug traffickers. But the real reason for their feelings, and what explains why Camarena so vehemently opposed the operation, was that Kiki had managed to infiltrate Caro Quintero's organization with the help of a repentant trafficker named Manuel Chávez. For the first time, Camarena had been able to converse personally with Caro Quintero and Ernesto Fonseca, and had established a significant trust basis with the traffickers. All this had enabled him, from the position of an undercover agent, to gather valuable information and evidence. Among other things, he had been able to obtain the addresses, telephone numbers, and bank account numbers of various men in the organization – information that could eventually lead to their arrests. But the haste of Ed Heath had jeopardized all that Kiki had accomplished; and there was something else that worried them even more. Among those who had been arrested was Manuel Chávez, who, after recovering his freedom within twenty-four hours, met immediately with Fonseca and informed him of Camarena's activities. The DEA agents learned through some of their informants that Rafael Caro Quintero, upon learning of the undercover operation, had put a price on the head of Enrique Camarena. The drug trafficker had never been bothered or put in danger by the authorities' investigations over the years; but this was different: a DEA agent had gained entrance to his home and had gained his confidence. For this he ordered that Camarena's life be taken.

Camarena, paying no attention to the warnings, largely due to his obstinate character and his obsession with combating the drug traffickers, continued with his work. Many of his colleagues advised him to ask Ed Heath or Francis Mullen in Washington to be transferred to a less risky country, but Kiki would not hear of it. Many agents not only feared for the life of their friend, but also for their own. Such was the case with Butch Sears, who requested an immediate transfer, and was replaced by Victor Wallace. The new agent, better known as "Shaggy," was a close friend of Camarena's, after having worked with him years before on the streets of California.

Kuykendall, Camarena and the rest continued looking for informants, and in September, 1984, a man named Gabriel[37] introduced himself to Kiki and told him his story. He had been working for almost twenty years in the drug business. He had begun as a smuggler for the Herrera family, and later started

---

[37] "Gabriel" is a fictitious name. His real name has been kept anonymous, in accordance with United States law, for security reasons.

his own distribution business. However, over the previous five years, as the cartel had come to be dominated by Caro Quintero, his business had been absorbed, and now he worked for them. His motive for coming to the authorities was revenge: his son had been murdered in the streets of Jalisco under the orders of Félix Gallardo, who wanted to send the message to all smugglers that his authority was never to be questioned. This situation was sparked when Gabriel had dared to try to negotiate his salary with the trafficker. Gabriel told Kiki that the traffickers had established a network of influence and complicity within the Mexican Federal Judicial Police and the Federal Security Office of the Ministry of the Interior of Mexico. Through this network, they coordinated operations to smuggle heroin, cocaine and marijuana to the United States.

The security agents, Gabriel told them, provided information to the traffickers and helped cover up and keep watch over their operations. Gabriel explained that the Federal Police "gave them protection and computerized print outs telling them when and where to cross the border, and sold them semi-heavy and automatic weaponry, arms normally reserved for military use." Several weeks before, Gabriel continued, he had driven a gas transport truck with the tanks loaded with 600 kilos of marijuana. Fifteen kilometers from the border, he was met by a patrol from the Federal Security Office and its commander accompanied him the rest of the way. When they arrived at the border, they received a more-than-cordial treatment from the Federal Police. After they crossed over to the American side, his companion handed $50,000 to a U.S. Customs officer. Their journey continued without incident until they reached their destination in Los Angeles. There, he turned in the truck and returned in a car that had been prepared for him. For his work, Gabriel earned $10,000, which was given to him personally by Ernesto Fonseca. But these sums of money were nothing, Gabriel pointed out, when compared to the funds that were spent supporting officials of the PRI (Partido Revolucionario Institucional or Institutional Revolutionary Party) which dominated Mexican politics. Gabriel's story was sent to Francis Mullen at the DEA office in Washington, who promptly ordered an internal investigation of the Customs Service.

On October 28, 1984, Camarena and Wallace drove to Gabriel's house. They were going to accompany him to the Guadalajara Airport were he would fly to the United States to give further testimony. As Gabriel was boarding the automobile, a burst of machine gun fire rattled his body. The DEA agents could not believe it – the traffickers had murdered him right in front of their eyes.

Less than a month after the tragedy, on November 14, Camarena discovered a hangar supposedly belonging to Miguel Angel Félix Gallardo, and its doors had been left open. Equipped with binoculars and a camera, he took what photographs he could and jotted down the registration numbers of the airplanes. In a few days, his work yielded results. On November 17, DEA agents in California found one of the airplanes in a field. To their surprise, the plane did not contain drugs, but rather $3.7 million in small bills. Then, on November 26, the sheriff of Mohave County, Arizona, discovered a small airplane landing on a dirt road. The sheriff immediately called for back up. When they finally searched the plane, they found 173 kilos of cocaine hidden in Christmas present packages. The plane's registration number was among those noted by Camarena in Félix Gallardo's hangar.

These findings pleased Kuykendall and his comrades, who celebrated at their traditional gathering place, *Camelot*. However, they all knew that it would not be long before the members of the cartel would respond. No one was more worried than Mika Camarena, Enrique's wife, who could not wait to get herself and her family as far from Mexico as possible. Enrique always answered the constant fearful comments of his wife by saying: "The traffickers won't be inclined to fire on an American. They've never done it before and they won't do it now." But on December 2, 1984, they bucked the trend. Two American citizens from California, Dennis and Rose Carlson, were killed when they were subpoenaed to testify regarding a payment Ernesto Fonseca made to another man. And on the night of December 3, a couple from Nevada, Ben and Patricia Mascarenas, disappeared when they went for a moonlight stroll in Miguel Angel Félix Gallardo's neighborhood.

These events worried the men of the DEA, especially since the Federal Police were doing nothing to investigate. And now, the idea that the traffickers would not have the guts to kill an American was left aside. In January, 1985, two investigators of the House Committee on Foreign Affairs were preparing to go to Mexico to gather information on the deaths of the Americans; but Marian Chambers and Richard Pena suspended their trip when they learned that they were to be accompanied by functionaries of the Department of State. Therefore, the only ones to make the trip were the latter. Kuykendall thought this would be a good opportunity to make them understand that the situation in Mexico was extremely complex. They met on four occasions with the DEA agents, but when the functionaries returned home to the United States, they decided not to file a report. Doing so made no sense, they concluded. Camarena's reaction was foreboding. Despite his strong constitution, the agent slumped into a chair in his office and said to his comrades: "Is it necessary for one of us to die in order to get someone to do something? Do they need to get one of us killed?"

ENRIQUE "KIKI" CAMARENA

During the 1970's, Enrique Camarena lived in Fresno, California. As a DEA agent, he spent much of his time tracking and catching drug traffickers that were distributing drugs originating in Mexico. Many of these smugglers would use abandoned roads in San Joaquin as makeshift landing strips. This swarthy man of Mexican descent, had, since his youth, dreamed of being an FBI agent. But as time passed, his interest in fighting drugs led him to join the U.S. Drug Enforcement Administration. This work impassioned him, especially when it came to high-speed chases on the highways and patrolling the streets at night.

Kiki Camarena was no ordinary man. The more dangerous his work became, the more he loved it. T his is not to say that he did not care for his own life or safety, but the constant action of fighting drugs simply left him with a passion for more involvement. Quite differently from his friends and colleagues, it was nothing for Kiki to spend successive nights without sleep doing his work. Rather than resting after work, Kiki could be seen in bars, talking over his experiences with friends to get their perspectives. His penchant for fighting drugs dominated his conversations. This would often seem monotonous to his friends. That is, whether the conversations centered around women, gambling, sports or even if they were playing cards, Kiki would always bring up the subject of drugs.

At the Fresno office, Kiki's work was exemplary. He rarely asked for back up help in making arrests. On more than one occasion, Kiki made four or five arrests at once and brought them in tied up with a rope or in cuffs. His superiors had, by then, lost count of his arrests. For some, he was a brilliant agent. For others, he was just crazy and someone to stay away from if they wanted to keep from winding up dead on some street corner along with this macho Latino. Camarena largely ignored these opinions. He just considered himself a narcotics agent who was simply doing his job.

Camarena often thought about issues far beyond the responsibilities of an ordinary policeman; for example, he would ask himself constantly: 'Who are the real drug traffickers? Who gives the orders? Who supervises the money or finances the gangs? How does one get to the heads of the gangs and how can all of this be resolved?' But Camarena knew well that the answer was not to be found in Fresno. The San Joaquin Valley was only a drop-off point on route to the real markets for the traffickers; Los Angeles and San Francisco were the real targets.

One morning in early 1980, Camarena received a call from Pete Hernandez in Mexico. Not only was Hernandez one of the best godfathers to his sons, but he was a DEA agent who had just been certified to work in Guadalajara. Hernandez had called him for a special reason. He wanted Kiki to join the team in Mexico. Camarena did not hesitate for an instant in accepting the offer. He could not wait to leave the streets of California. Besides, an assignment abroad would really enhance his career. DEA agents were not forced to accept assignments that would transfer them out of the country. These assignments were accepted on a voluntary basis, and if accepted would be pluses in their dossiers and would be significant when being considered for promotion. Hernandez also told him that Guadalajara was a beautiful city for his family to live in, and that there was an American school to which he could send his children. Moreover, the climate was spring-like almost the entire year round. Best of all, the government would give him a beautiful house and raises would be forthcoming.

Regarding the work, there was much to be done. Pete Hernandez related that Guadalajara had come to be the location where the main traffickers of Durango and Sinaloa had settled, as the Western Sierra Madre had become the center for marijuana and heroin. These traffickers had bought splendid houses, bars and hotels. Apparently, they were under the protection of the local or Federal authorities. This city represented what Camarena had always sought – action – and he was ready for it. However, all did not begin well. Rafael Davila, a commander of the federal authorities in

Mexicali, who had become friends with Camarena, had also been transferred to Guadalajara. As payment for not abiding by the rules imposed by the traffickers, he was killed by a burst of machine-gun fire outside a discotheque by two men. This served Kiki notice that Guadalajara was a tough place to be and that the law of the jungle was to be observed to some degree. But Camarena loved living life on the edge and maintained: "I am ready for action, and if the big money is in Guadalajara, that's where I want to be."

Mika Camarena, Kiki's 34 year old wife was expecting their third child. She did not oppose the transfer. On one hand, she was aware of some of the risks that were involved, but she was confident that together they would see things through. She also realized that there was no city in the world that was really safe for a DEA agent and his family. She was not affected by the fact that her husband's covert activities in Mexico were not under the auspices of Mexican law; that is, her husband did not enjoy diplomatic immunity. Mika basically thought that her family should remain together, and she would therefore follow her husband to any part of the world. Under no circumstance would she interfere with his career, knowing full well the passion that Kiki had for his work. The DEA was definitely an integral part of the family.

Enrique Camarena's transfer to Guadalajara became effective in June, 1980, the same year that Rafael Caro Quintero, Miguel Angel Feliz Gallardo and Ernesto Fonseca began to structure the production, distribution and marketing of marijuana, heroin and cocaine to the United States. This group of traffickers came to be known as the Guadalajara cartel. Even though Kiki Camarena shared the work with other agents such as James Kuykendall, Tony Ayala, Pete Hernandez and Butch Sears (who would later ask to be transferred), and with those that later joined the team, including Roger Knapp and Victor Shaggy Wallace, Kiki became the number one enemy of the traffickers.

In just a few years, Kiki Camarena had demonstrated his tenacity in the fight against the traffickers. He had even gone so far as to violate certain limits that had been put in place for political reasons between the two countries (including the prohibition of flying over Mexican territory and intervening in direct police actions).   Kiki confronted the Washington bureaucracy and, with a passion and bravery that had characterized his life, challenged any local or federal officer or functionary that got in the way of his goals – to end the drug trade and to arrest the leaders of the trafficking organizations. Kiki's position was not envied by anyone, however. For years Kiki had been writing an infinitesimal number of reports that not only mentioned known leaders of the cartel, but also implicated several high officers of the Federal Security Office (an organization under the Ministry of the Interior) and the Federal Judicial Police of Mexico. Meanwhile, heavy arms and revolvers were being distributed around the streets of Guadalajara as if they were harmless toys.

It was commonplace to see bodyguards in the rich neighborhoods of Guadalajara. The traffickers' chauffeurs and helpers always carried either Federal Police or Federal Security Office identification, and could often be seen nearby in cars with no identification tags. DEA agents, on the other hand, were always pulled over if they went over the speed limit or went through a red light or otherwise committed the slightest traffic violation.

The game was being played on uneven ground. Although Camarena and the others were well aware of this, they could not imagine what was to become of them. The slaying of four American citizens on December 2 and 3, 1984, was seen as a warning. However, what transpired soon afterwards would put them in a truly desperate situation. On January 3, 1985, while Camarena, Kuykendall, Knapp and Shaggy were having lunch at the *Camelot* bar, a man by the name of Antonio

Vargas[38] approached them. Antonio Vargas asked to speak to Camarena at another table. There, he told Camarena that he had documentation detailing regular monthly payments of $10,000 and $20,000 made by the cartel leaders to high-ranking government security officials.   During the unexpected encounter, Vargas handed Camarena an envelope containing the proof, but he asked Camarena to open it in private, once Vargas had left. Two blocks away from the bar, two men fired on him and Vargas was fortunate not to be killed. However, three of the eight bullets fired at him found their mark and were lodged in his spine. To this day, Vargas is bound to a wheelchair.

On January 18, 1985, eleven days after the attempt on Vargas' life, which was still being investigated, the first direct act of violence against one of the American agents occurred. At 6:50 in the morning, Roger Knapp was in his bedroom and his wife Carol was in the kitchen having breakfast with their three children. A husky man stood outside the agent's car and hurled an explosive device into the vehicle. Upon hearing the explosion, Knapp's wife, Carol, threw herself on the children and luckily had them lay flat on the floor. No sooner had she done so, than the stockily-built man began to spray the interior of the house with machine gun fire from an AK 47. In less than two minutes, the assailant had managed to pour almost 200 bullets into the house, leaving shattered glass scattered and bullet holes everywhere.   Fortunately, none of the family members was seriously injured, except for minor cuts and bruises. Immediately thereafter, James Kuykendall spoke to Francis Mullen to have Knapp transferred quickly.   Knapp, however, refused to accept another assignment.   For the American agents, although this was a clear warning from the

---

[38] Antonio Vargas is a fictitious name. His identity as well as the particulars of the evidence which he provided Camarena remain a secret.

traffickers to leave the country, none of them was willing to go. In fact, it was Camarena who lifted their morale by delivering their response throughout all of the bars, discotheques, restaurants and streets of Guadalajara. Camarena made sure that Caro Quintero and company would get the new message: that "from now on, this is total war. You don't fuck with the DEA. It's either them or us, and we'll see who is more of a man."

A great deal of tension prevailed after the attack on Knapp and his family. This was not only evident in the city of Guadalajara, but in Washington as well, where the bureaucracy had been shaken. Francis Mullen stepped down from his post and took leave for a few months for personal reasons. John Lawn was put in charge in the interim. Lawn was tough and of the same mold as Camarena, he too had built a career upon his experience in the street. Lawn, however, was also adept at handling politically sensitive issues with diplomacy. This is exactly what Secretary of State George Shultz was looking for.

For those involved with the war on drugs, the most lamentable tragedy took place on February 7, 1985. On that Tuesday, Camarena was in a bad mood, which became intensified by the oppressive heat. From his office, he called his wife Mika, and arranged to meet her for lunch in order to take a break. Following lunch, he was planning on spending some time with his family. At 2:00 p.m. sharp, Camarena took leave of his friends and coworkers, and left the Consulate building after storing in a drawer the revolver that he normally wore. Camarena walked along Libertad Street and then ducked into the parking lot under the Camelot bar, where his car was parked. Upon finding his car, he switched off the anti-theft device, started the engine and turned on the radio. From that point on, hundreds of theories have been offered to explain the mystery of Enrique Camarena's disappearance. Not only would his case make front page news in all of the major papers around the world, but it would become a central issue between the United States and Mexico.

Meanwhile, Mika Camarena waited for Kiki at the restaurant. She was anxious to talk to him about family matters and looked forward to spending some time with him, which was something that did not occur often. She waited for him for nearly two hours, feeling conspicuously alone at the table as people glanced at her. She assumed that something very important had come up at the last minute. Mika then called the Consulate and spoke to Kiki's secretary, who told her that he had left quite some time ago. Mika waited a while longer before having to pick up her children at school. She never suspected the worst.

At 6:30 p.m., Mika called Shaggy Wallace. The agent and friend responded with surprise: "Didn't you meet with him for lunch?" He knew Camarena would never be absent without telling anyone. Wallace immediately notified James Kuykendall, for Kuykendall and Camarena were virtually inseparable. The seasoned agent recalled what Kiki had been saying again and again: "Something's going to happen. Someone's going to wind up hurt." Kuykendall began calling the other agents, but nobody knew his whereabouts. At 8:30 p.m., Kuykendall called the American Embassy in Mexico City to inform John Gavin of the situation and finally expressed his looming fear: "I am convinced that our man has disappeared."

James Kuykendall left his home and drove at high speed to the Consulate in Guadalajara. On his way, he passed the Camelot, where he saw Kiki's car and noticed that the car doors were not locked, that the keys were still in the ignition and that the radio was playing. Camarena could still be somewhere in the country, or they might have taken him to Colombia or Bolivia or some other place in Central America or even Europe.

In a matter of minutes, the news reached the supervisor of the DEA team in Mexico, Ed Heath, who immediately relayed the matter to John Lawn, who was in charge of the DEA in Washington D.C. Lawn brought Francis Mullen back from leave and placed him in charge of the investigation. Within the United States, the matter was given a high priority and some 30 agents were dispatched to the West Coast, where the search for Camarena focused on the cities of Los Angeles, San Diego and San Francisco. The agents teamed up with local authorities in the intense search. The American authorities took their search to bars, restaurants and other places that presumed distributors of the Guadalajara cartel frequented. But the authorities' hands were tied. They could not initiate raids or make arrests. They were only to interrogate informants and make insinuations to suspects connected to the cartel that Camarena was to show up alive or there would be a terrible price to pay.

The matter was much more complicated in Mexico. Ed Heath and Kuykendall needed to convince the federal authorities to make a door-to-door search. The younger members of the Federal Police were trustworthy; the problem lay with the higher echelon. Shaggy tried to speak with the chief of the Federal Authorities in Guadalajara, Commander Alberto Arteaga, but he was away. He then tried to find the chief of Jalisco state authorities, Commander Carlos Acevez Fernández, but he was told that the Commander was too busy to speak with him. Wallace was intent on speaking with some high official, but nobody was available to see him. He was also ignored by the United States General Consul in Guadalajara, Richard Morefield and by the Governor of the State of Jalisco, Enrique Alvarez del Castillo. At 5 p.m., on the Wednesday after the disappearance, DEA agents met in Kuykendall's office in an effort to remain calm and to develop a strategy. A few minutes later, Ed Heath arrived and again called General Consul Morefield. This time he left precise instructions with his secretary that he was to either join the team or it would be the end of his career. In less than half an hour, the Consul showed up at the meeting. The decision was then made to call

Ambassador John Gavin so that he would pressure the Mexican government for a solution. At 8 p.m., the Assistant Attorney General of Mexico called to excuse his superior and the chief state prosecutor of Jalisco, who were both out of the country on business unable to attend to the matter. Notwithstanding his superior's absence, however, he promised to give the Federal Police orders to initiate an investigation of the matter and gave assurances that there would be total cooperation between Mexico and the DEA.

On Thursday, February 9, Shaggy searched 11 hospitals to see if anyone bearing any resemblance to Camarena had been admitted. Nobody. Meanwhile, Kuykendall and Pete Hernandez stayed in the office making calls, and throughout the day Knapp interrogated informants on the streets. Later that evening, they met again and the desperation on their faces was obvious. The accusing glances they shot at Ed Heath revealed that they blamed him for everything. Aside from the fact that the agents considered him inept for the position, he now wanted to take charge of the investigation. He knew very little of the situation at hand since he had not been with them when the crisis began. The meeting ended abruptly, as Heath tried to defend himself from the insults and accusations hurled at him for his mistakes. The agents pleaded with him not to interfere any further. At one point, Kuykendall grabbed Heath by the coat, lifted him out of his chair, and punched him twice in the jaw, leaving the commander stretched out on the floor. And for Pete Hernandez, this whole tragedy left him feeling like the lowest human being on earth; after all, he had been the one to convince Camarena to come to Mexico.

The Mexican Federal Judicial Police began the search late in the day on Friday, February 10. Approximately 80 officers participated in the search. Some went banging on doors in Guadalajara, while others were sent to comb the certain areas in Durango and Sinaloa. Their progress was slow, and they complained of not having enough vehicles and equipment with which they could communicate and coordinate the operation effectively. But when the DEA supplied them with everything they needed, Commander Armando Pavón Reyes, who had been sent from Mexico City to head the search, continued to complain that he needed more personnel. Moreover, regarding the rate of their progress, he explained that every decision had to first be approved by the chief of the Federal Police, Commander Manuel Ibarra Herrera.

On Saturday, February 11, at 2 p.m., the DEA was able to intercept a call between Miguel Angel Félix Gallardo and Rafael Caro Quintero. The latter was ordering Gallardo to leave the country due to the situation they were facing. Gallardo promptly had his plane prepared for him to leave immediately. Kuykendall had a list of planes that were owned by Gallardo, which he gave to Pavón Reyes so the Mexican Commander and American agent Salvador Leyva could go together to the airport and inspect the planes. Before Leyva left, Kuykendall took him aside and said, "Go with them, but be very careful not to let them out of your sight." When they arrived at Félix Gallardo's hangar, they observed four men preparing an executive jet belonging to Ernesto Fonseca, while five others stood watch with machine guns in hand. Pavón Reyes ordered his men to take their weapons out of their holsters and to surround the plane. The officers identified themselves as federal police. Minutes went by as tension mounted. Both sides knew that if anyone started shooting, they would all surely die. A strange man stepped out from inside the plane. The man wore loose-fitting black silk clothing, short, punk-style hair, an array of gold necklaces, rings, bracelets and sunglasses. He seemed to be in charge.

Leyva, the DEA agent, observed everything from inside one of the cars, some fifty yards away. Pavón Reyes walked over to the man in black silk clothing and stretched out his hand. Both men spoke calmly for a while. Pavón Reyes gave orders for his men to search the plane and the hangar. After the search, Pavón Reyes came over to Salvador Leyva and told him that the search had turned up nothing. As the pilot of the plane started up the engines, the "punk" gave Pavón Reyes a hug and a bottle of champagne. Laughingly, he told Pavón Reyes that he was at his disposal, but that the next time Pavón Reyes wanted to detain him, to come well armed and not with toys.

A few minutes later, the plane took off. On the way back to the city, Salvador Leyva questioned everyone about the incident. One of the young officers said to him, "Leyva, we all know that some of the boys are mixed up in this. We can't do a whole lot against the traffickers. The organization is very big and powerful. Maybe we're making a mistake, but we can't go against the grain."

Upon hearing the details of the incident from Levya, Ed Heath had the agent identify the "punk" through recently taken photographs. Anger and frustration overcame them as the man in question was none other than Rafael Caro Quintero himself, and he had slipped through their hands.

On February 12, the DEA agents held a meeting to outline the specific measures which were to be taken. Present at the meeting, were Ed Heath, General Consul Morefield, Ambassador John Gavin and the newly promoted Francis Mullen. Surprisingly, Mika Camarena was there also. She wanted explanations regarding the hundreds of reports her husband had made about the state of anarchy that prevailed in that region in terms of controlling the narcotics trade. She told them of the countless times her husband had described the situation in which DEA agents found themselves; that is, at the mercy of Mexican officials' corruption. Yet no one was doing anything about it. In her estimation, it was time that her government, the United States Government, intervene once and for all in the matter and pressure President de la Madrid.[39] Mika demanded that someone in Washington take this

---

[39] Miguel de la Madrid, President of Mexico, 1982-1988.

seriously and try to shed light on the matter. She wanted the newspapers to stop writing about the Colombian cartel and expose the Mexican cartel. She wanted those politicians who had visited them and those who had championed the war on drugs to resolve her husband's case. She insisted that the CIA, the FBI the State Department reveal the *real* drug situation in Mexico. In synthesis, Mika attacked them all. For her, politics meant nothing. She was determined to fight until the death of her children's' father was cleared up.

In defense, Heath told Mika that he understood her complaints and that he agreed to some extent, but that his job was not to watch over every move his agents made minute by minute, and that basically they were all just "little cogs in a big machine." Mika did not accept the excuses and began to insult him. Mullen then tried to calm her by relating that all who join the DEA are aware that they can be killed on any street corner or have their families attacked, and that on this occasion things had gone to the limit. Mullen promised her that he would do everything possible and would not rest until those responsible were caught. Mika looked at him straight in the eye, and between sobs begged, "I know that the Mexican government will never find Kiki if they are not pressured by the heads of our government. If the worst has happened, I will only live to seek justice. My children have the right to know what happened to their father. I want them to bring back Kiki if it is in a coffin. And if that's how it must be, I demand them to find and punish the guilty." No one dared say anything. Ambassador Gavin tried to get closer to her, but then Mika finished by saying, "Don't let my husband become just another statistic."

On the same day, Commander Pavón Reyes and a squadron of 40 policemen began searching the houses of drug traffickers, but as expected, no one was found. Mullen called Jack Lawn to update him regarding the Federal Police activities, and mentioned something that they had just discovered minutes before. There was an explanation for Caro

Quintero's 'new look' and his escape from the airport. A secretary to Commander Pavón Reyes, Rogelio Muñoz Ríos, had called to confess that his boss had just given him $270,000 to deposit in one of his bank accounts. This was payment for having let Caro Quintero escape. The money had been given to him by one of Caro Quintero's men. T his made matters all the more complicated; after all, Pavón Reyes was in charge of finding Kiki Camarena. Lawn was determined to put everything related to the Camarena case and Mexican drug trafficking before United States Attorney General William French Smith. The Attorney General responded with a cable to his counterpart in Mexico: "I am extremely concerned about the disappearance of Camarena. I request that you send me all the information within your power so that I may include it in the investigation I have begun. Regarding your government's immediate response in this matter, I expect to be informed as soon as possible." An obtained copy of the cable caused apprehension in the State Department, as they knew that this time a scandal could not be avoided.

On February 13, the Mexican authorities made some arrests and offered their theory of the incident: five men, probably led by José Luis Gallardo Parra, one of Fonseca's lackeys, had ambushed Camarena as he tried to leave the garage. Three of the men were disguised as federal police in uniform, which probably caught Camarena off guard. They then convinced him to get in their beige Volkswagen Atlantic. The DEA did not buy this theory. There was no further information on the car to which they had alluded, and those who were arrested, besides being individuals of very low income, were accusing the federal authorities of torturing them to get their confessions. The DEA agents began questioning potential witnesses who might have seen Kiki as he walked down Libertad Street or in the Camelot's garage, but no one claimed to have seen anything. This struck the agents as being very strange, because the incident took place in broad daylight on a street that was normally very busy.[40]

On February 14, Mullen traveled to Mexico City to talk in tough terms with the Chief of the Federal Police, Commander Manuel Ibarra Herrera. During the conversation, Mullen made this reply, "Every time you do a search, you find nothing." The commander would gave no satisfactory answers to Mullen, who by now was convinced that he was looking at a man who was on the other side. He left the meeting abruptly and went to the American Embassy in order to give a press conference. Before doing so, Mullen discussed the need for the press conference with John Gavin, who had recently arrived from Guadalajara. Both men knew that the decision to go ahead with the press conference would surely produce conflict between both governments. However, it seemed to them that the time had come for the world to be told the truth. Indeed, the time for negotiating was over. It was time to strike. They owed it to Mika.

The major Mexican and American press were present at the last-minute meeting. Seated in front of the reporters were Ambassador Gavin and Francis Mullen. With great detail, both revealed how the Guadalajara cartel operated. They gave the names of the three leaders. They described, in depth, the poppy and marijuana plantations that had been discovered, and told of the network that existed between the Colombian and Mexican traffickers in order to smuggle cocaine into the United States. They dwelled on the complicity of the Federal Police as well as of the Federal Security Office, and explained the problems encountered over the years by agents of the DEA. Finally, they described extensively the role of Enrique Camarena in the war against drugs, his disappearance and the subsequent activities.

---

[40] José Luis Gallardo Parra was released for lack of evidence four days after being arrested.

The following morning millions of people were shocked at the news. *The New York Times'* front page headline read "Enrique Camarena, DEA Agent, is Kidnapped in Mexico." The subtitle added, "Our people are usually treated badly or assassinated." One of the major newspapers in Mexico headlined its front page with, "National Drug Trafficking Scandal in the Government. Enrique Camarena, DEA agent, Kidnapped." All of the morning and daily newspapers carried the story. T he editorials accused the government of complicity and of being inoperative in dealing with the drug traffickers. *The Washington Post* dedicated a major column whose caption read: "Corruption in Mexico. Government Ties to Drug Trafficking. Enrique Camarena is Kidnapped." The Mexican Government denied the allegations made by Gavin and Mullen, and framed the issue as an internal matter that was beyond the jurisdiction of the Americans. They even went so far as to criticize the Americans for going around the world, arrogantly preaching about the so-called superior Yankee morality. The Director of the Anti-drug Division of the Attorney General's Office in Mexico, Jesús Antonio Sam López, declared the following to *Newsweek* and *The Washington Post*:

> *There are no drug-trafficking cartels in Mexico. There is no greater power than the government in our country, and there is no area in which the state is not in control. Drug trafficking is being fought as it should be, and the drug traffickers have never been nor will they ever be allowed to dictate the destiny of our society. Everything being said is an invention of the Americans meant to discredit the government. In spite of this, we will make the greatest effort to locate the missing agent.*

For his part, Kuykendall accepted being interviewed by scores of local and foreign television stations. To the astonishment of all, he showed photographs of the drug traffickers, as well as copies of film that showed the poppy plantations which were discovered in desert areas.   He exhibited pictures of the hotels, restaurants, mansions, bars discotheques that belonged to Miguel Angel Felix Gallardo, as well as photos of Ernesto Fonseca's properties and the last fortress that Rafael Caro Quintero had built. This "fortress" was a mansion equipped with the latest security technology, complete with an electrical energy generator. The mansion had nine apartments on the third floor alone. Also displayed were pictures of a park belonging to Caro Quintero that measured 8,600 square meters, with various exotic fishes, two swimming pools and two tennis courts. The whole park was surrounded by a wall almost three meters high, and guarded by some twenty heavily-armed men. These images certainly had an impact. Moreover, the American journalists hovered over their typewriters, telling how their hotel rooms were constantly being searched and their telephone calls recorded.

President Miguel de la Madrid's government was under attack. He therefore asked for the resignation of the director of the Federal Police, Manuel Ibarra Herrera.   Herrera was replaced by an ex-representative of INTERPOL, Florencio Ventura, who committed himself to solve the Camarena case. Nevertheless, Mullen viewed the Mexican strategy as one that merely tended to improve its international press image. He then decided to call Lawn on February 16, to suggest that they adopt a hard line stance against the Mexican Government. Lawn in turn called United States Attorney General William French Smith and they agreed to pressure their own government to urge President de la Madrid to intervene in the case. Smith called the White House and asked to speak to President Ronald Reagan, but was only able to reach Donald Regan, the President's chief of staff, who did not consider it prudent for the President to get directly involved. The next day, Smith called again and this time not only was he able to talk to the President, but also to Robert McFairlane, his national security advisor. Ronald Reagan told him, "Rest assured, the Mexicans will do much more than they have been to cooperate with us in solving the case. I give you my word on it." On February 18, Ronald Reagan sent a message to President de la Madrid in which he expressed his personal interest with respect to the Camarena case, and stated that he hoped that the interest was mutual.

On February 20, Jack Lawn was in his office with Francis Mullen when the telephone rang. It was Willy Von Raab of the United States Customs Service. Raab was from New York, and well connected to the Republican Party. He had left his studies at Yale to join the war on drugs. Raab hated red tape; that is, anything that would get in the way of his getting the job done, such as seeking proper authorization, judicial orders etc.

He offered to collaborate in every way possible to resolve the case. Lawn told him, "Willy, your help could really be of use to us. It would be interesting if you intensified the border control." Raab answered, "Control? I'll do better than that! From now on, nobody gets through." A few minutes later, Raab called his assistant and ordered, "I want you to personally see to a shut down of the southwestern border. Those that do get through get thoroughly get checked out. Delay them as long as you can and interrogate them thoroughly." His assistant complied, coining the operation Operation Intercept.

There were immediate results. Tourism was the second largest source of revenue for the Mexicans, oil being number one. As a result of the operation, hundreds of tourists were delayed at the border or at airports, causing them to cancel their reservations. Moreover, the Customs agents were telling the tourists entering Mexico that there was a strong possibility of a coup d'etat in that country, and that the entire nation would fall into the hands of either the guerrillas or the military. Quite naturally, people fled back to the U.S., frightened, to such a point that President de la Madrid called Ambassador Gavin, who would not attend him.

Moreover, Raab had a friend in the State Department by the name of Jon Thomas, who began to spread the rumor that the State Department would advise President Reagan to cancel a $250 million loan that the Mexican government had requested from the Treasury Department.

The United States Senator from Texas, Lloyd Bentsen, protested the operation immediately, labeling it as "interference with the inherent matters of a foreign state, and detrimental to the good relations of both countries." Bentsen called Secretary of State George Shultz, who defended the operation and especially Jon Thomas. However, Shultz had never been consulted in the first place and was furious. It was too late to undo what had been started, especially after calling Ambassador Gavin and hearing that the Mexicans had begun to cooperate. - On February 25, Jorge Espinosa, the Mexican Ambassador to the United States, communicated with Shultz to register a complaint, but the Secretary of State was adept at being evasive and promised that as far as he knew, nothing out of the ordinary was taking place on the border, and that ultimately those controls were the responsibility of the Customs Service.

On February 26, President de la Madrid called Ronald Reagan personally. Both heads of state spoke through their interpreters for approximately fifteen minutes. De la Madrid expressed that what the Americans on the border were doing did not serve any purpose in the war against the traffickers. He assured that the Mexicans were doing everything possible in the struggle against drugs, which had cost many policemen their lives. But Reagan explained to him, without mentioning Camarena, that the matter was about guaranteeing the safety of the American citizens in Mexico. His Mexican counterpart, however, insisted that it was not necessary for the Americans to continue what they were doing on the border. Reagan finally answered tersely, "We want more cooperation, and the only tangible way of showing us progress would be the immediate resolution of the Camarena case."

On February 28, Commander of the Federal Police Armando Pavón Reyes, still in charge of the search for Kiki, went to see Kuykendall. Upon arriving at Kuykendall's office, he produced an anonymous note indicating that Camarena was at a ranch called *El Mareño,* not located in the town of La Angostura, in the State of Michoacán. The ranch belonged to a State Congressman Manuel Bravo, of whom the DEA had no record even though Pavon Reyes maintained that he had connections to the cartel. Commander Pavón Reyes proposed to Kuykendall that he prepare for an early morning raid on the ranch: they were to meet at the central office of the Federal Police at 6 a.m. in order to board a helicopter. The DEA agent was suspicious. Why would the commander, who had always proceeded so slowly and erratically, be so eager to undertake such sudden action based solely on an anonymous note?

The following morning, Kuykendall and Tony Ayala arrived at the meeting place only to be met by Commander Alfonso Velázquez Hernandez, who informed them that the Federal Police had decided to leave two hours earlier. Tony Ayala was convinced that this was another of Pavón Reyes' ploys. He got in his car and sped off toward the ranch. When he arrived at 8:40 a.m., it was too late. Manuel Bravo and his wife were dead (the wife having been shot three times in the back), and two of his sons, Hugo and Manuel, were lying dead some 10 yards from the main house. Rigoberto, the third son, was in his bed, a bullet in his head. One of the Mexican officers was found with three bullets in the chest, which had been fired from a high-caliber automatic weapon. The version the Federal Police gave reporters and the DEA was that upon arriving they identified themselves and ordered the family to remain where they were and to allow access to the house. They were then fired upon by someone inside the house. According to the police, the Mexican officer was the first to die. They then were compelled to return fire and the ensuing battle lasted almost a half hour. Pavón Reyes produced automatic weapons that he claimed belonged to the Bravo family. However, a young worker had witnessed the operation from a nearby hillside some 300 yards from the house, and maintained that the family had been killed in cold blood. The witness declared on CBS News that his own foreman had been killed first by the Federal Police when they entered the property shooting. This caused the Governor of Michoacán, Cuauhtemoc Cárdenas, to protest, calling the operation "the Mareño Ranch Massacre," and to request an investigation.[41]

Because the ranch site was part of the investigation of the recent massacre, Pavón Reyes permitted the DEA agents to be on the premises. The American agents combed the ranch inch by inch in hopes of finding some trace of Camarena, but without any success, they later returned to Guadalajara. Nevertheless, at 8 p.m. that day, a field hand named Antonio Navarro was walking along a pathway when he noticed a foul odor coming from some nearby shrubs. His curiosity being pricked, he looked closer and there, sticking out of a bag of fertilizer, was a human foot. Navarro ran to the police station in town to tell of his discovery. The chief of police, Salvador Sandoval, informed Pavón Reyes, and then they both went to the site without informing the DEA.

On the morning of March 6, 1985, the Mexican television stations broadcast that Enrique Camarena's body had been found and taken to the city of Zamora in the State of Michoacán. DEA agents Kuykendall, Wallace, Hernandez and Ayala immediately went to the hospital to identify the body. The man fit the general description of Kiki, but it was impossible to positively identify him without an autopsy as the medical examiners estimated the body had been dead close to 25 days. The first autopsy took place that afternoon, with DEA

---

[41] On September 10, 1985, Mexican Attorney General Sergio García Ramírez accused various Durango police officers and 6 federal police officers, including Commander Alfonso Velásquez Hernández, of the homicide of the Bravo family.

agents present, including Ed Heath. The copse had three fractured ribs on the left side, numerous lesions on the right arm, a broken right wrist, bruises on the face and head, and the rectum had been violated with a blunt object. In the opinion of the doctors, death had been caused by suffocation.

Jack Lawn, Administrator of the DEA, knew that the place where Kiki's body was found had been combed by his agents. In addition, Lawn was not confident in the autopsy. He talked to Mika about having a second autopsy done in Washington at the Armed Forces Institute of Pathology. For that to take place, they would have to get permission from the Mexican authorities to transport the body to the United States, but the Federal Police and the Attorney General's Office of the Republic denied it, as they had yet to complete their own investigation, which could still take months or even years to complete. Because of this complication, Dr. Jerry Douglas Spencer, a Marine captain and a specialist in forensic pathology, and two other specialists from the FBI forensics laboratory stepped off the plane in Guadalajara on March 8. The pathologists positively identified the corpse of Enrique Camarena, and according to their analysis, his death had occurred on February 8. A dead man can indicate much more than one can imagine: the doctors maintained that there was no evidence of insect or rodent bites. If the original theory were true –that the corpse had lain where it was found for days– it would have been impossible for it not to have sustained insect or rodent bites. Therefore, the corpse had to have been abandoned only a few hours prior to being found. The analysis also found micro-organisms on the skin that could not exist in the area where the body was found, but grew in a higher, moister climate. Upon analyzing the condition of the internal organs, it was concluded that the body had been refrigerated for at least two or three days.

On the very same day, by executive order, President Miguel de la Madrid made Camarena's corpse available to the

American authorities, to be returned to the United States. An Armed Forces airplane transported his remains to San Diego. Once there, after the ceremony of honor performed by the United States Marine Corps, Mika Camarena decided to have his remains cremated. The following day, she joined James Kuykendall on a small aircraft that flew toward the Mexican border. There among the mountains she scattered his ashes, in hopes that Kiki's spirit would remain there to protect all who dedicated themselves to the war on drugs.

THE SEARCH FOR THE GUILTY

In March 11, 1985, Pavón Reyes, one of the high-ranking officers of the Mexican Federal Judicial Police, discredited by the Camarena case and suspected of being involved with the cartel, suddenly left Guadalajara. As his whereabouts were unknown, DEA agents urged the chief of the Federal Police, First Commander Florentino Ventura, to take measures to locate and interrogate him. On March 12, Ventura announced that his men had detained 13 men in connection with the assassination of Kiki Camarena. Seven of the men were federal police officers stationed in the State of Jalisco. The six others were local police officers from that same state. Two of the local officers, Victor Manuel Lopez and Gerardo Torres Lepe, confessed to taking part in the kidnapping of Camarena, as ordered by the drug trafficker Ernesto Fonseca. One of the others arrested, Chief of Police of Jalisco Benjamin Locheo Salazar, also confessed to his taking part in the kidnapping. He admitted to receiving $75,000 for granting logistic support to the traffickers and to having a close relationship with Rafael Caro Quintero, Ernesto Fonseca and Miguel Angel Félix Gallardo.

The Miguel de la Madrid Administration considered the Camarena case closed even though the traffickers were still at large.   By contrast, the American Government wanted to follow the matter to its conclusion, for once more, those held in custody were only secondary accomplices and not the real culprits.   Secretary of State George Shultz and Ambassador Gavin kept in close contact.   For them, the matter had become an integral part of foreign policy in regards to Mexico.   As a first step, they agreed that it would be advantageous to have United States Attorney General William French Smith replaced by Edwin Meese.   Although William French Smith had done an excellent job, Edwin Meese had a tougher character.   Meese was known for his public disapproval of the Mexican Government and its policy on migration.   In sum, Ed Meese profoundly rejected Mexicans residing in the United States, and his feelings for the Mexican Government were even more severe.

In this fashion, Secretary of State Shultz supported the public initiatives of Florida State Senator Paula Hawkins,[42] who never passed up the opportunity to speak about the death of Kiki Camarena on television, and to lambaste her nation's southern neighbor:

We never get anything from the Mexicans. Nothing. Our friendly relations should cease if they do not respond to our pleas to have the matter of Enrique Camarena resolved. They violated him, they tortured him, and then they killed him. Aren't we going to do anything? It's time we put a stop to this. We should turn things around and tell them to stop kicking us.

Senator Hawkins also had the support of several congressmen that sought to block Mexico's access to credit from the International Monetary Fund, which was crucial to Mexico's economy at the time.   Nevertheless, certain

---

[42] Paula Hawkins, Republican Senator from Florida, member of the Committee on Banking, Housing and Urban Affairs.

congressmen such as Senator Patrick Leahy were opposed to the drastic measures and spearheaded the defense of the Mexicans:

> *We are deeply saddened, but our DEA agents know what they face. Now they can't protest and ask our government to break relations with our neighbors. Certainly, the situation in Mexico is complicated. We need to resolve the issue, but to pressure and to extort another government through the loss of credits should make us ashamed. I believe it's time we took a look at ourselves and uncover the corrupt system we have. A large portion of the blame for this drug business lies with us.*[43]

On March 22, 1985, Administrator of the DEA John Lawn invited Mexican Attorney General Sergio García Ramirez to work out an agenda that would provide a solution to the drug trafficking problem and lead to the arrest of the drug leaders. The first point consisted of the need to have the DEA and Mexican Federal Judicial Police work in close cooperation to track down and arrest Rafael Caro Quintero, Ernesto Fonseca and Miguel Angel Félix Gallardo. Second, the Mexican Government promised to employ its security forces and capture those involved in the assassination of Enrique Camarena. The third item called for the capture and punishment of Armando Pavón Reyes. In return, the United States agreed not to interfere with Mexico's credit line with American banks or with any international institutions. Furthermore, Mexico would continue receiving financial assistance to fund its effort against drug trafficking and to bolster its security forces if it strictly complied with the aforementioned items. At the end of the meetings, Edwin

---

[43] Patrick J. Leahy, democratic Senator from Vermont, member of the Committee on the Judiciary and of the Committee on Agriculture, Nutrition and Forestry. Leahy delivered the above diatribe on four occasions.

Meese expressed his confidence that from that point on, the Mexican authorities would undertake the needed reforms to carry out the fight against the traffickers and track down those responsible for Camarena's death.

Toward the end of March, 1985, Don Clements, in charge of the DEA effort in Costa Rica, had been investigating the possible connections between the Medellin cartel, led by Pablo Escobar, and local drug traffickers. The muscular American agent, who sported a thick mustache, had been in the United States Marine Corps. He was in charge of verifying possible shipments of drugs that originated from Costa Rica's western Pacific coast, with Mexico as their destination. The DEA had received reports that Costa Rica was being used as a refueling station for shipments coming from Colombia or Panama, with their final destination being Mexico or cities in the western region of the United States. Don Clements' objective was to put an end to these operations.

Although Clements was occupied with personal affairs (his transfer to San Diego had just been approved, effective in a matter of weeks), he received a call early on April 3 from a local policeman, Victor Mullins. Mullins told him that some fugitive traffickers from Mexico were in the country. At 9:30 a.m., Mullins, Clements and DEA agent Sandalio Gonzalez met at the American Consulate in the capital city. The policeman informed the agents that Sara Cristina Cosío Martínez, Rafael Caro Quintero's girlfriend, had been observed casually walking around the streets of San José and shopping at the main stores.

It was known that Caro Quintero had kidnapped the long-haired, robustly-figured seventeen-year-old months before fleeing Guadalajara. The Cosío Martinez family, however, trying to preserve their reputation, had never publicly revealed the sequestration. The father had been the minister of education of Jalisco, and one of the most prominent members of the PRI (Institutional Revolutionary Party) in Mexico.

According to some sources, he had paid a million dollars to have the girl rescued, but this had not produced the return of his daughter since she had fallen in love with her captor.

Clements called Ed Heath in Mexico to inform him of the developments. It was suggested that the Mexican Embassy in San José be called to coordinate with the local law enforcement and DEA agents for the investigation and possible capture of Caro Quintero. Clements made the call and the organization came together smoothly. The CIA provided the Mexican authorities with sophisticated equipment with which to intercept calls between Sara and her family. Sara finally made the call to her family from San José and the number was traced. The number was then given to the DEA in Costa Rica, and Clements in turn gave the number to Victor Mullins to have it checked in the local directory. The trail did not take them far from the capital. The number corresponded to a plantation called "La Quintana," which was registered to Mexican citizens Inés Calderon Quintero and Jesús Gutiérrez, who had bought the property a month before with $800,000 cash.

Sandalio Gonzalez and Mullins boarded a plane and headed for the plantation to photograph it. It was a magnificent sight. In the center of the property was a two-story house that covered approximately 450 square meters. It contained a Jacuzzi, a swimming pool and a large cage with many types of birds. The rest was covered with vegetation of different kinds. Meanwhile, Clements, together with the local police, began to ask questions of the population surrounding the plantation to confirm the identity of the two inhabitants. The people in the area not only identified the couple, but they added that the two were arrogant and treated their neighbors with disdain. The couple would ride around in their fancy cars showing off their wealth. This confirmed what the DEA had suspected – the couple could only be Rafael Caro Quintero and Sara Cosío.

Clements turned in the detailed report to American Ambassador to Costa Rica Francis McNiel, but as McNiel had just been named ambassador to another country, he referred the matter to George Jones, who was in charge of relations at the local level. Clements and Jones met to discuss how to solicit the cooperation of the highest authorities so as to formulate a plan that would lead to Caro Quintero's arrest. Their cooperation was taken for granted being that Costa Rica was extremely legalistic in its policy. The head of the DEA communicated with the Minister of Public Security of Costa Rica Benjamin Piza. Piza was considered to be one of President Luis Alberto Monge's most brilliant officials. He was known to support any effort to modernize and advance the justice system. The minister listened quietly to Clements and then went right to the point: "What do you need from us?" Clements informed him that Caro Quintero was guarded on his own property by fifteen bodyguards, armed with sophisticated weapons. Clements doubted that the local police could handle the situation that would most surely result in a bloody fight. Clements was correct to the extent that Commander Luis Berrantes Aguilar, Chief of Police of San Juan, only had enough equipment to arm twenty men. Piza informed him that he had no qualms about referring the case to the Anti-Terrorist Command, which was under his authority. This organization was composed of a hundred men who had received training in the United States from the FBI. They maintained active training with the CIA. The organization was only used in cases of national emergencies, to the extent that they are not known to many of the citizens of Costa Rica.

Piza reasoned that if Caro Quintero was not a terrorist and that if this was not a terrorist situation, then the matter merited being considered a national security emergency. Clements was impressed by the Minister's decision, and commented to his fellow agents, "It's incredible. We have never been in such an advantageous position in terms of collaborating with local authorities. Now it all depends on us. There won't be any excuses for our mistakes."

While a group of policemen were dispatched to keep watch on the Caro Quintero property, Chief of the Anti-Terrorist Command Miguel Torres, Chief of Police of San Juan Colonel Berrantes Aguilar, Agent Clements and American Ambassador George Jones began to formulate a plan of attack. The plan was based along the lines of a SWAT team attack which would be carried out by the security forces. The problem lay in how to incorporate the DEA into the operation, since the agents were prohibited from direct action in a foreign country according to the Mansfield Law. Although it was a complicated situation, Jones was ready to go beyond the restrictions. Aware of the possible repercussions, two options were considered. First, the operation could be carried out by the special command forces, with the DEA stepping in after its conclusion; or the DEA could be directly involved without second thoughts of the consequences. Clements decided to take responsibility for any future complications: "I will do everything possible to stay within the rules that we have to bear on our shoulders, but in no way will I let Quintero get away. Regardless of the circumstances, I am going to arrest him. Whatever I have to do on the day of the assault, I do because I feel I have to." He later added, "I am certain that the entire DEA is behind us. They are counting on us and I swear I'm going to arrest that drug trafficking son of a bitch."

On April 7, 1985, the plan to capture Caro Quintero was set. The men of the Anti-Terrorist Command would carry out the incursion with the DEA providing logistical support. Everything was ready, except for one detail that would make the plan perfect. They needed to find a judge who would authorize the legality of the procedure and supervise the action.   They sought Judge Jorge Meza, a confidant of Commander Miguel Torres. He was a judge of great prestige and inflexible reputation. His only stipulation was that they wait until the next morning to initiate the procedure. In this fashion, the assault was carried out by the local security forces that penetrated to the heart of the plantation, while DEA agents Don Clements and Sandalio Gonzalez and a dozen others remained in cars at the entrance and along the periphery of the plantation. This was the way they could observe the Mansfield Law.

Everyone was confident the plan would succeed. For Colonel Berrantez, this was an excellent opportunity to show what his boys could do. The stillness was shattered by the explosion of grenades and the characteristic hum of high-caliber bullets. After ten or fifteen minutes, the DEA agents received word that the situation was under control and that they could proceed onto the property. A voice over the radio informed them that the special command forces had encountered more than twenty gunmen, in addition to those who fired from within. Given the circumstances, there had been no way of asking questions or distinguishing the innocent from the guilty as they fired in return. When Clements and Gonzalez entered the main house, they found the police pointing a gun to the head of a man stretched out on the floor as they interrogated him. Clements drew closer and asked the man of the whereabouts of Caro Quintero, but got no answer from the man claiming to be Marcos Antonio Rios Valenzuela. The passport he carried identified him as Mark Anthony.

Clements then decided to accompany the local police in the search of the smaller houses and other possible hiding places. While they searched they came upon an arsenal of rifles and automatic weapons with the Federal Security Office of Mexico and National Guard of Nicaragua insignias. They also found caches of expensive clothing, jewelry, and money. But as the houses and other potential hiding places became fewer, Clements became desperate. It seemed Caro Quintero had escaped again. Nevertheless, in one of the houses, on the second floor, they found Sara Cosío. She invited them in as though she were receiving guests in her house. Clements sat down and began to interrogate her when Gonzalez appeared. The replies she made were evasive, although they noticed that she responded with an unworried air, and with some irony and humor. They all were perplexed when she said her boyfriend was in the house, but that no one had recognized him. Gonzalez picked up a photograph lying on some furniture and they noticed that the man being interrogated at gun point resembled the man in the photograph, who had a happy Sara on his arm. They asked her what kind of relationship she had with the man. Sara simply relied, *"Its Rafael."* The two officials ran out of the house to within a few yards of the entrance of the ranch. There, seated with a policeman beside him, was the man who called himself Marcos Antonio Ríos Valenzuela. The man had a striking resemblance to Caro Quintero, although he had shaved his mustache and had changed his hair style. No one could explain how they had not recognized him earlier. Sandalio Gonzalez wanted to confirm what his eyes were beholding and after a few questions, he got the answer he had hoped for: "Yes, I am Rafael Caro Quintero."

The police photographed him on the spot. They read him his rights and then took him in handcuffs to an awaiting car. Before leaving the property, one of the officers of the Anti-Terrorist Command drew close to Clements and asked him, "When do you want us to kill him?" Even before the DEA agent could answer, he was interrupted by the officer who felt that killing him would be a just act, for they were all soldiers and as such, their mission was to terminate the enemy. Clements took a few moments to respond: "I am not a soldier. I am a policeman. My job consists in making the effort to arrest the criminals. I am not trying to moralize, but we're neither judges nor the jury. Nobody is going to kill Caro Quintero. I am going to take him in to face trial and have him sentenced to life in jail."

Clements knew that Caro Quintero could not be taken to the United States to stand trial. There was no case pending against him in any court in the U.S., nor was there a request for his extradition. The only country that had charges against him was Mexico. Meanwhile, he had to take the proper measures to ensure that the trafficker be transported quickly to face justice. At the same time, Caro Quintero was being held in a jail that did not seem like it would be able to contain him for very long. The trafficker could count on hundreds of gunmen to help with his escape. Caro Quintero needed to be returned to Mexico with haste, but red tape could delay that maneuver for months. For that reason, Clements considered having him deported for carrying firearms and for having entered the country illegally.

On April 10, 1985, Clements met with Minister Benjamín Piza to see if it was possible to extradite Caro Quintero in the near or mediate future. Since Piza was the head of the ministry charged with maintaining public safety, it was not unreasonable to consider accusing the trafficker of having endangered public safety and thus deporting him. Before ending their meeting, Piza said that before he could sign the deportation papers he would have to consult with the head of state. In less than twenty-four hours, Benjamín Piza informed Clements that the decision had been made, but that the DEA needed to make sure the Mexicans came as soon as possible for the trafficker.

On April 11, two Mexican airplanes arrived in San José. On board were members of the Federal Police, commanded by Florentino Ventura, who personally closed the door to the cell in which Caro Quintero was to be held. The place selected for Caro Quintero's detainment was a jail in northern Mexico called "Prison of the North," which, in recent years, had undergone improvements in its infrastructure. These improvements allowed Caro Quintero to enjoy a cell accommodated with a television, a small chamber for interviews, a private bath, etc.

The trafficker confessed on the first day of his trial, through a monologue lasting almost four hours, that he had internationally trafficked marijuana, cocaine and heroin. He also testified that he had paid Commander Pavón Reyes $20,000 to allow him to escape from the airport in Guadalajara when he was about to be arrested for the murder of Enrique Camarena. The trafficker gave a detailed account of all the businesses he had used to further his operations, and gave a list of police officials, mayors, governors, customs officers and lawyers that had collaborated with him.

In his testimony, Caro Quintero related the different methods he had used to advance his operations, and described the patrimonial position he had attained. He noted the exact banking entities used to launder his money, as well as the exact numbers of each of his accounts. Certainly, the trafficker named an overwhelming quantity of politicians, government officials of the PRI, local and international financiers, journalists, and people of Mexico's upper crust. His confession was total, except that he denied participated in the murder of DEA agent Enrique Camarena. He maintained that Camarena's murder had been organized and executed by his friend and associate Ernesto Fonseca.

On April 17, 1985 the DEA agents were able to smile again when they heard that Ernesto Fonseca had been captured by mere happenstance. It was an atypical week because of the Holy Week festivities and many Mexicans were taking advantage of the holiday by heading for the coastal cities. It so happened that in Puerto Vallarta the local police had been doubling their efforts to control the thousands of tourists on vacation. A police patrol unit observed four men carrying high caliber weapons under their clothing. They followed the men into the Pacific Beach Resort of Puerto Vallarta and watched them go into a small, guarded house near the beach. They could see that the majority of the tourists in the club had weapons and they were observed speaking to one another as though they knew each other well. The police informed their superiors, and in that manner the intervention of the Federal Police came about. The federal agents entered the place without resistance. There they found different types of arms, projectiles, some jewelry and a lot of money in cash. Then an incredible surprise occurred: when those under arrest were ordered to form a line, one of those to be identified said he was Ernesto Fonseca.

Fonseca immediately confessed to his role as one of the leaders of the Gulf cartel. Although he admitted having participated in the assassination of Camarena, he claimed not to be the main culprit. According to his statements, the idea of kidnapping the DEA agent was Caro Quintero's. The original idea was simply to take him for a ride in which they would frighten him enough so that he would drop his investigations. According to Fonseca's version, he claimed to have had strong words with Caro Quintero for having kidnapped and tortured him. After all, this was an American agent and who could tell what consequences might come of this action. Moreover, he claimed he never knew that they intended to kill him, and upon finding this out he got furious and had called his partner to reprimand him.

Among those arrested with Fonseca was his trusted gunman Samuel Ramirez Razo, a man who years ago had been a member of the Federal Police of Mexico. The ex-policeman, nicknamed Sammy, tried to make a deal with the agents for a lighter sentence in return for his cooperation in naming the men who had killed Camarena. The deal never was agreed to as Sammy decided to talk suddenly of his own will. According to his account, Ernesto Fonseca had ordered him to hire a gunman named Luís Parra to kidnap Kiki. It was carried out with the help of two policemen, Gerardo Lepe and Victor Lopez, from the State of Jalisco. Camarena was taken to the Mareño Ranch (where he was later found dead), where Caro Quintero was waiting for him in person. According to Sammy, Fonseca and an attorney from Guadalajara, Javier Barba

Hernandez, arrived and had a heated discussion with Quintero after which they left. Later, Sammy added that he knew from comments made by other gunmen that Caro Quintero had ordered Camarena to be killed.

Although the new testimony was important to the DEA agents, there still were some things that were not clear. In the first place, nothing was known of the participation (in Kiki's death) of Miguel Angel Félix Gallardo, who was the real trafficking boss in that region. He had been the focus of Camarena's investigations and it was felt that he must have played some role. Also, it was never specified who had actually killed him. Many American agents were not satisfied with the theory that he was killed out of revenge or after a quarrel with the drug traffickers. They suspected that his death was carried out very carefully by the Federal Police and the Federal Security Office, both of which had been publicly denounced by Camarena for having connections to the drug traffickers.

Another element that was missing in establishing what had really happened to Camarena was the whereabouts of Juan Ramón Matta Ballesteros. Matta, one of the closest collaborators of Felix Gallardo and Caro Quintero, was a Honduran chemist that had been with the traffickers since the formation of the grand society, or cartel. However, everyone was aware that finding him would not be easy, for his whereabouts were truly a mystery. DEA agents in Europe and all over America began the search to secure his arrest. At the same time, the effort was made to formally charge him of drug trafficking, which was done before the Federal Court of the State of California. This included a request to INTERPOL for his arrest.

At the beginning of June, 1985, reports surfaced that indicated the possibility that Matta Ballestero could be found in Spain. Some agents immediately made the journey to

Madrid but found nothing. No trace of his whereabouts could be found until an informant indicated to them that he could possibly be found in Cartagena, Colombia. The National Police of Colombia immediately cooperated with the American agents as the trail led them to a private section of that Colombian city.

On June 20, 1985, police surrounded the place in collaboration with the DEA. In less than two hours, they saw Ballesteros go out to the garden of one of the houses. He was arrested quickly and taken to a local jail.

According to accounts on file with the DEA, a group of Honduran businessmen anonymously offered the Colombian authorities $500,000 for his freedom. Although this could not be verified, the authorities needed to act with urgency. Meanwhile, Ballesteros admitted to his participation in trafficking cocaine, and revealed that after his arrest and that of Caro Quintero and Ernesto Fonseca, Miguel Angel Félix Gallardo's control was now being shared by René Verdugo and Francisco Jaramillo. Both men were close associates of the leaders in custody. On June 28, the Department of Justice of the United States formally requested the extradition of Matta Ballesteros. This never took place, however due to his having escaped from the Picota Prison, located in the city of Bogota.

It was April 5, 1988, when news of Matta Ballesteros reached the agents again. Chief of Operations of the Marshall's Service Howard Safir, stationed in Honduras, learned that the trafficker lived in a house located in one of the better residential areas of Tegucigalpa. Upon verifying the information, he notified his superiors, who in turn informed the DEA. However, Honduran law prohibits the extradition of its citizens. Therefore, certain officials of the Department of State contacted local authorities in order to arrive at an alternative plan to bring Ballesteros to American soil.

On April 10, local police appeared at the traffickers house and deported him to the Dominican Republic in a military plane. The Dominican authorities, however, denied his entry into their country and forced him to board a plane headed for Puerto Rico. During the flight, Ballesteros was arrested by American agents and later placed in the Marion Penitentiary in the State of Illinois.

Toward the end of 1988, Carlos Salinas de Gortari became President of Mexico. New hopes were born in regards to the war on drugs in that region. The flamboyant chief of state proclaimed the drug problem to be a battle in which the State would put forth all its energy. An indication of this could be observed during his speech before the General Assembly of the United Nations, in which he stated, "In time of peace, Mexico fights a war, the war on drug trafficking." The new leader of Mexican politics always proclaimed his fervent belief of finding a solution and constantly maintained that "the war on drugs goes forward, regardless of who falls." In reality, it was evident during his six years of administration that the Mexican State lost the battle, and that throughout his presidency the leaders of the traffickers were not eradicated. Only the names of the leaders changed. Some organizations grew in size and their routes were modified. The Mexican cartels now name the successor to the leader in case they are arrested, making it almost impossible to destroy the organization.

In addition, Mexican soil had become the route of passage for Colombian traffickers. Traffickers of both countries made pacts or created societies in order to further exploit the border with the United States, either by air, land or sea. Transporting over land does not present a major obstacle when one considers that the border between the United States and Mexico is the most traveled in the entire hemisphere. Moreover, the railroad routes, which have always been used to transport drugs, are not under strict vigilance.

This scenario has led to a surge in growth for the Mexican smugglers. Many of their organizations have become so rich and powerful that they can rival legitimate governments in terms of control and influence. In the past six years, the Mexican Government confiscated 246,800 kilograms of cocaine and approximately 62 million kilograms of marijuana. These statistics appear to be shocking, but the drug cartels go on undaunted. In fact, according to American specialists, the drug traffic of the cartels constitutes 30% of the total value of goods that enters the United States annually from south of the border. A prime example of this phenomenon was observed when one of the cartel leaders, Chapo Guzman, pursued his idea of digging tunnels at the border to transport drugs.

With the new power of these organizations, the traffickers initiated new campaigns of violence and new ventures of cooperation with police officials, which in turn enabled the traffickers to dominate markets along the border and in American cities.

Gradually, the leaders of drug trafficking changed: when Miguel Angel Félix Gallardo was arrested, the emerging Arellano Félix brothers began to fight with Joaquín Chapo Guzmán for the territory. Juan Guerra, before Félix Gallardo died, had delegated leadership to Juan García Abrego; and after the death of Pablo Acosta, Amado Carrillo emerged (alias "El Señor of the Skies"), and became the leader of the Juárez cartel.

During the presidency of Carlos Salinas de Gortari, various groups of police continued acting as armed instruments of the principal drug lords, providing them and their operations with protection and impunity. This scenario was exemplified in the arrest of Miguel Angel Félix Gallardo: when they captured the trafficker, he produced a Federal Police identification card. In this case, ex-Chief of the Federal Security Office José Antonio Zorrilla had been working as Félix Gallardo's laison. Another example is Santiago Tapia Aceves, the ex-Subsecretary General of Highway Administration, who, in exchange for $50,000, let Chapo Guzmán go free. Similarly, when seven of the eleven most important associates of Juan García Abrego, leader of the Gulf cartel, were arrested, various members of the Mexican Federal Judicial Police were with them. Among them was Guillermo González Calderoni, one of the highest-ranking federal policeman. González later escaped to the United States with $36 million, and despite not being able to explain where the money came from, the State of Texas denied his extradition to Mexican authorities. Moreover, García Abrego enjoyed the loyalty of Javier Coello Trejo, who in 1988 held the position of subsecretary of the war and struggle against drugs. Certainly, relations between the traffickers and high-ranking officials of the Salinas de Gortari Administration were exposed when three of the five attorney generals of the Republic were arrested, charged with collaborating with the traffickers. Arrested were Enrique Alvarez del Castillo, Ignacio Morales Lechuga and Humberto Benítez Treviño. Only Jorge Caprizo and Diego Valadés would demonstrate their innocence.

There were other arrests made during the Salinas Gortari Administration. These included drug traffickers, financiers who laundered drug money, policemen, state attorneys, and judicial officials who had used their positions to protect the drug barons. A summation of the arrests follows:

March, 1989: Miguel Angel Félix Gallardo arrested in Guadalajara, Jalisco;

August 21, 1989: Amado "El Señor of the Skies" Carrillo Fuentes arrested, but freed days later with all charges dropped;

February 8, 1990: ex-Commander of the Federal Police and Director of INTERPOL Mexico Armando Pavón Reyes is jailed. At the time of his arrest, he was working for the Arellano Félix brothers;

September 23, 1991: Mario Alberto González Treviño arrested, an agent of the Federal Police who had connections to Joaquín "Chapo" Guzmán's organization;

October 23, 1991: Gilberto "Matted Hair" Lucero arrested on a flight from Veracruz to Tamaulipas;

September 21, 1992: brothers Rafael and Eduardo Muñoz Talavera, members of the Juarez cartel, arrested in Tijuana, Baja California;

June 9, 1993: Joaquín "Chapo" Guzmán arrested in Chiapas;

June 17, 1993: Luis Medrano García, an associate of Juán García Abrego, apprehended in Ciudad Juárez;

December 6, 1993: Francisco Arellano Félix arrested in Tijuana, Baja California;

October 20, 1994: Humberto García Abrego, brother of Juan, apprehended in Monterrey.

Despite these arrests, the new drug czars continue walking the streets, and the level of drug traffic they produce is intolerable. Nevertheless, Mexico inaugurated a new president at the end of 1994, Ernesto Zedillo, and with this new administration in place, the White House renewed its confidence in its southern neighbor. The Zedillo Administration responded by arresting several drug traffickers –although they were persons of little importance within the cartels' hierarchies– and agreed to improve in areas such as the sharing of information and the extradition of persons suspected of grave crimes. However, Zedillo's greatest triumph on this front was the arrest of the head of the Gulf cartel, Juan García Abrego.

Over the years, García Abrego had been a symbol of the Mexican Government's impotence against the corruptive power of drug trafficking. At the height of its power, the Gulf cartel enjoyed an annual income of $10,000 million, which permitted them to buy the cooperation and loyalty of anyone necessary, or kill those who attempted to confront them or challenge their territory. García Abrego liberally distributed his money. According to case documents and testimony in a 1984 Brownsville, Texas money laundering case, his organization invested millions of dollars each month to obtain the protection of Mexican officials at the highest levels. As a result, in 1985, García Abrego became the first drug trafficker to be hunted by both the DEA *and* the FBI.

For the purpose of achieving his capture, Horacio Brunt, a commander of the Federal Police of Mexico, was placed at the head of the investigation. Brunt, whose life and actions clearly marked him as an honest man, had distrusted many of his colleagues from the very beginning. He therefore formed a team of 15 of his most trusted officials to minimize the possibilities of infiltration and leakage of information; and although they had vast files on García Abrego, they had resolved to start again from scratch.

They approached their task by going back to the basics of detective work: collecting information about the associates of the trafficker, ordering wire taps and trails, and collaborating constantly with the DEA. After months of investigation, Brunt and his men were able to give the final blow. On January 15, 1996, Brunt's men surrounded a ranch near the city of Monterrey, and, shortly thereafter, arrested Juan García Abrego. García Abrego had birth certificates claiming his origin in both the United States and Mexico, so the Mexican authorities immediately classified him as a United States citizen. Consequently, the day after his arrest, García Abrego was deported to the United States.

These events certainly earned Horacio Brunt the respect of the anti-drug forces in the United States, but in Mexico he was a hero. Meanwhile, the drug traffickers had put a $5 million price on his head.

After the arrest of Juan García Abrego, another scandal surfaced. The Mexican Attorney General's Office and the

National Institute for the War on Drugs discovered that Raúl Salinas de Gortari –the brother of Carlos Salinas de Gortari– had maintained ties with the leaders of Mexican drug-trafficking organizations since 1987. According to documents produced by the Attorney General's Office, the ex-President's brother held meetings with leaders of the Gulf cartel and with Joaquín "Chapo" Guzmán. The documents indicate that Raúl Salinas had guaranteed protection to García Abrego's organization if his brother were elected President of Mexico. It is also suspected that Raúl Salinas de Gortari hid García Abrego in his ranch and in other properties in order to conceal him from the authorities.[44]

The Attorney General's Office made public a communiqué, dated November 30, 1995, and registered SAP-1452-95, wherein the Mexican authorities asked British Attorney General Mr. Nicholas Lyell to conduct a corresponding investigation into Raúl Salinas de Gortari's involvement in "tax evasion, money laundering and illicit enrichment." Finally, an informant revealed that he had seen Raúl Salinas together with the traffickers García Abrego, Manuel Muñóz Rocha, Ricardo Aguirre Villagómez and some Mexican businessmen in June, 1987.

But, the Zedillo Administration is not doing enough in the war against the drug traffickers. On January 30, 1996, at a hearing to discuss Bill S-1547, which would have prohibited monetary contributions from United States sources to Mexico unless the latter stepped up its efforts against drugs, U.S. Senator Alfonse D'Amato expressed his opinions regarding that North American neighbor:

> *It seems that corruption extends to the very top of the Mexican Government . . . The drug traffickers supposedly have ties with a member of Zedillo's cabinet and with a PRI*

---

[44] See "Raúl escondía a García Abrego" (Mexico: *Reforma*, May, 1996).

congressman. I don't want to say that President Zedillo is not doing all he can, but what he is doing is not enough.

The same Senator demanded that Mexico extradite the 156 traffickers requested by the United States, and that Mexico fulfill its responsibilities in the agreement that was signed in 1978. D'Amato stated that "there are hundreds of individuals that are known and that are free in the streets . . . If President Zedillo wants to do something, then he should arrest and process them, and if there are real charges, extradite them."[45]

On May 7, 1996, the administrator of the DEA, Thomas A. Constantine was called to testify before a Senate banking committee, presided over by the republican from New York, Alfonse D'Amato. In his testimony, Constantine was pressed to respond to the drug situation in Mexico: "These Mafias utilize vast financial resources to co-opt governmental and commercial institutions. We have witnessed Colombia's struggle with this problem, and it would not be unexpected if the same problems were to root themselves in Mexico."[46] Constantine also testified that there exists a federation of Mexican organizations that, in terms of power, wealth and influence, is only superseded by the Cali cartel. This federation of more than 17 organizations and cartels operates under an "elastic, fluid and flexible" system. The DEA official then named the principal participants of the group:

The Tijuana cartel, run by the Arellano Félix brothers;
The Sonora cartel, led by Miguel Caro Quintero, whose brother, Rafael, is in jail;

---

45 See "Relacionan a políticos mexicanos con narcos," Maribel González, *Diario Reforma*, Mexico, May 7, 1996.
46 "Falta una Estructura contra Carteles," Maribel González, *Diario Reforma*, Mexico, May 8, 1996.

The Juárez cartel, headed by Amado Carrillo, known as "The Señor of the Skies;"

The Gulf cartel, managed by Juan García Abrego until he was arrested in January, 1996. It is presumed that the leadership has been assumed by either Sergio "The Czech" Gómez or Antonio Avila, who are both vying for control.

During these Senate hearings, both Constantine as well as Jim Moody, an assistant director of the FBI, agreed that the trafficking organizations in Mexico constitute a growing threat insofar as the volume of drugs they transport, the violent crimes they commit, and the rising level of corruption among officials on both sides of the border. Moreover, "they provide substantial financial support to their preferred political candidates in order to assure that their operation will march on without interruption." The American functionaries added that one of the greatest problems in Mexico is the lack of basic legal instruments to combat the traffickers: it is illegal to tap telephone lines, conspiracy laws do not exist, the police do not use informants, there is no witness protection program, and money laundering is not a crime.

V

Money Laundering and Money Launderers

I t is estimated that approximately $500 billion in drug money is laundered each year, a figure that clearly demonstrates the magnitude of the problem. However, is this a problem which centers around the banks of developing nations –Panamanian, Mexican or Uruguayan banks, for example– or is the international financial community equally involved? This can be a difficult question to answer as the accusatory finger has most often pointed directly at Latin American and Caribbean financial institutions, while the global financial establishment has kept itself in a state of deliberate blindness. Besides, in this interconnected world, the price of admission to the most important international organizations requires each country's explicit conviction to fight drug trafficking and money laundering. That is, each participating country must have laws and regulations in place to counter these crimes, and must also abide by reciprocity treaties and other international agreements. Nevertheless, in such a world, there are countries that stand out as caricatures of non-conformity.

THE SEYCHELLES ISLANDS

Seychelles is an island republic located in the Indian Ocean whose 90 small islands house 73,000 inhabitants spread out over 445 square kilometers. It has a gross national product of $90 million, a deficit of $22 million, and an annual foreign trade of $180 million. In addition, it has a law in place which has been described as the "Welcome Criminals Act."[47] The law establishes that any person who invests $10 million or more in the country will not be questioned regarding the origin of the funds, and will also enjoy complete protection in case of an extradition request by another nation. This law has become a veritable invitation to money launderers and other criminals to do their business with the utmost impunity, as one of its articles states that "The Seychelles government could grant diplomatic passports and other protections to such people, shielding them from international law enforcement agencies."

The President of Seychelles, France Albert René, in power since 1977, sustained that since tourism, their chief income-producing industry, had been devastated with the Gulf War, they had had to diversify their economy, and the "Welcome Criminals Act" was the best solution. However, the President and the Seychelles ambassador to the United States, Marc Marengo, explain that the objective of the law was not to protect criminals. They claim that each investor is investigated *before* they receive protection under the law. And so, despite the pressure which has been exercised by the United States, Great Britain and France, the René Administration continues to defend the law, letting the world's anti-drug and anti-money laundering agencies see the obscure intentions of a government that guarantees "Immunity of extradition or

---

[47] "Seychelles Offers Investors Safe Haven for $10 Million," Thomas Lippman, *The Washington Post*, December 31, 1995.

prosecution for all criminal proceedings, except for those crimes committed in Seychelles."

The Financial Action Task Force (FATF), which supervises the world's money markets, complained --with just cause-- about the act promulgated by the Seychelles Government and recommended that the European nations adopt concrete measures against this island country.[48]   The scandal that produced a significant outcry was when a journalist from the *Sunday Times*, pretending to represent a group of Russian companies involved in South American agricultural commodities, whose real income --he assured-- came from drug trafficking, was granted diplomatic immunity and money-laundering facilities if he invested the $15 million he claimed to have.[49]

ARGENTINA: THE POST OFFICE "BANK"

No less interesting is the proposed Postal Law of Argentina.   Its objective was to privatize the State Postal Service, and to regulate the existing privately-owned companies.   Although it was approved by that country's Senate in November, 1994, no Senator claimed the legislation as his own, nor did anyone publicly defend its text.   The Senators who voted in favor merely stated that if there were errors in the approved project, they could always correct them; however, nobody explained why the legislation had so many errors, in the first place. For example, two very peculiar ones are:

---

[48] The United States, for their part, announced that the American Government will not grant any type of economic aid or loan to the country, and that it will close the Seychelles Embassy in Washington.
[49] "Seychelles Forced to Drop Drug Dealers' Charter After Outcry," *Sunday Times*, January 21, 1996.

1) The privatized enterprise would be able to provide monetary services, including savings accounts, in a "secret " basis. But nobody explained what "monetary services" were. One can only deduce from the context that these services might involve savings accounts, money transfers and other such activities. These transactions, according to the wording of the bill, could not only be in Argentine pesos, but in any currency, and could involve national and international principals. Moreover, the transactions would be guaranteed inviolability under the Constitution. That is, it would be prohibited to divulge who made the transactions and how much money was involved. This information could only be obtained through the order of a judge. These terms are explicitly outlined in the text of the bill: "These operations are secret and are sheltered by the constitutional guarantee of inviolability of correspondence. Only the principals of the transaction are authorized to reveal its details, except in the case of a judge's order."

There is one caveat: although this postal entity would be prohibited from divulging information, the banks themselves are obligated to inform the Central Bank (Banco Central) of all transactions. If the Postal Service were exempt from this obligation, they could work as an "undercover bank," and who would prevent their illegal activities?

The final report of the House Commission on Communications, the body which considered this matter, was signed unanimously. The signatories included seven Representatives of the Unión Cívica Radical (Radical Party), five from the Partido Justicialista (Justicialist Party), and one from the MODIN (National '*Dignity*' Party). Such unanimity is rare on such controversial issues.

2) Another article states:

Postal shipments are protected by constitutional guarantees of inviolability of correspondence and of postal secrecy.

The guarantee of inviolability of postal correspondence includes the prohibition to open such correspondence, to seize them, to suppress or divert their delivery, to damage them, or to try in any way to determine their content.

The guarantee of secrecy includes the prohibition from determining the identities of the corresponding parties, which is an extension of the constitutional guarantee of personal privacy.

In real terms, this means that if a truck arrived loaded with 50 bags of letters and packages, some containing drugs, law enforcement officials could not delay or intercept their delivery, as these actions, as well as their very pretext for knowing the contents of the correspondence, would be illegal. The July 1, 1996 edition of *The Wall Street Journal* reported on another aspect of the issue:

At 1995, (former) Argentine Economy Minister Domingo Cavallo went public with accusations that legislators were tailoring the bidding specifications for a postal privatization so narrowly that only one person could win: a courier service owner whom Mr. Cavallo publicly accused of "Mafia-style" tactics, such as paying off legislators and beating up rivals. The lawmakers hit the minister with a flurry of lawsuits and then shelved the debate on the sell-off.[50]

Meanwhile, the Argentine press has interpreted these events as a personal fight between Cavallo and businessman Alfredo Nallib Yabran. Finally, no one commented on the article regarding *secret monetary services*.

---

[50] Matt Moffett and Johnathan Friedland, *The Wall Street Journal*, July 1, 1996.

THE NEW MEXICAN LAW

Another salient topic is the new Mexican anti-money laundering law which was promulgated in May, 1996.

The law does not require banks to report large currency transactions.[51] Furthermore, according to a paper that former FBI chief James Moody delivered to a CIA-FBI symposium on drug trafficking in 1994, "The FBI notes that many of these firms (related to Mexico's program to privatize) are purchased by Mexican and Colombian drug trafficking organizations . . . These semi-state firms are comprised of significant financial institutions, factories which are worth billions of dollars." Moody's paper was obtained by the Mexico City daily El Financiero.

"It is no exaggeration to say that drug money is invested in industry, banking, agriculture, tourism and possibly in the Mexican stock market," said a report on Mexican drug trafficking issued in April 1996 by the Washington Office on Latin America. The report listed a variety of companies and individuals it said were tied to drug traffickers, including a former president of the Mexican Banking Association; a Ford Motor Co. Agent; an air taxi business and a luxury hotel in the Pacific beach resort of Puerto Vallarta.

In Mexico, opposition to currency-transaction-reports is being led by banks and financial institutions, some of which allegedly have been infiltrated by drug Mafias. In fact, "DEA sources report that many Mexican traffickers have purchased large shares of banks and placed members on the board's directors, . . . as a result, many banks keep two sets of books and bank examiners are paid off by corrupt bank officials."[52]

---

[51] "Drug Profits Crossing Border Plague U.S., Mexican Officials," Molly Moore and John W. Anderson, *The Washington Post*, July 8, 1996.
[52] Wankel, DEA congressional testimony, *The Washington Post*, op.cit.

Still, the Mexican Congress has not given security forces better laws with which to combat money laundering. "The problem is that you have nineteenth-century tools trying to deal with twenty-first-century criminals," DEA chief Thomas Constantine told members of Mexico's Congress.

In fact, it is hard to imagine the day when Mexico passes an effective law to deal with money laundering. According to an undercover DEA agent, the bank accounts of Raul Salinas de Gortari were used to launder the Gulf cartel's money. Salinas, in addition to being connected to Mexico's political elite, was an associate of Ricardo Peralta Quintero, the cellular telephones magnate, and of Ricardo Salinas Pliego, the current owner of TV Azteca. Raul Salinas transferred to the. latter, from his bank account, $29.8 million in 1993, at the same time as the privatization of the TV channel took place. Televisa, another TV channel, criticized this privatization harshly. Before long, their news director was replaced by Abraham Zabludovsky, who was also an associate of Raúl Salinas de Gortari.

Also, Jose Madariaga Lomelin became the most important banker in Mexico after having purchased Multibanco Mercantil de Mexico, and he admitted to being parteners with Raul Salinas in this venture. In sum, we see the spectrum of Raul Salinas' interests: banks, transportation, journalism, television, and communications. That's all.[53]

---

[53] Information taken from the testimony of Raul Salinas against Valentin Roschacher, Chief of the Central Office of Narcotraffick of the Swiss Federal Police. Acording to Salinas, these persons had formed business partnerships with him, although at first they denied it. cf. *Ignacio Rodriguez Reyna* (Mexico: Reforma, July 4, 1996).

THE TOP TEN

We see below that the ten countries that proportionately launder the most money are Liberia, Norfolk, Ireland, Malta, Paraguay, Cayman, Mexico, Sierra Leon, Panama and Grenada. Liberia

Country	%	Country	%
Liberia**	75.83	Cayman Islands****	29.79
Norfolk Island	55.39	Mexico***	29.66
Ireland	44.68	Sierra Leone	29.51
Malta and Gozo**	31.47	Panama****	29.10
Paraguay	30.79	Grenada***	28.56

Source: Doctors **Simon J. Pak** and **John S. Zdanowicz**, *Florida International University*, Miami.

*Based on comparisons to U.S./world average prices.

**Listed as a "Tax Haven" (Paraiso Fiscal) by government of Spain. (Spain requires special reports from financial institutions which conduct transactions for residents of 48 designated "tax havens" [Money Laundering Alert, Feb. 1996])

***Listed as "High Priority" on money laundering activities in the U.S. State Department's 1996 International Narcotics Control Strategy Report.

****Listed on both of the above lists

occupies the top spot, with its ratio of laundered money to total annual exports ($390 million) being the highest of the group. Norfolk Island takes the second honor; this small archipelago dependent on Australia, according to official reports, features tourism and flower and vegetable sales as its top industries.

The American media have given much attention to the issue of drug trafficking and money laundering; however, the subject is treated differently depending on the country or financial institution involved. For example, if the scandal involves a developing nation, a Latin American bank for instance, the news is treated in a spectacular exposé-like fashion; however, if the money laundering story relates to a major U.S. bank or financier, the news is presented cautiously.

There are some countries which are rarely questioned or criticized. One of them is Switzerland. However, this unique nation has developed a money-laundering system as sound and efficient as its world-famous watches. Although not often, this country's rigorously confidential numbered accounts attract a complaint or two from the United States. For this watch-making country, their financial services industry has indeed enabled them to reach a new level of economic independence.

To the northeast of Switzerland lies little Liechtenstein, a territory with 9,000 inhabitants, although unofficially, another 48,000 reside within its borders. Although Switzerland controls the foreign affairs of this state, Liechtenstein has a parliament comprised of 24 legislators, a constitution and an internal separation of powers, and since 1993 has been a member of the United Nations. Contrary to belief, Liechtenstein is most characterized not by tourism, but by its banking system, which is similar to that of the Swiss. In Liechtenstein, the confidentiality of transactions is carefully guarded not only by the banking institutions, but by the judges of the country. Therefore, whenever the Helvetic countries become hampered with money-laundering investigations, they funnel the funds in question to their neighbor Liechtenstein, where their secrets are always well-guarded.

Stanley E. Morris, Director of the Financial Crime Enforcement Network (FinCEN), expressed with absolute clarity that "now banks are seen as the first line of defense against financial crimes." His comments were sparked specifically by the money-laundering scandal involving

Citibank that took place in the U.S. during the first months of 1996.

Jack Nelson, a journalist for the *Los Angeles Times*, explained that "Citibank in New York, for example, cooperated with federal authorities in an effort to assist Mexico's investigation of Raúl Salinas de Gortari. "[54] However, as we will see later in the chapter, Citibank was involved in this money-laundering operation in far greater a degree than merely cooperating with authorities. In fact, Citibank was a central part of the initial inquiry, which illustrates the double-standard mentioned earlier; that is, when the culprit is Liberia or Seychelles, the condemnation is absolute, but when a money-laundering case is linked to a prestigious bank of New York, "the institution is cooperating."

To take care of this matter, the United States Government created in April, 1990 the Financial Crimes Enforcement Network. The FinCEN, the result of Treasury Department Order No. 105-08, was given a special mission: "to provide a government-wide, multi-source intelligence and analytical network in support of the detection, investigation, and prosecution of domestic and international money laundering and other financial crimes by federal, state, local and foreign law enforcement agencies."

But some members of Congress do not agree with the function and existence of the FinCEN. Such is the case with the Chairman of the Senate Banking Committee, a long-time activist on the money-laundering issue, Alfonse D'Amato, who wrote, on January 24, 1996, a letter to Secretary of the Treasury Robert Rubin. In it, he states that the FinCEN "should serve solely as a support office to the enforcement community and not a regulatory or investigative agency." This was based on the fact that, in June, 1994, the Department of the Treasury had announced a restructuring of its Money Laundering Division,

---

[54] *Los Angeles Times*, June 6, 1996.

assigning to the FinCEN the responsibility and authority to dictate the regulations of the Bank Secrecy Act. That is why Senator D'Amato asked Rubin to provide a "concise description of FinCEN's mission."[55]

REPORT OF THE DRUG ENFORCEMENT ADMINISTRATION

On February 28, 1996, Special Agent of the DEA Harold Wankel met with the House Banking and Financial Committees in order to inform and bring the Representatives up to date on the issue of the laundering of drug money in certain countries. This testimony did not contribute much to the congressmen's knowledge of the subject since he was merely giving an overview and was addressing long-standing issues.

"As we know, the laundering of illegal drug profits is an integral part of drug trafficking, as important and essential to drug trafficking organizations as the distribution of the illegal drugs themselves. Drug organizations are truly international businesses, and like any business, these organizations are fueled and motivated by huge profits that are their lifeblood."

Drug trafficking is a multibillion-dollar cash business, and drug money is essential to these enterprises. Without it, they cannot finance the manufacturing, the transportation, the smuggling, the distribution, the murder and the intimidation that are essential to their illegal trade. Drug money laundering organizations are established to ensure the cash flow to these illegal businesses. Profits from the sale of illegal drugs are recycled through laundered investments, which take place across many borders and often involve international financial institutions, banks and money exchange houses. With today's

---

[55] See: *Money Laundering Alert*, March 1996, volume 7, number 6.

sophisticated banking techniques, including the electronic transfer of money, once the money enters the banking system, it can be transferred among dozens of banks within a 24-hour period, making the paper trail either impossible or extremely time-consuming to follow. Globalization of the drug trade has necessitated an expansion and sophistication of the laundering of illegal drug profits.

As the international drug markets have been expanded across all continents and into virtually every nation, so too have methods used to launder — or make legitimate – illegal profits of the global drug trade. Methods of laundering drug money vary by country and region of the world, and are driven by a number of factors, including the sophistication of banking and financial centers, the existence of underground banking systems that operate largely along ethnic lines, and strength of enforcement pressure.

We want to give an idea of the magnitude of the problems law enforcement officers face with international drug money laundering and the progress that has been made with international partners toward putting a choke hold on the flow of profits back to the illegal drug trafficking enterprises. Therefore, we will concentrate the discussion on those countries and areas of the world where law enforcement is seeing the majority of drug money laundering activities, beginning with the epicenter of the cocaine trade, Colombia. The Cali Mafia is still one of the primary recipients of drug proceeds from the United States. Until just recently, they were responsible for 80 percent of the cocaine sold on the streets of the United States.

Money Laundering Chart
INCSR 1996

High Priority	Medium High Priority	Medium	Low Medium	Low	No Priority	No Priority
Aruba	Antigua	Bahamas	Australia	Afghanistan	Albania	Madagascar
Canada	Argentina	Bahrain	Cambodia	Andorra	Algeria	Malawi
Cayman Isl	Austria	Belgium	Cote D'Ivoire	Anguilia	Angola	Maldives
Colombia	Brazil	Belize	Cuba	Barbados	Armenia	Mali
Germany	Costa Rica	Bolivia	Denmark	Bermuda	Azerbaijan	Marshall Isl
Hong Kong	Cyprus	Bulgaria	Egypt	BVI	Bangladesh	Mauritania
Italy	India	Burma	Portugal	Cook Islands	Belarus	Mauritius
Mexico	Israel	Channel Isl	South Africa	Estonia	Benin	Micronesia
Netherlands	Japan	Chile	Trinidad	F W Indies	Botswana	Moldova
N Antilles	Liechtenstein	China	Vanuatu	Finland	Burkina Faso	Mongolia
Nigeria	Luxembourg	Czech Rep		Ghana	Burundi	Mozambique
Panama	Pakistan	Dominican R.		Haiti	C African Rep	N Marianas
Russia	Paraguay	Ecuador		Honduras	Cameroon	N Korea
Singapore	UAE	France		Indonesia	Cape Verde	Namibia
Switzerland		Gibraltar		Iran	Chad	Nauru
Thailand		Greece		Iraq	Comoros	Nicaragua
Turkey		Guatemala		Ireland	Congo	Niger
UK		Hungary		Jamaica	Croatia	Oman
USA		Korea		Kenya	Djibouti	P N Guinea
Venezuela		Kuwait		Laos	Dominica	Qatar
		Lebanon		Latvia	El Salvador	Rwanda
		Macau		Lithuania	Eq Guinea	Saudi Arabia
		Madeira/Azores		Malta	Eritrea	Senegal
		Malaysia		Monaco	Ethiopia	Slovenia
		Montserrat		Nepal	Fiji	Solomon Isl
		Morocco		N Zealand	Gabon	Somalia
		Peru		Norway	Gambia	Sudan
		Philippines		Romania	Georgia	Swaziland
		Poland		Seychelles	Grenada	Tajikistan
		St. Vincent/G		Sierra Leone	Guinea	Tanzania
		Slovakia		Sri Lanka	Guinea-Bissau	Togo
		Taiwan		St. Kitts	Guyana	Tunisia
				St. Lucia	Iceland	Turkmenistan
				Suriname	Jordan	Turks / Caicos
				Sweden	Kazakhstan	Tuvalu
				Syria	Kiribati	Uganda
				Ukraine	Kyrgystan	US Virgin Isl
				Vietnam	Lesotho	Uzbekistan
				FR Yugoslavia	Liberia	W Sahara
				Zambia	Libya	W Samoa
						Yemen
						Zaire
						Zimbabwe

Colombian economists conservatively estimate that each year $4.5 billion is repatriated to Colombia by drug traffickers. The arrests of the Cali leaders in 1995 and the emergence of crime syndicates from Mexico have impacted somewhat the amount of U.S. dollars flowing back to Cali, but the long-term impact has not yet been determined. These dollars are controlled by a cadre of well-educated, skilled accountants, who follow the rules of business drawn up by Cali Mafia leaders to literally keep track of every dollar in their worldwide trafficking network. The city of Cali stands as a monument to the billions of narco-dollars the Cali Mafia has returned to Colombia. Majestic, modern skyscrapers fill the skyline of the city many of which remain unoccupied– none of which has outstanding mortgages. The alliance of the Cali Mafia with the trafficking organizations in Mexico has created a highly effective method of repatriating Cali profits. Money laundering has evolved from the late 1970s and early 1980s, when traffickers simply showed up at U.S. banks with suitcases full of money, deposited it in accounts, and then had it transferred either back to Colombia or to safe havens in Europe and offshore banks.

After legislation in the U.S. forced the reporting of deposits over $10,000, "structuring" became the method of choice for many money launderers. One form of structuring is "smurfing," in which individuals recruited by the Colombians run from bank to bank and deposit just under $10,000 in cash. An organization of 10 smurfs, each hitting 10 banks a day, can convert about $1 million in cash each day into a small stack of cashier's checks of $9,000 to $9,900 each, which are much easier to get out of the United States.

This system was cumbersome, however, and not without substantial risk. As the Cali Mafia began to monopolize the cocaine trade in the 1990s and their profits began to soar, they turned to bulk transfers of cash in commercial shipments. To solve some of their money transfer problems, Colombian traffickers bought a fleet of large planes, such as Boeing 727s, Caravelles, and the Turboprop Lockheed Electras, gutted them, and used them to transport multi-ton loads of cocaine to Mexico, Canada, Portugal and West Africa for sale in the United States and Europe. Once they offloaded the cocaine, they reloaded the planes with U.S. cash, sometimes as much as $20 to $30 million in drug profits, to return to Colombia.

Bulk shipments of cash, whether in cargo planes or commercial shipments, continue to be the primary method of smuggling cash; however, another increasingly popular method of laundering drug proceeds is "dollar discounting." This method involves a broker approaching a legitimate businessman in Colombia that needs U.S. dollars to buy goods in the United States. The money broker simply sells the drug proceeds, which are already in the United States, to the businessman at a discount rate of up to 20 percent. The businessman then deposits the equivalent sum in pesos in the trafficker's bank account in Colombia and his or her agent in the U.S. picks up the U.S. dollars. The discount rate of 20 percent is a dramatic increase in the cost of doing business for Cali money launderers. Previously, Colombian brokers paid between 6 and 10 percent to move funds into Colombian accounts.

We've also seen an increase in the shipment of large quantities of postal money orders. The money orders, with names left blank, are sent directly to Colombia and Panama. There, the funds are sold to *casas de cambio,* or money changing houses, for cash that will be deposited into the traffickers' accounts. The money orders are then sold and resold through the networks of *casas.* They are finally redeemed at banks outside Colombia. When the U.S. Post Office began to detect this money laundering pattern and began to seize these funds, the money movers began to send the money orders back to the United States to be deposited into bank accounts.

More sophisticated alternatives to the banking system have also surfaced, such as the laundering of drug money through import-export businesses and other front companies. Elaborate import-export schemes are being used to make drug proceeds appear as legitimate income. Falsified export documents, bills of lading, and invoices for goods being shipped out of Colombia to the United States are used to justify large payments sent to Colombia. The use of payable-through-accounts held in U.S. banks by foreign banks makes it difficult for law enforcement to trace the money. These accounts can have hundreds of sub-account holders in foreign countries who have complete access to these accounts but who are unknown to the U.S. bank and maybe even to the foreign bank. The goal of all these schemes is to get the money into the banking system unchallenged. In 1995, Colombia passed a law requiring Colombian banks to report large currency transactions; however, once in the system, the money can be wire-transferred into a labyrinth of worldwide accounts at a moment's notice.

The arrest and continued incarceration of major Cali drug lords have disrupted the financial safe haven status Colombian traffickers have enjoyed at home for many years. The enforcement of currency requirements and anti-corruption police efforts have also placed drug assets at risk in Colombia.

The international net is continually drawn tighter, limiting opportunities for Colombian traffickers to conceal their assets with a minimum of risk. For example, organized crime is believed to control 20 percent of the commercial banks in Russia,[56] however, the lack of stability in the country, as well as no long-standing basis of trust, has precluded major investment in that alternative. Recent seizures and forfeitures

---

[56] President Clinton said that while Russia no longer posed a serious threat to U.S. security, "the bad news is that once you strip the veneer of Communist control off Russia with nothing to replace it, within five years you have half of the banks run by organized crime." *Los Angeles Times*, June 6, 1966.

in Europe, particularly the $142 million seizure from Colombian trafficker Julio Nasser David in Switzerland, have caused considerable concern on the part of Colombian drug lords about putting their illegal money into European banks.

The key to future success in Colombia and Mexico is promoting strong money laundering laws that are strictly enforced in all countries, and maintaining strong ties with foreign officers in the financial centers around the world. Under Presidential Directive Decision (PDD) 42, The United States is addressing those countries that are the most egregious in offering safe havens to traffickers' illegal money. On October 21, 1995, President Clinton used the authority given him by the International Emergency Economic Powers Act to invoke economic sanctions against 97 companies and individuals who are involved with four members of the Cali drug Mafia. It is now illegal for any U.S. company to trade with these businesses or individuals.

Southeast Asia

Unlike cocaine organizations, which are largely Latin-based and concentrated in the Western Hemisphere, heroin traffickers are more diverse and they operate from bases all over the world, including Southeast Asia, Southwest Asia, the Middle East and now Colombia.

International law enforcement efforts are frustrated by the fact that opium cultivation and heroin manufacturing primarily take place in countries with extreme political turmoil and developing governments. Because of this, our nations have limited access and influence on the key heroin source countries of Southeast and Southwest Asia.

Money laundering in this area of the world is conducted through a complicated maze of trusted confidantes who have done business together for generations. These underground banking systems go back years and years to a time when family members worked away from home and needed to get their wages back to their families in other provinces. That same system exists today and is used to launder millions of dollars in drug money for Southeast Asian traffickers.

I'll confine my remarks to the most active of the money laundering countries in Southeast Asia: Singapore, Thailand, and Hong Kong.

Singapore

Although there is neither cultivation nor processing of drugs in Singapore, it is an important financial center for narcotics-related proceeds. Along with Hong Kong, Singapore plays a key role in the transfer and concealment of proceeds from the sale of Southeast Asian heroin.

While Singapore is a not a signatory to the Vienna Convention of 1988, it is a member of the Financial Action Task Force (FATF) and continues to maintain a tough stance towards drug trafficking. In 1993, Singapore passed the Drug Trafficking (Confiscation of Benefits) Act, which provides for seven years incarceration and a fine of $100,000.

Officials in Singapore believe that between 1989 and 1992 a drug trafficking group funneled approximately $100 million in U.S. currency through one underground bank in Singapore to Bahrain and ultimately to the organization's worldwide bank accounts. Singapore's Commercial Affairs Department has frozen the equivalent of $20 million U.S. dollars from previously arrested and convicted members of this hashish and marijuana organization.

Thailand

Thailand has an extensive and efficient network of banks and financial institutions which are used by drug traffickers to move and hide their proceeds throughout Asia. Thailand had a number of significant accomplishments in the past year in terms of fighting drug-related money laundering. In 1995, approximately 138 investigations were initiated under Thailand's asset seizure law, and last fall, the first criminal convictions and forfeiture actions were handed down. As of mid-December, over $9 million had been frozen, compared to $1 million just one year ago.

Thailand has enacted narcotics conspiracy and asset forfeiture laws. The asset forfeiture law stipulates that the suspects are required to prove their assets have been acquired through legal means.

Thailand has taken major steps to become an important financial center in Asia. The country has established offshore banking and has issued a number of licenses. Those banks can take deposits in foreign currencies and borrow in foreign currencies from local and foreign institutions. Thailand has proposed a new money laundering law that addresses only drug proceeds. The law will require recording and reporting of significant and suspicious transactions, as well as provisions that protect bank employees who comply with the law from retribution.

Real estate continues to be a widely used means for investing drug proceeds. Drug traffickers have also invested in companies involved in rubber processing, seafood packing, food products, import-export businesses, hotels, and jewelry shops. Underground banking uses these businesses to send money around the world.

Hong Kong

With its flexible corporate laws, sophisticated banking industry and currency and exchange controls, Hong Kong is a prime location for the laundering of illicit proceeds by narcotics traffickers. Hong Kong, however, has implemented asset seizure, money laundering and organized crime legislation. The law requires that bankers notify authorities of suspicious transactions.

Other legislation allows the United States to request civil forfeiture of identified proceeds of drug trafficking. Another law allows the Hong Kong government to identify and seize proceeds generated from any crime, not just those linked to drug trafficking.

In 1995, Hong Kong concluded its first successful money laundering prosecutions. Two members of the Chinese Triad were convicted of laundering $56 million of heroin-trafficking proceeds.

Emerging Threats:
Nigeria

This country is a home base for major trafficking groups who smuggle Southwest Asian and Southeast Asian heroin into the United States and Europe. The Nigerians are using South Africa as a transshipment point as well. Although Nigeria is neither a significant regional or international financial center, nor an important tax haven or offshore banking center, drug traffickers have laundered money in Nigerian financial institutions.

Drug profits are being pumped into the economy, as well as being laundered for reuse in other countries. The Nigerians use a variety of methods, including bulk smuggling in electronic car traps, refrigerators, and other merchandise which is later sold; wire transfers to Hong Kong and Thailand; couriers; and the purchase of "junk commodities" that are later sold for high prices.

Foreign currency accounts in Nigerian financial institutions are not prohibited, nor do banks have to disclose the source of the funds. The law prohibits attempts to hide drug proceeds as well as the transport of drug profits internationally. Money laundering is also illegal and carries prison terms of 15 to 25 years.

Nigerian heroin traffickers appear to be capitalizing on the vulnerability of South African borders to create a new drug pipeline for heroin coming out of Southwest Asia destined for the United States. Local criminal groups with histories of drug running are immigrating into South Africa and using that country as a staging area for smuggling heroin into the United States. The DEA believes that South Africa may also be targeted by drug lords from Brazil and Colombia as a potential market for cocaine and other drugs. Nigerians are involved in smuggling cocaine into Europe and distributing it to middlemen who sell it in South Africa. According to INTERPOL, an increasing number of South Africans are being arrested throughout Europe and Africa for drug offenses. We should anticipate that South Africa will be used by money launderers as well.

Russia

Over the past several years there has been an increase in drug trafficking by organized crime elements in Russia. The country has emerged as a transit route for heroin from Southwest and Southeast Asia to Europe and the United States, as well as for cocaine from South America to Europe. There is an increased threat of international drug money laundering by criminal elements in Russia as well as by criminal elements among Russian émigrés located in such areas as Europe and the United States.

The enormous amount of money associated with the drug trade has attracted Russian organized crime elements who now are involved in all aspects of the opium and hashish industries, including cultivation, production, distribution, and money-laundering operations. Criminal groups in Russia are exploiting the open access to the West and the lack of regulations in the banking, financial and commercial sectors of their country. The lack of regulatory controls and legislation inhibits Russian Government efforts to target drug money-laundering operations. Russian officials speculate that criminals have taken control of some banks and are laundering proceeds from a wide variety of criminal activities, including drugs. Some experts estimate that 25 % of Moscow's commercial banks are controlled by organized crime, and there is speculation that Colombian cocaine traffickers and the Sicilian Mafia may be using Russian banks to launder funds.

Mexico

As drug organizations from Mexico become more powerful in the international drug trade, so does their influence in money laundering. Mexico returns more surplus currency to the United States than any other country. Law enforcement officials are now seeing millions of dollars laundered by Mexican organizations. The primary reason for this is that the Colombians are paying the Mexican transportation organizations in cocaine. Considering 80 % of the cocaine smuggled into the United States comes through Mexico, the Mexican Federation is indeed a major player in the drug trade and must find ways to launder and conceal the profits from their cocaine sales.

In Mexico, between April and October 1995, Mexican authorities made three seizures of U.S. currency that totaled nearly $20 million. Last April, $6.2 million was discovered inside a shipment of air conditioners at the Mexico City Airport. The following month, Mexican authorities seized $1.5 million from a Colombian money launderer at the Mexico City Airport. And in October, Mexican officials found $12 million inside suitcases taken from a private plane that is believed to belong to the Amado Carrillo Fuentes drug organization.

Each year, over 500,000 bank drafts drawn on Mexican banks enter the U.S. One bank in Arizona determined that the average Mexican bank draft was valued at $65,000, but that it was not unusual to clear drafts in excess of $200,000 to $400,000. Mexican bank drafts, which were not subject to U.S. reporting requirements, now must be reported and the implementing regulations are being written. Previously, this was a significant method of reintroducing drug profits back into the United States. Although illicit enrichment is illegal and money laundering is a fiscal offense in Mexico, money laundering is still prevalent and not a criminal act. Banks are also required to keep records of transactions and make them available to law enforcement authorities upon request. However, DEA sources report that many Mexican traffickers have purchased large shares of banks and placed members on boards of directors. As a result, many banks keep two sets of books and bank examiners are paid off by corrupt bank officials. In addition, much of the money that is going back into Mexico is being invested in the infrastructure of the Mexican economy and is not subject to seizure. Money is also invested in U.S. institutions, as well as financial institutions throughout the world.

As a fiscal offense, money laundering charges provide for fines and sentences of up to 5 years. In Mexico, the money laundering law targets any illegal act, including tax evasion, illicit enrichment, corruption, as well as drug trafficking. In May, 1995, Mexican Attorney General Antonio Lozano announced that his office would be drafting a new money laundering law aimed specifically at Mexico's major drug trafficking organizations. The bill, which is to be presented before Congress in 1996, criminalizes money laundering under the penal code.

Currency Transaction Reporting (CTR) requirements unfortunately are not part of the proposed legislation; however, the pending bill attempts to fill some of the loopholes of the existing law. For example, it provides for penalties for banks which fail to report suspicious transactions. The bill would also reverse the burden of proof in asset forfeitures related to drug cases. As in the United States, the defendant would have to prove that his or her possessions were derived from legitimate sources. The primary opposition to this proposed legislation comes from the banks and financial institutions, as well as the close-knit community within Mexico that has controlled the vast majority of business in Mexico for years.

Each year criminal drug organizations accumulate war chests filled with billions of dollars from the sale of drugs in the United States. This money equates to power and the ability to produce more illegal drugs, which are sold in countries around the world. Over the years, one of the things we have learned is the power of financial investigations. Drugs are a cash business and drug traffickers must find ways to make their vast wealth appear legitimate, and money laundering is the only way they can do that. The drug trade is a vicious cycle, and by attacking the financial base of these organizations, we can have a direct impact on their ability to do business.

We could see the potential of financial investigations in two recent global law enforcement operations to disrupt the financial operations of the Colombian cocaine cartels, in Operation Green Ice in 1992 and Operation *Dinero* in 1994.

In Operation Green Ice, law enforcement from Italy, Colombia, the United Kingdom, Canada, Spain, Costa Rica, the Cayman Islands, and the United States cooperated together to expose the financial infrastructure of the Cali Mafia. During the first phase of Operation Green Ice, over $50 million in cash and property were seized and almost 200 people were arrested worldwide, including seven of Cali's top money managers. In addition, valuable information was obtained when law enforcement gained access to financial books and records, as well as computer hard drives and disks containing financial transactions and bank account information. During the second phase of Green Ice, nearly 14,000 pounds of cocaine, 16 pounds of heroin, almost $16 million in cash were seized, and over 40 people were arrested.

During Operation *Dinero*, a two and a half year undercover investigation involving the DEA and the IRS, as well as law enforcement and police organizations in Italy, Spain, Canada, and the United Kingdom, law enforcement penetrated the drug money laundering networks and followed the money trails that led to the top echelons of the Cali cocaine organizations.

Through this investigation they further established direct links among the criminal organizations of the Italian Mafia and the Colombian cocaine Mafia. This was an historical operation also because it was the first time a law enforcement agency established a private bank, operated by undercover agents, as an investigative tool to gain insight into the seamy netherworld of drug money laundering. The results of Operation *Dinero* made it an overwhelming success. Over $52 million and nine tons of cocaine were seized, and 88 people were arrested worldwide. This was cocaine that did not end up on the streets of our cities. This is money that will not be used to further the production and distribution of more illegal drugs. And these are criminals who will not continue to pursue the deadly cycle of drug-related crime and violence.

Special Agent Wankel concluded his testimony by explaining that the most important aspect of "both operations, Green Ice and Dinero, was the message it sent to the drug Mafias, that the number of safe havens for their drug money is quickly dwindling. Law enforcement agencies will continue to use financial investigations like these two highly successful operations against traffickers and money launderers. As is the case with all crime, money is the motivating factor. For enforcement to be effective, we must attack the money of these multibillion dollar drug enterprises. We must continue to work with and strengthen our international partnerships, and maintain strong ties with our counterparts in the financial centers of the world. We must continue to urge all countries to ratify the U.N. Convention and to pass more effective money laundering and forfeiture laws. Above all, we must continue to identify the points where the money is most vulnerable and identify what we can do to separate traffickers from their ill-gotten gains."[57]

THE DIRECTIVES OF THE INTERNATIONAL COMMUNITY

Despite the continuous efforts of the agencies in charge of fighting drug trafficking and money laundering, it is calculated that the gains from cocaine trafficking in the United States alone are $29,000 million. A great problem in fighting these cartels has been the traffickers' abilities to develop new techniques to legitimate their capital.

Within the process of money laundering, the traffickers necessarily must rely on a bank or financial entity with which they can pour their illicit money through the sieve of legality. The banks most used for this purpose are located in Switzerland, Liechtenstein, Luxembourg, the Bahamas, the Turks and Caicos Islands, and the Cayman Islands; nevertheless, in recent years, many other banks in other parts of the globe have become important money laundering centers. Most crucial for the drug traffickers is that they be able to quickly deposit or transfer money to a place that exercises tight banking confidentiality and that does not care whose money it has.

---

[57] Statemant by Special Agent Harold D. Wankel, DEA Chief of Operations. House Banking and Financial Committee, February 28,1996.

In 1986, President Ronald Reagan included the problems of drug trafficking and money laundering among his most important international priorities. Within the domestic sphere, he signed National Security Directive No. 221, which identified drug trafficking and money laundering as the top national priority, and which improved the mechanisms with which to deal with the problem (an important regulation – that banks report to the Department of the Treasury any transaction exceeding $10,000 – had already been established in 1980).

This heightened supervision of banks resulted, at the very least, in bad publicity for institutions such as E.F. Hutton, Merrill Lynch, The Chemical Bank of New York and The First National Bank of Boston.   Even though in some cases the laundering of money could not be proven, the suspicions of the congressional committees and other entities that investigated them were certainly reasonable. In other cases, such as that of BCCI, banks were directly ordered to close their doors.

Many money laundering investigations end in Switzerland. An important case became public when ties were discovered linking Minister of Justice Elizabeth Kopp and her husband with the Medellín cartel and the Turko-Lebanese Mafia. Minister Kopp, using her position, hid or directly denied requests to extradite certain drug traffickers living in Switzerland; meanwhile, her husband acted as the attorney for these men. In addition, on several occasions Kopp denied the freezing of accounts belonging to the traffickers. As a consequence to the resulting scandal, in 1989 the Swiss Parliament defined the act of laundering money as a crime, and began to support international efforts to regulate bank secrecy and to establish requirements to "know the client."

Subsequent to the crack down on money-laundering organizations, banks and other financial entities have raised the price of their work. In 1990, those responsible for laundering illegal money charged a 6% commission. Currently, the commission ranges from 20-25%. Considering the increased difficulties the launderers face to do their job --

the necessary constant improvement of techniques-- and the raise in the quantity of money to be laundered, the ascending rates of commission are certainly justified.

Although many countries have now assessed what they can do to fight the laundering of drug money, the solution lies in a global approach. As it is a problem that confronts all countries, it is necessary to increase international cooperation and to develop global standards in the form of multilateral treaties or conventions. Global policy must be homogenized. Many countries have been seduced by the billion-dollar illegal drug industry, but at a high social and political cost. As corruption weeds its way through the highest levels of government, justice and law enforcement, those who walk along that road must accept responsibility for the assasinations and acts of terror which the traffickers impose upon those who oppose them.

The 1988 Vienna Convention on the Illicit Traffic of Narcotics and Psychotropic Substances, ratified by 99 countries, consitutes a good beginning. But what is needed now, especially for the other countries, is a new international convention, to be enacted as soon as possible, which deals solely and specifically with the crime of money laundering. After all, we all seek the same thing: to achieve a multilateral effort.

The United Nations has committed to such a goal, providing a platform for international debate. Meetings of experts, politicians and state representatives have taken place one after the other, and their resulting worthless statements and proclamations have resonated like official mandates or like an official voice of the world. However, it seems that many have forgotten that the true objective is to find *a solution*. In each meeting, recommendation, and presentation, the participants discuss issues like car theft, prostitution, trafficking of children, lack of education and a never-ending list of problems as if they were directly linked to drugs and money laundering. This *official voice* has defined the over-arching issue as follows:

The problem of drug trafficking is considered a part of transnational organized crime. The most important transnational crime organizations are the following:

a) The Italian Mafia, also known within their territorial jurisdictions as "*Cosa Nostra*" (in Sicily), "*Camorra*" (in Naples), and "*Ndrangheta*" (in Calabria);

b) The Russian Mafia, which flourished as a result of the fall of communism, and took advantage of the economic, social, institutional and judicial collapse during the transitional period that confronted the countries previously behind the Soviet iron curtain;

c) The Chinese triad, whose headquarters is in Hong Kong;

d) The Japanese Yasukas;

e) The Colombian and Mexican cartels.

The transnational criminal organizations base their illicit activities on the following:

a) The traffic of nuclear material and conventional and military arms;

b) Terrorism;

c) The traffic of minors, newborns;

d) The traffic of organs for transplant or ablation;

e) The traffic of narcotics;

f) The laundering or legitimization of capital.

To confront these organizations, the international community has generally subscribed to bilateral agreements. The results of these tactics, when measured against the growth of the above criminal organizations, are sparse. The following treaties can be seen as examples:

a) The 1984 agreement between the United States and Italy for the creation of a Task Force to Combat Criminal Drug-trafficking Organizations. The agreement incorporated mutual assistance and the exchange of information.

b) Protocol of Cooperation, signed in 1993, between Germany and Russia. The object was to exchange information regarding the various criminal organizations that operated in both territories.

c) Other bilateral agreements of reciprocal assistance, cooperation, extradition, information exchange, etc.

Regional agreements also play a role against organized crime. This represents a new approach to the problem, especially in the areas of drug trafficking and money laundering. Within this sphere, significant advances have been made, including initiatives of the Inter-American Drug Abuse Commission (IADAC, created by the OAS) and the recommendations of the Financial Action Task Force (FATF).

To responsibly deal with the continuing advance of criminal organizations, the international community must go beyond the distinct United Nations conferences and hold a world-wide conference to specifically establish clear rules and global strategies.

Taking the advice of the *official voice*, hundreds of experts from around the world met again and again to find solutions to the problem. In various corners of the globe, numerous issues related to money laundering were examined, and as if it were a universal truth, they shouted out their new discovery: "the problem must be approached globally, and the only solution is the diplomacy." Whether through a multilateral treaty or through a global convention to make existing legislation compatible,   the   acceptance   of   the   appropriate recommendations must be made a de facto condition for belonging to the United Nations and to the international community in general. The specific conclusions and concrete recommendations that were reached, as a result of this flurry of meetings, are as follows:

Conformation to the United Nations Convention Against the Illicit Traffic of Narcotics and Psychotropic Substances (signed in Vienna in 1988) must be obligatory for all United Nations participant countries.

The recommendations of the FATF, the "Group of Seven" (Canada, Germany, Italy, Japan, Great Britain, and the United States), and the Presidents of the European Community must be considered. For example, Sweden, Switzerland, Austria and Australia have joined this group in their support of the principle of "knowledge of the client" and of the limitation of banking secrecy. In addition, diplomatic efforts are being made to incorporate Finland, Norway, Turkey, Hong Kong, New Zealand and Singapore to this list.

All countries must, within their legal frameworks, define the money laundering as a crime, limit banking secrecy, and adopt the principle of "knowledge of the client." That is, countries must keep track of those who open bank accounts, regularly verify the patrimonial state of these persons, take note of the sums of capital involved in their transactions, identify the destinations of capital transfers, prohibit codified accounts, improve institutional and personnel standards of financial operations, permit the utilization of confiscated funds toward drug traffic prevention and repression programs.

However, all these principles and declarations will be of no use if the proposed measures are not adopted and enforced. The United States has relied on anti-money laundering laws since 1970, and the Department of the Treasury and Congress have been revising and perfecting these laws and regulations, which now number in the hundreds, every year since then. In this way, the United States appears to be headed in the right direction; nevertheless, events in reality do not correspond to this legal trail blazing.

The news media and official agency reports reveal on a daily basis the struggle that the Americans have on their hands with money laundering. It has become commonplace to hear that some trafficking organization has utilized this or that bank to clean their money. Many officials tell only partial stories or details, but the time has come to tell the rest of the stories and take a look at *all* the books on the shelf.

The story of the struggle against money laundering is replete with cases like the one which occurred in Texas in 1989. In this story, U.S. Customs officials discovered that First City Texas Bank was being used by Mexicans to launder drug money. The officials received reports that two banks located in the Rio Grande Valley and a Monterrey, Mexico firm, Cologne Currency Exchange, were using the bank in McAllen, Texas to advance their illicit business interests. According to the investigation, various persons would cross into the United States and, without having had declared the money they carried at the border, would go to the bank and deposit cash or other monetary instruments in the name of Cologne Currency Exchange. After making the deposit, the exchange house, from their home city of Monterrey, would order weekly transfers of 5 to 10 million dollars to other exchange house branches that Cologne had outside of Mexico. When the money finally returned to Mexican soil, it was clean. With this information, officials of the U.S. Customs Service in McAllen initiated an operation called *"Casa Rico,"* in which two agents, posing as traffickers, contacted the banks in the Rio Grande Valley and Cologne Currency Exchange. The operation culminated in 1992 with the arrest of 25 persons, all high-level functionaries of Mexican banks as well as the owners of Cologne Currency Exchange. Proof had also been obtained showing that approximately $30 million were laundered through First City

Texas Bank. The success of the operation, of course, delighted many; however, nobody ventured to point out in more than a whisper that no Americans had been arrested, and that First City Texas Bank suffered not the slightest of consequences. But above all, having discovered the laundering of $30 million did not warrant much satisfaction; that is, within the world of money laundering, this figure is minuscule.

One of the most important operations against money launderers was called Operation Tracer. In 1982, the Federal Reserve Bank in New York sent its counterpart in Puerto Rico, *Banco de Ponce* (Ponce Bank), a report that showed an enormous increase in the currency flow in Puerto Rico from 1980 to 1982. During this period, Puerto Rico had 16 banks which increased their funds approximately from $1,600 million to $11,740 million dollars. However, the report's most salient point was that the Puerto Rican banks were not complying with the Bank Secrecy Act since they had not filed Currency Transaction Reports (CTR's).[58] The Internal Revenue Service

---

[58] The Bank Secrecy Act and its implementing regulations require, with certain exceptions, that banks and other financial institutions file a Currency Transaction Report -CRT- with the Internal Renueve Service for each deposit or exchange of currency in excess of $10,000 and that any person transporting monetary instruments of more than $5,000 into or out of the United States must file a Currency or Monetary Instrument Report -CMIR- with the U.S. Customs Service. The federal agencies that oversee the operations of financial institutions have responsibility for monitoring compliance with the Act and its regulations. The Department of Treasury has overall responsibility for implementing the Bank Secrecy Act. Treasury has deligated responsibility for assuring compliance with the reporting and recordkeeping requirements of the Act and its supporting regulations as follows (see 31 C.F.R.-103.46): Office of the Comptroller of the Currency, for all National Banks; Federal Reserve System, for all state-chartered Federal Reserve member banks; Federal Deposit Insurance Corporation, for all other federally insured banks and branches of foreign banks operating in the United States; Federal Home Loan Bank Board, for all federally insured savings and loan associations; National Credit Union Administration, for all federal

had complained to the various Federal Reserve Banks regarding the missing CTR's for transactions involving Puerto Rican banks.

As a result of these irregularities and unfulfilled responsibilities, the Justice and Treasury Departments joined forces and participated in the above-mentioned investigation, which had already been initiated by the DEA. Undercover DEA agents had infiltrated diverse Puerto Rican groups in an effort to find out who ran the heroin distribution ring that linked Puerto Rico and Chicago.[59]

The investigation required interviews with and interrogations of representatives of ten of the principal Puerto Rican financial entities. They also had to consult with managers and examiners of the Federal Home Loan Bank Board and with Federal Deposit Insurance Corporation investigators, who in turn met with the Puerto Rican Secretary of the Treasury and the U.S. Attorney for Puerto Rico. The investigation fell on seven of the most prominent Puerto Rican banks, and a complete audit was done on each, which included a review of their procedures for processing cash and of the training that bank officials had in regard to dealing with laundering operations for drug money. One of the first conclusions of the investigation was that this Caribbean island had become a paradise for North and South American tax evaders, who, with the help of bankers, would open up

---

credit unions; Securities and Exchange Commission, for securietes dealers and brokers; Internal Revenue Service, for all other financial institutions; and U.S. Customs Service, for transportation of currency into or out of the country.

[59] President Ronald Reagan created the Task Forced Program in 1982. Within this program, the Florida-Caribbean Task Force was created, which, in 1984, took charge of Operation Tracer. Typically, their principal objective was to combat national and international drug-trafficking organizations, but in this case, they collaborated in the investigation of Puerto Rico's financial institutions.

accounts under false names. These functionaries had fallen to the enticing life style that the drug traffickers could provide; after all, dealing with tax evaders and traffickers was not exactly+ legal. Their primary maneuver was to help those who wanted to launder their money to buy winning lottery tickets for amounts over $100,000. In this way, dozens of known traffickers won the Puerto Rico Lottery.

The finale of Operation Tracer came when two undercover agents managed to infiltrate a group of bankers and were offered the opportunity to buy a winning lottery ticket. On June 6, 1985, about 200 federal agents raided the ten most important financial institutions in Puerto Rico; 17 persons were arrested, charged with conspiracy to defraud and to commit other offenses against the United States, and with failure to file and causing failure to file currency transaction reports on transactions exceeding $10,000 in cash or its equivalent, as part of a pattern of illegality involving transactions exceeding $100, 000.

This case would neither be the only nor the last against perpetrators of money-laundering laws. American agencies still had ahead of them their most difficult and controversial campaigns, that is, those cases against the largest and most prestigious banks of the country for violations of the Bank Secrecy Act.

THE FIRST NATIONAL BANK OF BOSTON

On February 7, 1985, The First National Bank of Boston, one of the best known American banks, pled guilty to a felony charge that they failed to file appropriate forms on $1.2 billion in international currency transactions in violation of the Bank Secrecy Act. However, the case was shrouded in contradictions and confusion. Therefore, the Senate Permanent Subcommittee on Investigations began an investigation, Senator William V. Roth clearly expressed its objective:

We are here today to try to discover several things. First, we want to have a factual accounting as to how a bank the size and prestige of the First of Boston could find itself in this situation. Secondly, we need to explore, to the degree possible, how pervasive this type of non-compliance is. Frankly, I wish we could have held this hearing earlier. At least perhaps we could have prevented some of the unfortunate leaks that have occurred in this case. In fact, I find it reprehensible and the height of irresponsibility that such things as the Treasury list of nine Massachusetts banks has been made available to the press. As we will see today, this list has little significance as to whether or not the banks named are actually in non-compliance with the Bank Secrecy Act. Yet, I am afraid, the banks on that list have had their reputations damaged apparently for the sake of headlines.

We also want to find out why the enforcement agencies, specifically the Comptroller's Office, have failed to detect and report violations during their regular bank examinations. Finally, we want to know what changes may be necessary in the law or regulations to insure compliance.

In 1983, the Permanent Subcommittee on Investigations held extensive hearings on offshore banking and the use of offshore facilities to launder illegal funds. There have been many developments in this area since our hearings. I will not dwell on these here as they will be detailed in the Subcommittee's final report on this subject to be issued soon. Though our previous work has concentrated on the offshore aspect of money laundering, we are intimately aware of the domestic problems as well. The two cannot be separated.

I want to commend Senator Rudman, our Vice Chairman, for initially bringing the Bank of Boston issue to the attention of the Subcommittee. Senator Rudman was an active participant in our offshore bank investigations and *immediately realized the significance of the Bank of Boston's noncompliance and recommended that we get the complete facts.*

There is no question in our minds that the Bank Secrecy Act is an indispensable link in the prosecution chain of major crimes; particularly those involving organized crime, drug traffickers and major frauds. We, on this Subcommittee, have seen the ravages of these crimes that take the life savings from some and even the lives of others. And we have seen that the Act is one of the most effective tools in the arsenal of U.S. prosecutors. Therefore, we do not take the Bank Secrecy Act lightly. Nor do we consider it a technical regulation to be enforced in an agency's spare time or between other more pressing matters. We are going to hear testimony today that unfortunately indicates to us that our view of the importance of the Bank Secrecy Act is perhaps not as widely shared as it should be – either within the government or in the private sector.

Now many people have asked how the First of Boston could find itself in its current situation. I will tell you how. They did not take the Act seriously, either as a corporation or as individuals within the corporation. They ignored it. They may as well have thrown the Comptroller's notices, the law, and the regulations in the trash.

And the bank examiners – where were they? They were in the bank. They were even sent back to the Bank of Boston by the Treasury Department to specifically check on Bank Secrecy Act compliance. They were even told where to check and what to check.

I can understand that 50 bank examiners with primary concerns of bank solvency spending weeks in a bank the size of First of Boston could perhaps not deem it important to spend a great deal of time on the Bank Secrecy Act. But how could they miss a violation of the size and scope of this one when they were told specifically where and what the violation was? The answer to that question is what we seek today.

This is not the first time that bank regulatory agencies have been called to task for the lack of adequate enforcement of the Bank Secrecy Act. In 1977, during the Carter Administration, hearings before the House Committee on Government Operations revealed that the bank regulatory agency examiners had failed to detect reporting violations at the Chemical Bank of New York prior to the prosecution in that case. In 1979, the Treasury Department conceded to the House Banking Committee that there were very few referrals by the banking regulatory agencies. In 1980, at hearings before the Senate Banking Committee the enforcement efforts of the banking regulatory agencies were described as "dismal" and "lackadaisical." And a 1981 GAO report found that the compliance monitoring of the bank regulatory agencies was inadequate, cursory or nonexistent.

As to the question of how widespread this total disregard – this almost scornful disregard of the Bank Secrecy Act is . . . I hesitate to ask the question. What we know already indicates the problem is probably pandemic. In Boston alone, three financial institutions have been prosecuted, a fourth is under investigation, and I understand a fifth is receiving close attention by federal prosecutors.

We thought our investigators should take some time while in Boston to discuss Bank Secrecy Act compliance with another major bank, the Shawmut Bank of Boston. After we served a subpoena for records on the Shawmut Bank on March 1, 1985, to our utter dismay, we found that the Shawmut had not filed Currency Transaction Reports on almost $200 million of international currency transactions covering the past five years . . . I will say this about the Shawmut Bank. It is to their credit that they took the initiative, shortly after the First of Boston plea, to determine whether or not they were in compliance with Title 31. When they discovered they had not filed, they informed both the Comptroller and the Treasury Department. They did this several days before our initial contact with them . . .

The Wall Street Journal reported that the Bank of New England, the second largest bank in Boston, had failed to file reports on several international currency transactions. Thus, Boston's three largest banks have failed to comply with this provision of the Bank Secrecy Act.

But we are not here simply to point accusing fingers at two or three banks. This is, as I have said, not a new problem. The First Bank of Boston did not invent non-compliance with the Bank Secrecy Act. **Twenty-eight banks have been prosecuted for Title 31 violations since 1976,** *according to a list provided to us by the IRS. That list begins with the Chemical Bank and ends with the First National Bank of Boston, two of our country's largest banks. At present, the IRS has 188 ongoing Title 31 investigations encompassing 41 banks. Fifty-three of these 188 cases are in the Northeast United States. An additional 81 cases are with various U.S. attorneys awaiting prosecution decisions. These are very disturbing statistics, more so because of the types of banks represented.*

I consider the epidemic of drug abuse to be one of the most serious problems confronting this country. We could lose an entire generation of youth to the drug problem. I have said it before – money laundering is the glue that holds all this together. We cannot tolerate our major banks providing the vessel for that glue by ignoring the provisions of the Bank Secrecy Act. This is society's problem, not just law enforcement's. Banks can no longer hide behind the assertion that they are not law enforcement agencies. Banks are part of this society, and as such they have a responsibility to assist in this battle. While I do not believe in burying banks in massive regulations, I do not think it is too much to ask that they follow simple instructions. I do not think it is too much to ask that they inquire when customers are bringing grocery bags full of small bills through the front door.

One of the first witnesses to testify before the Subcommittee was John P. Hamill, President of Shawmut

Corporation and Executive Vice President of the Shawmut Bank of Boston. The banker took the stand and, after taking the oath, began his testimony: "The bank has 29 branches, all located in the Boston area, and we provide financial services principally to individuals and local and regional businesses. I want to describe, if I might, Mr. Chairman, how we discovered our reporting deficiencies and how these deficiencies came about."

But Senator Roth interrupted him and, to clarify the situation, asked, "Excuse me. When was this again?" Hamill, answering the question, continued with his testimony:

After February 7, 1985, when the Bank of Boston situation came to light, our people came to me. We began an invtigation. We concluded the bank had inadvertently continued to treat certain customers as exempt which, after the 1980 changes in the regulations, we were not authorized to exempt without specific Treasury authorization.   Those customers included seven foreign banks with longstanding relationships with Shawmut as well as 20 well-known local institutions and commercial firms in the Boston area. The list of those customers include   churches,   cultural   organizations,   educational institutions, and scheduled airlines.

At that point, we asked for meetings with the Treasury Department and the Comptroller of the Currency.   Those meetings took place on February 19, 1985, pursuant to telephone conversations that we had with both the Treasury and the Comptroller's offices late February 14 and early in the morning on February 15.

On February 19, in those meetings, we presented the conclusions of our internal review, and we submitted CTR's for foreign transactions going back to 1980. In addition we submitted exemption applications to the Treasury Department for 20 customers of the bank – the scheduled airlines, the churches, and the educational institutions – under a procedure whereby we believe those customers are eligible for an exemption.

Our review confirmed that we had made an error. We did not properly comply with the Bank Secrecy Act. As I will describe, this is not a case where no one at the bank saw the regulations. In fact, the branch division of the bank did receive the regulations and applied them diligently, if not perfectly, from the time that they received them in 1980. In fact, the branch division filed over 800 CTR's during the period of 1980 through 1984.

The bank's currency department, however, did not see the regulations. Let me explain a little bit, if I might, the distinctions between the branch division and the currency department. The branch division is the main point of contact with the customers and the commercial customers of the bank. The currency department, however, is separate from the branch division, and it is in the currency department where we deal with domestic banks, foreign banks, major corporate customers, and institutions which normally have cash transactions. These are among the same 20 companies and institutions that I have mentioned already.

Some of this goes to the question of why the currency department did not get the regulations. If I might go back to 1972 when the Bank Secrecy Act became effective, transactions with foreign banks, as well as domestic banks, were exempt as were transactions with customers who in the ordinary course of their business were customarily depositors of large amounts of cash.

These exemptions basically meant that all of the customers of the currency department were not affected by the Bank Secrecy Act for the 8-year period between 1972 and 1980. The 1980 amendments removed the general exemption for foreign bank transactions and limited the domestic customer exemption. When the 1980 changes became effective and were received by the bank, they were routed to that part of the bank that had dealt with the Bank Secrecy Act for the prior eight years; that is the branch division of the bank.

. . . The branch division then complied with the amended regulations through the regular updating of the exemption list and periodic reminders of the importance of full CTR compliance to the various branches.

The currency department never received a copy of the change in regulations, and it continued to treat the customers it had been dealing with as it had for the prior eight years.

In 1983, as a result of changes in the operation of branches, the currency department began to deal with certain of the deposits of certain customers of the branches so that at that point in time, certain customers were sending deposits to the branches which would forward those deposits directly to the currency department.

At that time, the currency department became aware of the fact there was a requirement to put together a list of its customers, basically, the customers it dealt with, and to provide that list to the branch division so that it could be kept in one place for regulatory inspection. The two lists came together for the first time in 1983. As it turns out, incorrectly, the currency department continued to believe that its requirement was merely to keep a list of its customers because those customers were the ones that it normally did business with in the course of its business and, therefore, were exempt from reporting.

When we commenced our internal review, we found that the exempt list would, in fact, satisfy the requirements of the CTR regulations with the exception of those 20 customers and the seven foreign banks.

. . . The foreign banks that Shawmut treated as exempt are also long-standing customers of the bank. The vast majority of the transactions with these customers were transactions in which they sent money to us, cash deposits. In turn, Shawmut transferred funds by wire to accounts maintained by the foreign

banks at other U.S. banks. That is, the cash would come in to us and in turn be wired out to other U.S. banks.

The foreign banks in the group included one in Spain, two in Portugal, one in Ireland, and four in Canada. All are long-term customers, and some for as many as 50 years; none less than 20 years. Deposits of currency from foreign banks from 1980 to 1985 totaled $157 million and withdrawals totaled $33.9 million.

Since the internal review of our compliance procedures commenced last month, we have taken a number of specific steps to improve the level of our compliance with the CTR requirements.

. . . Mr. Chairman, we have done as well as we should have. We should not have missed this particular regulation, but we think the error was localized within the currency department. As we look back as to why it happened, we think we understand why it happened. It is unfortunate, and we regret that we did not find the error, but we have always sought to be fully cooperative with the Office of the Comptroller and the Treasury Department with regard to the enforcement of the CTR requirements, and also with regard to this particular matter. We voluntarily brought it to the attention of both the Comptroller and the Treasury Department within days after having found the error ourselves. We have never sought to withhold or delay the giving of any information with regard to the requirements as we understood them, and we believe our new compliance program will continue to improve our program as we go forward over the course of the coming years. We stand ready to cooperate with the subcommittee, with the Treasury and with the Comptroller, and I will be pleased to answer any questions you might have at this time.

CHAIRMAN ROTH: Mr. Hamill. Do I correctly understand your corrective action was initiated by the banking management, that this is not the result of any inquiry or investigation on the part of the Government?

MR. HAMILL: That's correct, Senator.

SENATOR RUDMAN: I want to refer to one part of your statement that says:

"The foreign banks that Shawmut treats as exempt are also longstanding customers. The vast majority of transactions with these customers consist of deposits. In turn, Shawmut transferred funds by wire to accounts maintained by the foreign banks at other U.S. banks."

I assume you had a corresponding relationship with some of those banks, or did this just as a service to these other banks.

Did any of these wire transfers in behalf of the foreign banks that you deal with go to other than deposits in the name of those foreign banks in those various U.S. banks? In other words, were some of those wire transfers to an account of an individual or corporation?

MR. HAMILL: Senator, the vast majority went to accounts of the foreign banks in other U.S. banks. There were some. We don't have the whole detailed list. There were some that went to corporations, and we're looking at some of those instances.

The Senators continued the session, not only asking questions about the bank's exempt list, but most of all questioning Hamill regarding the Office of the Comptroller's investigation. The banker explained that since 1980, the Comptroller had performed inspections of the bank just about every year, but had never called their attention to violations of the Bank Secrecy Act. Finally, Daniel Rinzel, Subcommittee Majority Chief Counsel, took the floor and, getting right to the heart of the matter, asked, *"Are you familiar with the Deak-Perera firm?"* After Hamill responded in the affirmative, Rinzel interrogated him about the type of relationship that existed or had existed between Shawmut of Boston and Deak-Perera. The questions clearly made Hamill uncomfortable. This line of interrogation ran deeper than just wanting to know if Shawmut had reported its transactions with that firm; that is, there was no one in the room who was not familiar with the activities of Deak-Perera.

During those first days of March, 1985, various U.S. newspapers revealed a scandalous relationship between Deak-Perera and two banks –Shawmut of Boston and First National Bank of Boston.   Deak-Perera was controlled by Gennaro Angiulo.   Angiulo, together with his four brothers, ran a money-laundering operation in New England through a collection of firms which they managed.[60]

Moreover, it was suspected that in addition to his money-laundering activities, Angiulo was also responsible for bringing vast quantities of heroin and cocaine into the Boston area from Mexico.   Nevertheless, the only proof against the man was related to the charges of money laundering. In April, 1985, Angiulo, after the completion of a federal investigation ˙and trial, joined several other members of his family who were already in prison serving long sentences which had been handed down by the United States District Court for Massachusetts.

Hamill limitedly responded that "we have had some dealings with the Deak-Perera firm where we may buy or sell foreign currency, where we have customers who are going to be traveling abroad and are in need of foreign currency . . . ." Rinzel questioned further into the matter, asking whether the transactions with this firm were reported or not reported. Hamill responded bluntly: "when we have bought foreign currency from them we have generally not reported a Deak-Perera transaction. I think we have done about $1 million over the five year period, and we are looking at that particular situation in order to determine the reporting requirements."[61]

---

[60] "Steps Must Be Taken to Clog Money-Laundering Pipeline," by William Safire, *The Atlanta Constitution*, March 28, 1985, p. 17-A.
[61] Shawmut Bank of Boston, the third-largest in Boston, told the Treasury it had failed to report more than $190 million in large cash transactions with foreign banks and had improperly exempted 27 customers from currency reporting rules. Boston of New England has

Although the senators were starting to get at the information they wanted, they decided to let Hamill end his testimony, but not before requiring him to send the results of his internal investigation (especially those results pertaining to dealings with Angiulo's notorious firm) to the Subcommittee.[61]

The ball was now in the court of Todd Conover, Comptroller of the Currency, who convened a hearing which was attended by Joe Selby, Senior Deputy Comptroller for Bank Supervision, and Jordan Luke, Deputy Chief Counsel (Policy). After taking the oath, Conover requested the floor:

> *I am here today to discuss compliance with the reporting provisions of the Bank Secrecy Act. The recent conviction of the First National Bank of Boston for currency transaction reporting violations has raised concerns regarding the implementation of that act. The Office of the Comptroller of the Currency (OCC) shares these concerns.*
>
> *In September 1982, this Office was notified by the Treasury Department that a review of currency flows at the*

---

admitted to two sets of unreported cash transactions. The functionaries of both banks deny having solicited immunity from the District Attorney's Office, but admitted that they hoped to encounter an understanding attitude on the part of the Department of the Treasury. See: "Money Laundering: The Defense Gets a Star Witness," Blanca Riemer and Loris Therrein, *Business Week*, March 25, 1985.

[61] On March 18, 1985, C. Keffe Hurley Jr., Senior Vice President and General Counsel of Shawmut Bank, sent a note to the Subcommittee, informing them that records of cash deposits which were transfered to foreign entities were not available since they could not find documentation showing these transactions. In the same note, Hurley indicated that, regarding the deposits which were not reported by the bank, the difference between the Subcommittee's numbers and those of the bank was $13 million, a figure which corresponded to the missing documentation. With respect to transactions with Deak-Perera, Hurley promised to send a report as soon as he was able to find the corresponding records.

Federal Reserve Bank of Boston had indicated that several Massachusetts banks, including the Bank of Boston, exhibited a large volume of currency activity. At this time the OCC was in the process of conducting a regular examination at the Bank of Boston as of September 30, 1982. The Treasury was aware of this and requested that we report back to them with our examination findings regarding Bank Secrecy Act compliance.

In response to this request, our examiners focused their investigation of the Bank of Boston's Bank Secrecy Act compliance specifically on the Treasury's concern, and they were able to explain more than 95 % of the currency flow that concerned Treasury based on the bank's failure to include domestic banks on its exemption list. They cited the Bank of Boston for this violation of the Bank Secrecy Act regulations, and a bank official promised corrective action.

During the examination, a bank official also expressed some confusion as to the reporting requirements for international currency transactions and confirmed that the bank was in contact with the Treasury regarding this issue.

.... In late April 1983, the Internal Revenue Service began an investigation of the bank. As is not unusual in these situations, the Treasury notified us to suspend examination of the bank for Bank Secrecy Act compliance On February 7, 1985, the Justice Department brought charges against the Bank of Boston for failing to report over $1 billion in cash transferred between the bank and various foreign banks.

We have drawn several conclusions from our initial review of these events. First, while we provided some support to the investigation and conviction of the Bank of Boston, we are not satisfied with our performance overall. We have learned that we could have been more effective in applying our procedures, in training our examination staff, and in responding to information from the Treasury Department regarding potential compliance problems in certain banks.

We now recognize that we could have done a more vigorous compliance review during the 1982 examination. The enhanced examination procedures put in place by the banking agencies in November 1981 represented a substantial improvement in our ability to monitor Bank Secrecy Act compliance. However, it has recently become clear that the examiners that were involved in the Bank of Boston examination were not familiar with the 1981 procedures and the specific reporting requirements as revised in 1980. It is also clear that while this Office did respond to the Treasury's notification of potential problems with the Bank of Boston, the attention and follow-up we devoted to the issue were less than sufficient.

To many Senators, especially Chairman William Roth, the Comptroller's excuses and statements were almost intolerable. That is, those who were present all agreed that the private sector was not giving the necessary priority and importance to Bank Secrecy Act regulations; however, it was a very different issue when a government entity like the OCC was not doing its job correctly and was not, for one reason or another, paying heed to the regulations dictated by their own government. What infuriated the senators was that the examiners did not have precise knowledge of the requirements and regulations of the Bank Secrecy legislation.

Conover defended himself and his office. The Comptroller maintained that each member of the Office had the necessary aptitude and knowledge for his or her position. In the case of the examiners, they were always professionally evaluated before being promoted to the next level, and part of the evaluation dealt with the Bank Secrecy Act. Moreover, at each of the district offices there were a number of mandatory training sessions each year. In fact, he explained that the OCC spent $14 million annually on training, which composed 9% of their annual budget. With these funds, investigators took specialized university classes dealing with banking and finance. Furthermore, 90 different training seminars were kept active and current, the majority of which involved aspects of the Bank Secrecy Act.

But the Comptroller's defense upset the senators even more. They could not understand how, in the face of so much training, it was possible for the examiners to perform so unsatisfactorily. After all, even Conover himself described their performance as such. Chairman Roth asked for an explanation. Conover responded that if perhaps there was no valid explanation, one only had to look at the work load of these examiners to understand any shortcomings. He explained that in recent years the examiners had an overflowing case load of audits and inspections of banking and financial procedures. He noted, moreover, that the crisis involving American businesses and the banking infrastructure had even further bogged their schedules. The Comptroller explained that the examiners could not and cannot be present in the banks 365 days of the year, and neither could they completely inspect each of the millions of transactions which every bank makes. Their function was basically to contact bank managers and directors in order to monitor bank policy in each area, analyze their procedures, and work in conjunction with their internal auditors. However, Conover said that the Bank of Boston experience would help them avoid this type of "human error" in the future; he let it be understood that his office was working with the Federal Financial Institutions Examinations Council to develop better procedures for training and educating examiners with respect to the Bank Secrecy Act.

The members of the committee were astonished once again when Senator Rudman introduced another issue to the hearing. The Senator had in his hands a report drafted by the same Comptroller of the Currency. Paragraph 26 of this document stated that "during the OCC's review of its handling of the Bank of Boston matter, the staff has had several discussions with the Assistant U.S. Attorney in charge of criminal investigation. He informed us that he has been dissatisfied with the level of cooperation he had received from the two examiners." Although Conover asserted that in reality the problem had been minor –just a case of differing criteria, a situation that had not come up again– the Senators would not let the issue drop so easily.

In fact, Rudman insisted to Conover that "your office did nothing to cooperate in any meaningful way with the U.S. Attorney in Boston. As a matter of fact, your office gave the U.S. Attorney misleading information.   I am not saying deliberately, but the information they gave was misleading." Jordan Luke responded in a limited way to this attack by maintaining that he had always acted in collaboration with the Attorney, and moreover, that the disagreement over criteria had led to the formation of a task force.   According to the Deputy Chief Counsel, the Attorney had access to the documents, including the reports of the examiners of the First National Bank of Boston; and although these documents were not handed over with the urgency with which they should have been, this was because permission from Washington to turn over the reports had likewise been granted in a tardy manner.

Senator Rudman then wanted to know the names of those who investigated the First National Bank of Boston.   The names of Steve Conners and Thomas Rollo were immediately offered as all those present were familiar with these two men; moreover, the two investigators were in the waiting room preparing to testify.   But Senator Rudman wanted to know specifically if those investigators sent to the First National of Boston had been familiar with the Bank Secrecy Act and the rest of the regulations stipulated under Title 31 of the U.S. Code, and if they had known what they were supposed to be looking for when they passed through the doors of the bank. Although, Jordan Luke had claimed that both examiners had perfect knowledge of the regulations surrounding Title 31, testimony which infuriated all those on the Subcommittee, it turned out that in 1982, when the men had investigated First National Bank of Boston, at least one of them, Thomas Rollo, was not familiar with the legislation. In fact, he hardly knew anything about it.

Upon this revelation, tones in the room once again grew restless and angry. Luke, for a second time, attributed this unfamiliarity to shortcomings in OCC training. Senator Rudman turned quickly to the Comptroller and responded:

> *Well, Mr. Conover, I suppose if a New Hampshire State Policeman passed a body in a gutter with two holes in the forehead and did nothing about it and told the police he didn't know there was a law against homicide, I suppose that is a lack of training too. This seems to me an absolute basic requirement. You have examiners going into the Bank of Boston not even knowing that $1 million in currency transactions are required to be reported. You say that is training, I say that is gross negligence.*
>
> *"I can't justify it, Senator," Conover dully responded. Rudman then summed up the situation perfectly:*
>
> *I think we have here really an abysmal performance by examiners, I don't say I can blame them; maybe they didn't know. I suppose if the captain of the Titanic had survived that incident, he would have testified that he should have looked for icebergs. The fact of the matter is, your navigator, the Treasury Department, told you specifically in 1982 to look for the icebergs. You went ahead, you crashed into them; as far as I am concerned, you sank. I think it is a sorry performance, Mr. Conover. I hope you do a better job in other areas. I don't have much faith from what I have seen in this investigation.*

Senator Alfonse D'Amato then requested the floor with the object of clearing up a point that remained cloudy. He wanted to know if the unsatisfactory results were owed to more factors than just the lack of training. Specifically, the Senator asked Luke if the examiners were using a evaluative procedure known as "module 1." Luke answered in the affirmative, explaining that "module 1" was a procedure commonly used in comptroller investigations, and was a basic technique in evaluating banks. And although Luke described the details of the "module 1" procedure in very technical terms, the senators, through the jargon, were able to understand the underlying backbone of this approach. Those of the Subcommittee, shocked once again, had never heard anything like it. The procedure consisted of interviewing the bank management and asking them if they were complying or not with cash transfer regulations and other laws. D'Amato, cutting to the chase, asked, "you ask the bank if they are in compliance?" The answer once again was in the affirmative, but Luke tried to explain that this was only one part of the module 1 investigative process. D'Amato interrupted him: "What is the other part? If the banks say 'yes, we are in compliance,' what do you do thereafter?" Luke only repeated the same explanation he had just given –that module 1 was common control procedure– and promised to submit as soon as possible reports regarding other financial institutions which were made using the same procedure.

Nevertheless, the senators repeated their disgust in the work of the examiners, of Conover, and of his office in general. They informed him that their report would be rigorous in its critique of OCC operations, especially since the First National Bank of Boston had managed to launder about $1.2 billion right under their noses.

The members of the Subcommittee then ushered in those who had been seated in the waiting room: Stephen Conners, Former Senior National Bank Examiner, Comptroller of the Currency, and Thomas Rollo, Bank Examiner, Comptroller of the Currency. The senators were anxious for their testimonies as these men were the ones who had directly investigated the First National Bank of Boston from within.

The first to speak was Steve Conners, who was now working for the Patriot Bank Corporation. First, the Conners confirmed that he had indeed been in charge of the investigation of the Boston bank, and that this investigation was based on the regulations of Title 31 as of September 7, 1982. The former examiner then indicated that he had assigned Mr. Rollo the task of reviewing the cash program of the bank. From there forward, much of Conner's testimony did not correspond to the statements of those who had testified earlier. For example, Conners said that Thomas Rollo had hardly begun his investigation when he told his superior that he had already found some problems. Rollo explained that before he had even arrived, the Department of the Treasury had returned to the Bank of Boston an immense quantity of CTR forms which had been sent in incomplete, and that he had not obtained a response from bank officials regarding this matter. The data which was consistently missing in the CTR's was the addresses and the ID numbers; and although the Treasury Department had returned the forms and had indicated what information needed to be added, the bank had never done it.

Another issue, and perhaps the most important, dealt with the exempt list. The bank had included on this list *individuals and businesses without prior authorization from the Treasury Department.* On September 21, 1982, Robert Powis, Treasury's Deputy Assistant Secretary, sent a memorandum to the Office of the Comptroller of the Currency. In this memo, Powis informed them that the preliminary reports that were arriving regarding the Massachusetts banks' currency shipments to and from the Federal Reserve Bank of Boston, their exempt lists and their Currency Transaction Report filings, should be expounded upon as soon as possible. Powis also included in the memo a list of new banks which had made transactions with the First National Bank of Boston, but whose corresponding CTR's had not been filed; the total of the unreported transactions with these banks came to

$1,218,682,281. This list of banks included the following institutions:

Swiss Credit Bank; Zurich, Switzerland
Swiss Bank Corporation of Basel; Basel, Switzerland
Union Bank of Switzerland; Zurich, Switzerland
Barclays Bank International; New York
Bank of Boston S.A.; Luxembourg
Bank of Lev; Zurich, Switzerland
Die Erste Oesterreichische; Vienna, Austria
Canadian Imperial Bank of Commerce; Ottawa, Canada
Standard Chartered Bank Limited; New York.

Daniel Rinzel took the floor to ask Conners to comment on those individuals and entities included in the exempt list. Conners, however, claimed that it had been a few years since he had been involved with this matter, and that he could not remember any of the names or businesses who were exempted by the bank from having to report transactions over $10,000. Nevertheless, Conners did remember that the bank would mark which banks were to be included in this list by placing an "X" next to their name, a practice which had seemed strange to Conners, but he personally was never able to get a clear picture of what it meant since Thomas Rollo was the one who had analyzed these books.

However, despite not having been the one who personally reviewed the bank documents, as supervisor he had ordered that additional investigations be done on all areas of the bank, resulting in the involvement of 50 additional examiners in the case. The final report prepared by Thomas Rollo indicated that the First National Bank of Boston did not comply with the Bank Secrecy Act and with regulations stipulated under Title 31.

Thomas Rollo spoke next and confirmed Conners' testimony. He also confirmed that in the very initial stages of the investigation he had recognized grave problems in the bank's international coin and currency reporting operations. Consequently, he summarized these problems in an October 8, 1982 memo, which he sent to Conners. Conners, in turn, gave it to the regional office, and from there, it was sent to the central office in Washington. As far as he knew, the memo was brought to the attention of the Treasury Department – a fact that he had personally confirmed with Karen Wilson, Chief National Bank Examiner of the Treasury Department, and with Robert Powis, Deputy Assistant Secretary for Enforcement from Treasury. According to Rollo, thanks to his memo, these individuals were able to understand the problems surrounding the First National Bank of Boston. Consequently, they had told him that from then on, the Department of the Treasury would see to it that the financial institution complied with the regulations and requirements of the Bank Secrecy Act.

On December 8, 1982, Powis sent another memorandum to the Office of the Comptroller, asking them for a complete report on the situation of the First National Bank of Boston. He also requested reports on the other six Massachusetts banks which were under investigation. However, when the reports arrived on April 5, 1983, the information pertaining to the audit of the First National was not among the folders.

Despite the missing folder, the Subcommittee was able to discover another Bank Secrecy Act non-compliance situation at the Bank of Boston's North End branch which involved violations of the Act's exempt list requirement. For many years, Gennaro Angiulo and various members of his family had made transactions with the bank without these transactions being reported. Angiulo's companies, Federal Investments Inc. and Huntington Realty Company, had been included in a list of exemptees before Bank Secrecy Act regulations were changed in 1980. However, after the new regulations were instated, the bank continued to include them on the exempt list as if nothing had happened. Obviously, they neglected to inform the Treasury Department of this situation.

This discovery and the ex-employee admissions that followed placed the bank in a tight spot. Howard Matheson, an ex-manager of the North End branch who retired in 1985, publicly confirmed that "Angiulo controlled Huntington Realty Co. and Federal Investment Inc.. They were among only 10 or 15 companies on the Bank of Boston's exempt list. I used to see them all the time." Even worse, another ex-employee of the bank explained that "the Angiulo brothers would regularly walk into the branch with more than $10,000 in a paper bag and use the cash to buy cashier's checks in 1982."[63] This was confirmed when a federal investigation of this notorious family discovered that they had bought $1.7 million of cashier's checks in 1982 alone from Bank of Boston branches.[64]

---

[63] See: "Banking by Paper Bag," by Tom Nicholson, *Newsweek*, February 25, 1985.

[64] In this Justice Department investigation of the Angiulo family, it was discovered that in addition to their transactions with First National Bank of Boston, the family also did business with the Boston branches of E.F. Hutton & Co. and Cowen & Co.. An affidavit filed by Justice's New England Organized Crime Strike Force revealed that the Angiulos bought $520,000 worth of cashier's checks, payable to Cowen, from the First National Bank of Boston and the Provident Institution for Savings. Cowen says that no transactions occurred in its one account directly controlled by the Angiulo. But the firm does acknowledge handling the Angiulos' checks in eight other accounts controlled by persons related to or associated with the Angiulo family. Lawrence Leibowitz, Cowen's general counsel, said that an ex-manager of the firm, Robert Jaffe, inherited the Angiulos' accounts from a colleague at E.F. Hutton and brought them with him when he transfered from E.F. Hutton's Boston office to Cowen in 1980. Paul Crabtree, Regional Vice President for E.F. Hutton in Boston, confirms that "members of the family did have accounts here in the past." However the accounts in question were inactive and those responsible at both institutions deny having violated any laws. Also,

The Senators who comprised the Subcommittee felt that their objective – that of uncovering the truth about what had happened in the Bank of Boston case – was almost complete. Although they continued hearing the testimony of other functionaries, many were really waiting to hear the Chairman of the Bank of Boston provide them with satisfactory explanations.

However, when William Brown did testify, he merely stated that this experience of the First National of Boston was an example of what happens when bank management makes a *wrong decision.*   The bank president lamented that his management team had erred in their judgment in including questionable parties in their exempt list. Brown asked the Senators for their forgiveness and, with nothing more to say, excused himself.

To a certain extent, William Brown did not have much more to say, but neither did he want to say anything more. In January and February, 1985, the Bank of Boston had achieved, through long negotiations with government attorneys, an agreement whereby the bank would admit guilt only to one count – that of not having sent in CTR's for $1.2 billion of its international cash transactions with nine foreign banks.[65]

---

in the opinion of Mark Kleiman, senior analyst at Harvard University's John F. Kennedy School of Government, "If the Angiulo's accounts were closed, it would have been a violation of their civil rights, and to suggest that brokers have the obligation to eliminate the accounts is a grave error." See: "Two Brokerages Get Tangled in the Money-Laundering Net," by Alex Beam, *Business Week*, March 11, 1985.

[65] The First National Bank of Boston was fined $500,000; however, prosecutors have not accused the bank of laundering money, a more serious offense. But federal officials implied that intentionally or not, laundering was taking place. Federal prosecutors say that between 1980 and 1984, First National received $529 million mainly in small bills – a weight of at least 20 tons – and sent out $690 million in bills generally of $100 or more.

UNITED STATES DISTRICT COURT
DISTRICT OF MASSACHUSETTS
UNITED STATES OF AMERICA
THE FIRST NATIONAL BANK OF BOSTON
INFORMATION

COUNT I: (Currency Violations – 31 U.S.C. SS1081 and 1059, superseded by 31 U.S.C. SS5313 and 5322 (b)).

The United States of America, by William F. Weld, United States Attorney and Jeremiah T. O'Sullivan, Chief Attorney, New England Organized Crime Strike Force, its attorneys, charges:

1) At all times material herein, The First National Bank of Boston, (hereinafter "Bank of Boston") defendant herein, was a financial institution organized under the laws of the United States of America, with its principal office located in Boston, Massachusetts. Bank of Boston was at all times a National Banking Association, and was a "financial institution" as defined in Title 31 U.S.C. Section 5312 (formerly section 1052).

2) At all times material herein, Bank of Boston was required to file with the Internal Revenue Service (hereinafter "IRS"), Currency Transaction Reports of United States currency in excess of $10,000 in order that the IRS may gather information concerning large cash transactions, for use in criminal, tax and regulatory proceedings.

3) From on or about July 1, 1980 and continuing through on or about September 30, 1984, In the District of Massachusetts, the defendant, Bank of Boston, a banking institution engaged in the business of dealing in currency, knowingly and willfully failed to file, and caused the failure to file, Currency Transaction Reports (IRS Forms 4789) with the Commissioner of the Internal Revenue Service, for currency transactions it engaged in, as required by law, as summarized in Appendix A, attached hereto and incorporated herein.

4) That the defendant Bank of Boston was required to file a Currency Transaction Report for each of the currency transactions set forth in Appendix A below; and willfully failed to file said Reports, in violation of Title 31, U.S.C., Section 1081 on transactions occurring before September 14, 1982, and in

violation of Title 31, U.S.C., Section 5313 for transactions on or after September 14, 1982, and in violation of 31 Code of Federal Regulations, Sections 103.22(a) (1980) and 103.25 (1980), which offenses were committed as a part of a pattern of activity involving currency transactions exceeding $100,000.000 within a twelve-month period, to wit:

1980 -	$194,410,422.00
1981 -	$544,721,484.00
1982 -	$269,307,393.00
1983 -	$161,378,672.00
1984-	$ 48,864,310.00
TOTAL	$1,218,682,281.00

All in violation of Title 31, U.S.C. Sections 1081 and 1059, and Title 31 U.S.C. Sections 5313 and 5322(b).

Respectfully submitted,

WILLIAM F. WELD
United States Attorney

JEREMIAH T. O'SULLIVAN
Special Attorney

By:

PATRICK M. WALSH
Special Attorney

DATE: February 7, 1985

The Congressmen were finally satisfied that they had come to grips with the case of the First National of Boston. On one hand, there was the judicial aspect: the famous and prestigious bank had admitted its guilt several days before, and, through paying a $500,000 fine, they had avoided a major scandal; above all the American public was now aware of what had occurred. On the other hand, there was the regulatory side: the government entities charged with detecting and preventing money laundering, either through negligence or criminal intentions, had permitted the First National of Boston to launder money.

The Senators wrote up their conclusions in an extensive 250-page report. In it, they severely criticized the performance of the government control organizations and espoused the need to improve the legal mechanisms with which to prevent the laundering of money. The report also expressed the fervent mandate that such a situation as the one involving the First National of Boston 'never' again occur within the borders of the United States. To their credit, an advance in pertinent legislation has occurred since 1985; however, their hope that such an event "never again" happens is certainly far from realistic.

Although the First National of Boston denied having laundered money or having been used for this purpose, the reputation and prestige of this 100-plus year-old institution was clearly damaged. One example can be seen in the reactions of the cities of Malden and Medford: both withdrew their municipal deposits from their local Bank of Boston branches. "Public confidence in the bank has been totally shattered," said Medford City Counselor Robert Penta, who sponsored the resolution that called for pulling Medford's money out of the bank.

Furthermore, Boston's mayor, Raymond Flynn, expressed: "I just didn't think it was right that a municipality should continue to have a relationship with a bank with that kind of cloud over it at this time." He immediately met with his financial advisors and with bank officials to discuss the withdrawal of $45 million in city funds.

In the face of these measures, a spokesman for the First National Bank of Boston declared: "we do not discuss who may or may not be our customers."[66] Meanwhile, all functionaries of the bank were putting maximum effort into restoring the bank's public image. Nevertheless, U.S. Attorney of Massachusetts William F. Weld said that as a result of the

---

[66] *Newsweek*, February 25, 1985.

First of Boston windfall, other banks in New York, Los Angeles and Chicago would be investigated and probably charged.

For many of the bankers, the storm of accusations would evaporate with the passage of time. For the government functionaries, charged with fighting the laundering of drug money and immersed in a debate over procedures, they count on one foregone conclusion: time will tell.

RAUL SALINAS DE GORTARI AND CITIBANK

Raúl Salinas de Gortari, the older brother of ex-President of Mexico Carlos Salinas (1988-1994), occupied an unimportant public position with an annual salary of $190,000. However, he quickly became famous as "Mr. 10%."

Although Raúl Salinas' ties with Mexican drug cartels have not yet been proven in court, the Gulf cartel used his accounts in Citibank to channel their profits. Statements by an ex-attorney for the cartel and DEA informant confirm these actions, and that "Salinas will always be able to handle Mexican officials if they ask questions."[67]

Raúl Salinas de Gortari deposited the money under his own name and under two aliases: Juan Guillermo Gómez Gutiérrez and Juan José Gonzalez Cadena. An ongoing investigation is trying to determine the point in time at which a Citibank employee told Salinas that such a procedure was unnecessary. At that juncture, it is believed that Salinas began using a much better mechanism. He would deposit Mexican pesos in Cremi Bank, which were then converted into dollars by the Tyler Corporation, an affiliate of Citibank in Mexico City. From there, the money was wired to the international division of Citibank's "private bank" in New York. Next, the money was sent to one of three destinations:

---

[67] *Newsweek*, June 10, 1996.

1) The Cayman Islands: an account of a company called Trocca Ltd (the only evidence of this Cayman company's existence is bank records of Citibank in London);

2) The London branch of Citibank;

3) Switzerland: an account of the Confidas Company (an affiliate of Citibank in Switzerland, but headquartered in Panama, with offices in Zurich).

In November 1995, Raúl Salinas' third wife, Paulina Castañon, was arrested in a Swiss bank while she was trying to withdrawal $86 million. One of the charges against her was based on the false documentation that she presented. This documentation, pertaining to her husband, though under the name of Gómez Gutiérrez, and included a drivers license, a passport, and a birth certificate.

For Mexico and Switzerland, it was a simple investigation. But for the United States Treasury Department, it was not so simple. That is, neither Mexico nor Switzerland had sufficient laws in place to combat money laundering. Consequently, it is not surprising that money flow into Mexico exceeds that country's exports of goods and services by 29.8%.

Recently, undercover DEA agents have traveled from San Diego to Tijuana with $35 million in small bills, and the bank not only accepts the cash without a problem, but does so adeptly and discretely. And despite all the information the DEA agents have given the Mexican district attorney, nothing has changed.

On March 25, 1996, the American press pointed the accusatory finger inward instead of outward.[68] That is, rather than focusing on the shortcomings of Mexican or Swiss laws, United States' non-compliance with its own laws was cited. Furthermore, it was reported, these United States laws, even if they were complied with, were not sufficient to do the job.

---

[68] *The Miami Herald*, Andres Oppenheimer, March 25, 1996.

This is what was happening. Rather than passing from Mexico to Switzerland, perhaps making stops in Spain or France, the bulk of Raúl Salinas' money was entrusted to Amelia Grovas Elliott, a vice president of Citibank, who utilized offices in New York, London, Mexico and Switzerland for the transfers. A federal grand jury in Washington had been gathering evidence in the case. Until this time, there had only been evidence implicating the ex-vice president of Union Bank of Switzerland, José Oberholzer, who had been investigated for his alleged ties to the Medellin cartel. But this investigation was also expected to "shed light on whether, in addition to the money deposited without documentation into his investment accounts by Mexican magnates, part of Salinas' money came from Mexican drug traffickers."[69]

Amelia Grovas Elliott, the Citibank official responsible for transferring millions of Salinas' dollars to his bank accounts in Switzerland, testified in the U.S. Government case against Antonio Giraldi, the presumed "launderer" working for Juan Garcia Abrego, the leader of the Gulf cartel. Giraldi, who was found guilty in the United States for his participation in the laundering of $35 million, was an employee of Elliott's at Citibank in New York. On May 12, 1994, Elliott testified about the rigorous procedural dictates of United States laws regarding the thorough knowledge that bank officials must have of their clients. The following text is part of her testimony:

> *Q: . . . (W)hat (are) your duties as vice president at Citibank?*
>
> *A: I head the Mexico team for the international private bank of the bank . . . Since June of '83, so 11 years.*
>
> *Q: (W)hat (are) your duties. . . in that position?*

---

[69] *Money Laundering Alert*, April 1996, volume 7, number 7. *Money Laudering Alert* is a specialized monthly publication edited by Charles A. Intrago.

A: I manage a team of 10 people with responsibilities . . . Primarily to manage accounts for Mexican high net worth individuals.

Q: How do you define a high net worth individual?

A: Usually an individual who has a net worth of at least $5 million and that has liquidity of at least a million to invest with us.

"White-gloved" banking

Q: What is international private banking?

A: Private banking is the area of the bank . . . That deals with clients with more money than the general public, that does it on a more white gloved kind of environment . . . In the private bank of a bank, you are a name. The person knows you, knows who you are, knows your family, they recognize your voice . . . (I)t is basically a more personalized kind of banking relationship.

Q: . . . (T)he laws which govern your conduct as an international private banker are the same laws that govern the conduct of bankers in the retail bank, commercial bank, the domestic private bank, they're the same laws, is that correct?

A: They're the laws, the banking laws, correct.

"High-profile" clients

Q: Is it reasonable to assume that bank officers . . . such as yourself who have extensive experience with international private banking clients in Mexico would be more likely to spot something improper or to have funny feelings about a prospective client than a relatively inexperienced relationship manager?

A: Yes.

Confidentiality for clients

Q: Are any of your international private banking clients concerned about the confidentiality of their holdings?

A: Most of them are.

Q: So that the Mexican government will not know?

A: Not so much the Mexican government – I don't know. I have never asked the question of a client. It's not – the Mexican government can know. A lot of my clients have reported it to – when they took the money out and continue to report it now and pay taxes there. A lot of my clients have taken money back and then reported their entire holdings outside . . .

Q: . . . With respect to the issue of confidentiality. . . would it be safe to say that . . . one of the concerns of international private banking for legitimate reasons – and I'm not suggesting for a moment that you would do anything for an improper purpose – is to conceal the source or ownership of a particular client's funds from people who have no reason to know?

A: Yes.

Q: What is your level of trust with Mexican authority, do you trust Mexican officials of any kind?

A: Some, some not.

Q: And how do you determine which you trust and which you don't?

A: If you get to know them – I mean, it's fairly obvious, I think. Mexican officials are talked about a great deal.

Q: They have a history of becoming fabulously wealthy while in office, would you agree?

A: Some . . .

Q: Does you team manage funds in some assets, regardless of the investment or the fiduciary vehicle, for former Mexican political leaders or their family members?

A: No.

Q: . . . (F)rom your decade or so of experience dealing with Mexico, are the people . . . who have the bulk of the wealth well-known in Mexico?

A: Yes, they are.

Q: Is it unusual for someone to appear in Mexico all of a sudden with a large amount of wealth that hasn't been previously known?

A: It can happen. . . . Mexico is a very big country but, but the people who hold the wealth, the bulk of the wealth of the country are not a handful, but a number that is . . . Manageable. And so, . . . you have to either meet them or know of them or recognize the name. That is not to say there can't be others but, generally speaking it is a fairly tight and fairly small upper crust.

Q: Have you ever accepted a client, heard of a client who said, 'I have $12 million I want to invest, but I have not had prior banking relationships?'

A: No.

Q: Have you ever in your experience. . . have you ever had a situation where a wealthy person gave you control of $2 or $3 million without having met you?

A: No.

Due diligence – "The way we do things"

Q: . . . Are you aware of any specific statute or regulation in the U.S. which specifically requires a bank who is in the process of accepting a prospective clien . . . to do any particular amount of due diligence or to follow any specific steps before they can accept the client?

A: I don't know if it's a statute. I don't know if it's a law. I just know that is the way we do things.

Q: Precisely. Would you agree that the due diligence process developed – was developed by the banks to protect the banks?

A: Probably.

Q: Would you agree that the objective of the due diligence or "know your client" policy is for the bank to achieve some level of comfort with a prospective client before accepting the client's funds and engaging in a banking relationship?

A: . . . It's too risky not to do the due diligence, not to know who you're dealing with.

Citibank's "methodology"

Q: (I)n your. . . international private banking group . . . how would a relationship manager learn that he or she had either cut a corner or shaved a little too close on the due diligence process after that had been brought to your attention?

A: The relationship manager would be discussing the prospective client with his or her supervisor throughout the entire process . . . (I)t's a complex kind of sale, so it has a fairly long, especially if you're not . . . in Mexico, it has a fairly long lead time. You would be discussing this with somebody else for no other reason than just to check yourself. 'So-and-so referred this person to me. This person does this and this. I have got to visit that person.' . . . And then that person will say, 'Well, you do this.' So that's the methodology that we use. So by the time the client is accepted, all those things have been basically ironed out . . .

Q: . . . (D)idn't you describe yourself as being terribly conservative when you were before the grand jury?

A: . . . When I was in front of the grand jury, I described myself as a conservative investor.

Q: Conservative as an investor, inflexible as a –

A: Inflexible in the way I do thing . . .

"Know Your Customer" as "part of the culture"

Q: Now, when you hired Mr. Giraldi and when this 'know your client' policy that you described was in effect, did you provide him with this information, train him about it and instruct him upon it?

A: . . . The 'know your client,' at least in our bank, is part of the culture. It's part of the way you do things. It's part of the way you conduct yourself. If you come in with a prospect and/or name of a prospect, you will be sure to be asked, 'Who is this person, what do they do, who introduced them to you?' by at least three or four people higher than you. It's just the way it is . . .

Q: And . . . your bank caused your international bankers to engage in extensive efforts to know your client before you accepted them?

A: Yes.

Q: . . . What's the purpose of having the bank officer verify the signature of the customer?

A: The signature card is probably the most important document in a banking relationship because a relationship manager, such as what I do, knows the client and usually gets to know the client's voice, a client's signature, the client's everything . . .

Q: . . . Now as part of this 'know your customer' . . . policy, procedure, . . . is there a requirement to obtain bank references?

A: We require two bank references . . .

Q: Did you accept oral references or did you require written references?

A: We required written references.

Q: Is the 'know your client' due diligence process . . . something that is ongoing and continuing or, once you have made the decision to accept a client, that's it, he's in or she is in and you never give your comfort level another thought?

A: . . . We visit our clients 10 to 12 times a year in their country. They come back three or four times to New York. We see the clients a lot. It's obviously a growing kind of thing and not just in knowing your customer as (to) make sure you know what's going on, but because the relationship can grow deeper the more you know this person. This is why we go to their homes, this is why we visit with their family, this is why we go to their business, this is why we remember birthdays. It just increases the depth . . .

Q: . . . You said that one of the things that you try to do in getting to know your client and exercising due diligence and following up with your clients is that you encourage your relationship managers to try to visit them at home.

A: At their home or their office, yes.

Q: And another thing . . . that you said you liked your relationship managers to do is to get to know everybody in the family.

A: Yes.

Q: Everybody from the wife, daughters or sons, to sisters and brothers-in-laws and things like that, correct?

A: Sisters and brothers-in-law if it's relevant, but certainly close members of the family, yes.

Attraction of Swiss bank accounts

Q: Are you aware that there are people who find some attraction to Swiss bank accounts –

A: Yes.

Q: -- or Swiss portfolios?

A: Yes, yes, for confidential reasons.

Q: Why do you believe that there is that perception or . . . feeling about something being special about Switzerland?

> *A: . . . (B)ecause Switzerland is known for having numbered accounts. Switzerland is known for having . . . very strict confidential laws. Switzerland did have some law changes in that – and we have seen in – in that they will not maintain confidentiality anymore if there is a criminal reason and/or they've been asked to provide information. A Swiss banker can, in fact, be put in jail if they divulge the confidentiality of the name of an account . . .[70]*

After this testimony, Antonio Giraldi was jailed for having used his position in American financial institutions such as Citibank and American Express to launder drug money.

Citibank lost its position as the nation's largest banking institution when Chase Manhattan Bank and Chemical Banking Corporation merged. Nevertheless, in the early 1990's, William Rhodes, Vice President of Citicorp, headed the committee of bank creditors that negotiated an agreement with Mexico to reduce that country's debt.

Under U.S. law, one can open a bank account under an alias; however, the bank is obligated to keep a record of the true identity of the account holder. Consequently, in December, 1995, "Amy" G. Elliott was interrogated by a Prosecutor. The news was published by Andres Oppenheimer, who had been doing research in Mexico for the previous three years.[71] The *New York Times* also published a feature article on the story, once again confirming its character as a serious and independent newspaper.[72]

---

[70] *Money Laundering Alert*, April 1996, volume 7, number 7.
[71] *The Miami Herald*, March 25, 1996.
[72] Anthony de Palma and Peter Truell, *The New York Times*, June 5, 1996. Truell is an expert in the area of money laundering, as he co-authored with Larry Gurwin the book *BCCI:False Profits: The Inside Story of BCCI, The World's Most Corrupt Financial Empire* (Houghton

Meanwhile, other newspapers partially reported the story. One of these, in the small article it dedicated to the story, repeated seven times that *"Citibank is not being investigated;"* however, in actuality, this is what was taking place. Finally, the official word from the Department of Justice put things in clear perspective, as spokesman Carl Stern stated that *"neither the Mexicans nor the Swiss have shared the results of their investigations with Washington as their laws prohibit them from doing so. . . . Obviously, Citibank is within the boundaries of the investigation."*

According to the *New York Times*, the goings-on within the bank were as follows:

> *During 1993, every few weeks a mysterious envelope would arrive to the 16th floor of the crystal-walled Citibank building in Mexico. The envelope would contain a cashier's check in Mexican pesos for a value between three and five million dollars. The clerks accepted the checks, which were drawn from a subsidiary of Citibank, and converted the pesos to dollars. The money was then wired to the bank headquarters in New York, and from there, placed in Swiss accounts. All this was done with no questions asked.*[73]

Significantly, these transactions were not reported to the Treasury Department, as was required by law.

Raul Salinas de Gortari told Swiss investigators that in 1989, shortly after his brother was elected President, he had opened accounts abroad under false names "in order to avoid a political scandal." He had needed client relations managers like that of Ms. Elliott, who attended to rich customers, to provide him with both discretion and personal attention.

Mifflin, 1992). It is one of the best treatments of the theme of money laundering available.

[73] Antonio de Palma and Peter Truell, *The New York Times*, June 5, 1996.

Once Raul Salinas was able to attain this exclusive status, Citibank officials in New York "completely outlined a strategy" by which no aliases would be needed, according to what he told Swiss investigators. Instead of using personal aliases, the funds would be transferred to European banks and deposited under the names of fictional companies located in the Cayman Islands or in Switzerland.

Raul Salinas affirmed that his personal manager, Amy G. Elliott, arranged all the details and moved his money from one country to another in search of the best interest rates. Elliott continued to consult with Salinas' wife months after Salinas was jailed for murder in order to consolidate the family fortune in a trusteeship in Europe. This trusteeship, a company called Confidas, was directed by Hubertus Rukavina, the executive vice president of Citicorp.

CONFIDAS AND RUKAVINA

Special investigators confirm that Raul Salinas de Gortari could have had accounts in more than two dozen U.S. banks. Salinas claimed that the money was the product of credit, advances and legitimate financial operations; however, Mexican prosecutors report that Salinas has not presented proof of any such operations. Ronald K. Noble, ex-Undersecretary of the Treasury, who now heads an international task force dedicated to fighting money laundering, asks, "How can someone with the last name Salinas de Gortari deposit in his own name millions of dollars without anybody ever questioning him?"

Richard Howe, a spokesman for Citibank, confirmed in July, 1996 that Elliott continues in her position of bank vice president, and that she maintains her good standing within the organization. When Howe was asked if high-level bank officials had known of Salinas' accounts during his three years of patronage, he responded that "the corporate management did not participate in any manner in the opening or management of this account."

But Confidas, of course, is at the center of the investigation. The primary issue is determining exactly whose money is in Confidas. If the company is not a subsidiary of Citibank, why doesn't the bank clarify this issue? This is still unknown. However, one does not have to be a genius to understand that the funds invested in Confidas are not only those of Raúl Salinas de Gortari.

For its part, Citibank neither confirms nor denies the content of the hundreds of newspaper articles mentioning this matter. The bank only provides a bland career history of Hubertus Rukavina, and mentions nothing regarding his role as director of Confidas:

> *Hubertus Rukavina is Executive Vice President of Citicorp and its principal subsidiary, Citibank, responsible for the Investment Products and Distribution Group. He was named to this position in January 1996. Previously he had been responsible for the worldwide Private Banking Group, based in Zurich, since January 1993. Mr. Rukavina joined Citibank as a trainee in October 1973. In 1975, he was based in Panama with responsibilities for planning and liability management in Central America, . . . He was assigned to the Private Bank in June 1987 as country business head for Switzerland and Luxembourg. In 1989, he was given additional Citibank responsibilities as Country Corporate Officer for Switzerland.*

Jane Wexton

Although Citibank had begun an internal investigation, they denied Jane Wexton, Vice President and attorney for the bank, from participating in the inquiry. The exclusion of Wexton was strange since she was the bank's money laundering specialist, affectionately called by her colleagues "Mrs. Money Laundering." Citibank declined to comment on why, during such an important internal investigation which involved such crucial personnel, they would isolate the person most expert on the subject from these matters. Moreover shortly after Raúl Salinas was arrested for masterminding the murder of José Francisco Ruiz Massieu, Secretary General of the PRI (Institutional Revolutionary Party), Citicorp began their internal investigation.

Despite affirmations by Citibank that they had done nothing wrong, the bank had taken some very strange measures related to the case. The high-ranking officials of the private bank, the department that had worked with Raul Salinas, were assigned other posts in January, 1996. Included in this reorganization was the head of the private bank, the Argentine Hubertus Rukavina, and the legal advisor of the private bank, George Baxter. The bank reassigned Rukavina and Baxter after internal audits of the private bank in 1995 revealed an abominable level of risk control, especially in the areas of new accounts and awareness of client background.

Wexton, Vice President and legal advisor on bank policy and regulations, had established an anti-money laundering program, and her efforts had won her an excellent reputation within the bank. In addition to training employees how to recognize illicit funds and designing an advanced system of information management, Wexton was also frequently consulted by bank executives and other individuals when they came across suspicious activities. However, in December, 1995, when problems arose with Mexican accounts, they informed her that she would be assigned to another area in the bank and did not permit her any questions regarding the matter.

Michael Zeldin, advisor to Decision Strategies International and ex-Director of that division of the Justice Department, characterized well the unusual nature of the situation:

> *In the banking sector, Jane Wexton is considered among the best professionals specialized in judicial regulations of any bank in the United States.*
>
> *If there was a problem, she would have been one of the persons with whom they would have had to consult; however, there apparently was a problem and I am led to believe that they did not consult her.*[74]

Indeed, among her legal-watchdog colleagues and within Citibank, Wexton was known as an "exemplary policewoman." Moreover, she was considered a frank person who would probably tell the authorities if she discovered any illicit operations. Wexton dedicated the majority of her time to issues related to money laundering, and traveled extensively throughout the world during her seven years with Citibank. As a member of the Advisory Board on Banking and Treasury Secrecy, Wexton attended numerous conferences and meetings with others who shared her interest in combating money laundering.

Meanwhile, Citibank is one of the most international institutions in the world. They annually move $98 billion in bank transfers through 98 countries. However successful, the fault seems to rest with this large international bank. According to experts, unless the individual comes from a traditionally rich family such as the Rockefellers, politicians

---

[74] Cited by Laura Hays, *The Wall Street Journal*, June 6, 1996. *The Wall Street Journal*, one of the best newspaper sources on the theme of money laundering, is owned by Dow Jones & Co. Carlos Salinas de Gortari, younger brother of Raúl, is a director of the company.

connected in any way with money laundering are typically considered immediate suspects.

The Mexican daily *El Norte*, in an extensive but anonymous editorial, labeled the whole process as *intentional blindness*. If it had not been for the work of Argentine journalist Andres Oppenheimer, *The Miami Herald* and *Money Laundering Alert*, we would continue to be ignorant of these developments.

BAD ADVICE

On November 23, 1995, Paulina Castañon, wife of Raúl Salinas de Gortari, upon following the advice of a Citibank executive to withdraw funds from an account in Switzerland, was arrested by police in the offices of the Pictet Bank of Geneva.

The arrest and subsequent findings revealed that Salinas had $80 million, used false passports, etc. Moreover, after the arrest of his wife, the accusations that Raúl Salinas was behind the murder of José Francisco Ruiz Massieu received more serious consideration. In addition, the ensuing drug corruption investigation was the most damaging inquiry ever for a Mexican presidential family. The paradox is that the same person that helped Salinas in his multi-million dollar maneuvers is the same person that sunk him with the piece of bad advice: Amy G. Elliott.

At the end of 1995, the DEA launched an investigation of Raul Salinas de Gortari. Although confidential, this information circulated quickly among high-status circles. Elliott acted rapidly, calling Paulina and advising her to go to Switzerland and withdraw the funds; but it was too late – the Swiss police were waiting for her. And at that point, there was nothing Elliott could for her client. In comments Raúl made to Swiss investigators in 1995, he appears to have felt betrayed by his bank: "I suppose that Ms. Elliott was looking to keep Citibank out of this problem, or that she had heard reports about drug trafficking, or perhaps was directly involved with the arrest of my wife."[75]

Raúl had been using false names to withdraw his money when Carlos Hank Rhon advised him to work with Citibank toward a better arrangement. That is, Rohn had developed a scheme of financial engineering involving trusteeships which would allow the brother of the president to stop using aliases, while at the same time guaranteeing the strictest banking confidentiality possible in the United States and Switzerland. No one would know who the principal of the accounts was.

The Vice President of Citicorp's private bank was assigned to executing these maneuvers. Most important, however, is that it is still unknown exactly who assigned this role to Elliott – surely she did not stumble upon it by herself.

"Elliott put the strategy together and knew the first investor that made money transfers," Raúl Salinas told Swiss prosecutor Carla del Ponte.[76] Elliott created two trusteeships in Zurich, Trocca Limited and Novatone, into which she deposited Raúl's money. She gave orders to the Mexico City branch to accept without question checks from Raúl's emissaries for amounts up to $5 million. S he arranged transfers to the Cayman Islands, London and Switzerland, and advised Raúl and his confidants. Then, under pressure, she made a wrong move and misadvised Raúl's third wife, Paulina:

> *Beginning in 1990, Switzerland passed legislation that punishes bankers who knowingly accept money that comes from a crime. The laws also give bankers the right to ignore Switzerland's bank-secrecy rules and tell police about suspicious transactions.*

---

[75] Cited by Ignacio Rodríguez Reyna, *Reforma*, July 1, 1996.
[76] Cited by Ignacio Rodríguez Reyna, *Reforma*.

"The progress accomplished by Switzerland in the fight against money laundering deserves recognition, and many aspects of the Swiss system could serve as an example to others," says a report by the Financial Action Task Force, a Paris-based group made up of countries fighting money laundering. The exact numbers remain a secret, but some estimate that Swiss banks manage about $2 trillion, or 40% of all "offshore" bank accounts.

Laurent Kasper-Ansermet, a former prosecutor in Geneva, said bankers tell him two-thirds of the money in Switzerland could stem from tax evasion. Another estimate puts the amount of drug-related money in Switzerland at 400 billion to 500 billion Swiss francs, he said.

Switzerland is popular among tax cheats because it refuses to help other countries prosecute tax evaders. That is significant for the money-laundering trade because the same channels used to shelter tax money are used to hide money for the Mafia or corrupt dictators.

Banks in such banking havens as the Isle of Man and the Cayman Islands can offer bank secrecy and an array of mutual funds, just like the Swiss. But they cannot always offer the rock-solid financial strength of Switzerland.

Swiss banks enjoy some of the world's highest credit ratings. Switzerland's 17 private banks, concentrated in Geneva, are partnerships. That means the owners put their own money at risk. Another reason depositors flock to Switzerland is the country's political stability.

The advantages explain why everyone from Iraqi dictator Saddam Hussein to Raul Salinas de Gortari, brother of former Mexican President Carlos Salinas de Gortari, have stashed money in the country. The new laws have made it harder for dirty money to get into Switzerland. But crime fighters say the banks could be applying the laws more diligently.

In 1994, when Swiss banks were first allowed to ignore bank secrecy laws to report suspicious deposits, joint Swiss-

American law enforcement efforts froze $265 million held in Swiss banks.

Prosecutors say the banks should be reporting even more information to authorities. Only about 30 reports have been filed in Geneva under the new disclosure law even though the city is home to about 150 banks.

Of those cases, most arose only after officials had already begun investigations. The investigations often began in the U.S.

The Swiss parliament is considering legislation forcing banks to report suspicious deposits instead of just giving them the right to report. Bankers complain the measures will bog them down with paperwork.

But Switzerland's chief prosecutor, Carla del Ponte, said she doubts that the banks will overload her with information. 'I know the banks,' she said. 'They will only announce when it's proper.'[77]

THE PARTNERS OF RAUL SALINAS DE GORTARI

Indeed, it was a prestigious thing to be a partner of Raúl Salinas de Gortari while his brother occupied the presidency in Mexico. The problem they have now, however, is that nobody knows where the money originated, and police and prosecutors appear to be following the money trail to a Mexican cartel. Now, no one is Raúl's partner.

Basically, Raúl had three lines of investment: communication, media (especially TV), and transportation. For example, TV Azteca was a state-owned entity, Imevision, before it was privatized in 1993. And, according to the complaints of journalist Joaquín Vargas, owner of MVS Multivision and Stereo Rey, to get in on this privatization, it was necessary to be Raúl Salinas' partner.

---

[77] *The Wall Street Journal*, July 2, 1996.

Vargas submitted a number of bids to acquire Imevision (now TV Azteca), but a group headed by Ricardo Salinas Pliego finally won out on July 18, 1993. Ricardo Salinas Pliego defended the nature of his success:

> *I definitely do not have any business relationship with Raul . . . I think it's just the juicy gossip of people going around saying 'Hey, did you know that Ricardo Salinas is partners with Raul Salinas?' Great gossip, isn't it; but being great doesn't make it true.*[78]

However, after having denied on numerous occasions that he had received a $30 million loan from Raul, calling such gossip a joke, he finally admitted the truth: "In mid-1993, when all this occurred, Raul Salinas was the brother of the Mexican President. If he did come and ask me to help him invest this money, well, I don't think any other businessman would have refused to do it."[79]

It was understood that to participate in the channel's privatization, one first had to side with Raul. If one tried to do it another way, he would be seen as jeopardizing the business pursuit:

> *There were many public officials who told him: 'Joaquín, you're making a mistake. The only thing you need is a partner – Raúl Salinas de Gortari. To this, Joaquín Vargas responded, 'It's possible that you all perceive that I am making a mistake,*

---

[78] Statements of Salinas Pliego to *Reforma*. He also alluded to the problematic coincidence that he had the same initials as the brother of the President. However, Raúl Salinas, from his jail cell, contradicted him before Valentín Roschacher, Chief of the Central Narcotrafficking Office of Switzerland, and Martín Zbinden, an inspector of this Office, on March 20, 1996.

[79] *Reforma*, June 7, 1996.

but as I see it, it is you who are making it. Later you will all see that I was right.'[80]

During this time, Raúl Salinas de Gortari withdrew $29.8 million from one of his accounts and deposited it in one of Ricardo Salinas Pliego's accounts, under the name of Silvestar, a company which was legally headquartered in Panama. From there, the money passed through the United States and the Cayman Islands, before finally arriving at Servicios Patrimoniales Integrados (Integrated Estate Services), another of Salinas Pliego's companies. Certainly, Salinas Pliego took this money for a tour of the world for a particular reason. Salinas Pliego also failed to indicate that Impulsora de Frequencias, a company owned by Raúl Salinas de Gortari, is the majority shareholder of TV Azteca, controlling 51% of the shares.

Raúl Salinas is also a partner in the passenger transportation company Mexicana de Autobuses (MASA) with the journalist Abraham Zabludovsky. Zabludovsky is the political commentator for a rival private channel. In this way, although the television industry is typically seen as a war of the channels, what it really demonstrates is the absolute determination of money launderers to control certain modes of communication. This practice is common in many parts of the world. As a response to whomever may affect the traffickers' interests, hundreds of journalists are ready to defame and discredit those who try to investigate or denounce them.

Incidentally, MASA was also a state-owned company until it was privatized in 1988. Following the privatization, MASA was the recipient of a plethora of state government contracts. A final note is that Abraham Zabludovsky's father, Jacobo, is the president of News Division (División Noticias), which includes Information System ECO (Sistema Informativo ECO).

---

[80] Pedro Ferriz de Con, cited from *Reforma*, op.cit.

Raúl later sold his MASA stock to the director of *Epoca Magazine*. For some reason, he became uninterested in the transportation industry.

Another of Raúl Salinas' partners is José Madariaga Lomelín, the current president of the Mexican Association of Bankers. On June 10, 1991, Madariaga Lomelín acquired Multibanco Mercantil de México, an institution with a long history in Mexico. This bank, under its new ownership, issued a credit card to Juan Guillermo Gómez Gutierrez, alias Raúl Salinas, with which to launder money.

Another partner is Adrian Sada Gonzalez, President of Serfin Financial Group.[81] According to documents obtained by the DEA, Raúl Salinas de Gortari transferred millions of dollars from a Swiss account to Sada González. The U.S. Embassy sent Assistant Special Prosecutor Pablo Chapa Bezanilla a letter informing him of the operation.

Shortly after Serfin Bank was awarded to Sada González, "this financial institution opened a $783 million line of credit to Raúl Salinas de Gortari."[82]

Businessman Carlos Peralta, Vice President of Grupo Iusa (Iusa Group), revealed that in 1994 at least 20 businessmen were invited by Salinas de Gortari to participate in an investment fund. Among them, Peralta mentioned Roberto González Barrera and Adrian Sada Gonzáles. The president of the Serfin Group, however, denied having been invited to participate.

But Carlos Peralta, the owner of a cellular phone company, had no trouble admitting that he had transferred $49,727,000 to four of Raúl's accounts in New York. These funds, in addition $23,000 in so-called *night deposits*, could be withdrawn the following day. According to what Peralta told the Swiss prosecutor, the transfers were done in the following manner:

---

[81] *El Financiero*, July 7, 1996.
[82] *El Financiero*, July 7, 1996.

$20 million were transferred to Citibank account number 021000089, sent to the attention of Amy G. Elliott. Elliott, who in cooperation with Mexican and American bank officers, managed Salinas' accounts.

$15 million were sent to Chase Manhattan Bank account number 676-015140147.

$10 million were deposited in Bankers Trust Co. account number 18043738.

Another $4,727,000 were deposited in Citibank in New York by means of a transaction with Bear Sterns.

According to a letter signed by Peralta on April 21, 1994, the transfers were executed by Langness Investment Ltd., a business of Peralta located on the Isle of Man, a British financial paradise.[83]   According to Peralta, no documentary evidence existed which cited the destination of this investment.

A BANKER IN COMMON WITH THE MEDELLIN CARTEL

Raúl Salinas de Gortari shared the services of José Oberholzer, the ex-Vice President of the Union Bank of Switzerland (UBS), with the Medellin cartel. The name of this banker surfaced in the documentary evidence used in the Raúl Salinas trial.

Oberholzer, whose origin is uncertain, managed huge Latin American funds and served as the contact in Switzerland for Salinas' multi-million dollar transfers. That is, Oberholzer deposited funds in the account opened by Juan G. Gómez Gonzalez, alias Raúl Salinas. The Swiss police were able to

---

[83] Andres Oppenheimer, *The Miami Herald* and *Reforma*.

verify that there existed agreements between Raúl Salinas, Carlos Hank Rohn, and Oberholzer, and that the latter served as Raúl's treasurer and confidant.

José Oberholzer, as vice president of UBS, advised his Latin American clients in the shady game of moving money and in creating fronts to conceal the money's origin. Currently, Oberholzer is being tried for laundering about $150 million of the Medellin cartel's money. He was arrested in Zurich on February 23, 1994, together with his client Sheila Arana de Nasser, wife of Julio César Nasser David, one of the late Pablo Escobar's operatives. Recently, information obtained in the investigation of Raúl linked Oberholzer to these laundering operations.[84]

The detention of the ex-vice president of the UBS lasted 48 hours, and Oberholzer is now confined to his home under house arrest. At first, the UBS defended him, and afterwards, retired him at 65. According to the 1990 reforms to the Swiss Penal Code, José Oberholzer can only be sentenced to a few months in jail.

Maribel González, a *Reforma* correspondent in Washington, questioned Citibank on various occasions in search of information regarding a meeting held between Amy G. Elliott and ex-Mexican President Carlos Salinas de Gortari. However, the bank always responded in the same manner: "Citibank is not being investigated."

Mike Wallace, of the CBS program "60 Minutes," commented:

> *Two powerful men, Carlos Salinas de Gortari, President of Mexico, and John Reed, head of Citibank, are supposedly ignoring what the third man, Raúl Salinas de Gortari, did to accumulate an enormous personal fortune in Swiss and British*

---

[84] Jorge Luis Sierra, Rossana Fuentes-Berain, Luís Vasquez and María Idlaia Gómez, *Reforma* (Mexico: May 27, 1996.

banks. As in the times of Watergate, the press and society have to ask the tough questions in order to know who knew what and when they found out. The presidentof the bank, John Reed, and the adjunct president in charge of Latin America, Bill Rhodes, have the fiduciary responsibility of making sure that no money laundering operations are executed under Citibank auspices.

VI

LEGALIZATION

T o date, no one has told us how we are to *end* the war on drugs. Not even the most optimistic prognosticator predicts a victory; to merely gain control of the situation seems to be the best that is hoped for. However, as only between 5 and 10% of the drugs and between 2 and 3% of laundered money is confiscated, to gain this control seems far from possible with such proportionately low results.

The legal system in place against drugs is basically constructed from a criminal point of view. The laws in force impose grave penalties on those who are sentenced for the sale, possession, importation, or cultivation of drugs. These structures, sanctioned by the different countries' legal and judicial systems, amount to criminal prosecution without considering the problems to public health and to the social order. However, it is precisely the consideration of these important issues that leads to the growth of organizations which oppose the politics of repression, postulate new concepts in the war against drugs, and propose different strategies to achieve the same objectives.

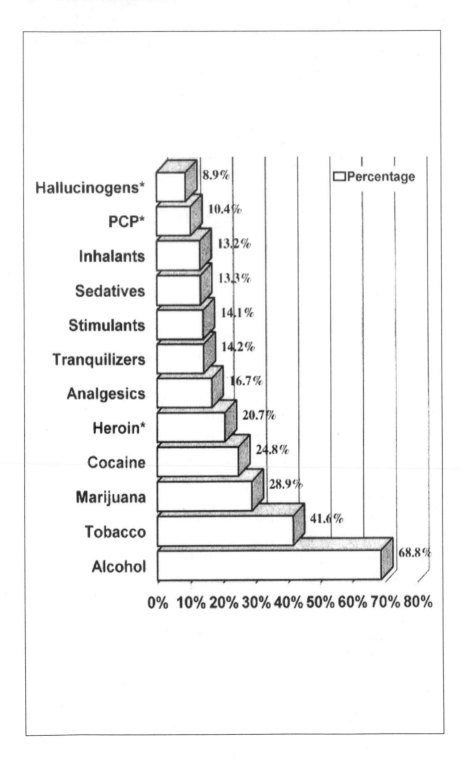

Once such groups dedicated themselves to this task, it was found that the official stance was what most undermined the war against drugs. These groups maintain that the majority of harmful elements come from exactly those national, legal and judicial orders that are in place to fight drugs.

The first proposal to legalize drugs was made by Ernesto Samper Pizano in 1985, while he served as president of the National Association of Financial Institutions of Colombia (ANIF). On June 29, 1985, before an audience of bankers and politicians who were trying to agree on ways to stop the utilization of Colombia's banks to launder drug money, Samper expressed:

> *Our nation must reject the traffic and use of drugs. However, I want to stress that in this struggle we must stand united instead of divided. The problem is very serious. The epidemic today is worse than when we began this war – a war that will continue into the future. Each one of us, because of our responsibility to our society, must offer solutions.*
>
> *Tainted money has a strong corrupting influence on the democratic institutions of the nation. We are obligated to look for adequate means to stand up to this threat. Money laundering is the most complex illicit business of the current array of financial crime, and it originates from the drug-trafficking industry. It is there where we must take aim. At the base of the issue is the fact that drugs are a business, and while they continue to be so, the situation will remain the same. From here, one of the most apt tools for eliminating this business is the legalization of drugs. The war we have today is extremely costly. We waste too much on prisons, planes, fumigation to eliminate poppy plantations, and even on conferences – all of which, in the long run, will not benefit us as long as the enemy persists and their businesses grow. If the prohibitionist approach against drugs were a success, we would not be gathered here today.*

Therefore, I think it is opportune that we change our direction and, without pre-judgement or negative attitudes, consider seriously the possibility of fighting by means of legalization. Those who are not in agreement with legalization are obliged to provide concrete proof of the benefits society is receiving from the illegality of drugs.[85]

The tough criticism of Samper's character for proposing such a project undoubtedly modified his thinking and principles. In a 1990 report, Samper declared that it was not the time to pursue such legislation. Although Samper's political savvy is clear, it is not clear whether he had actually changed his mind.[86]

THE DEBATE

In mid-1988, there arose among young people in the United States a strong movement in favor of legalization. This movement was supported by human rights activists as well as some legal research and public health groups.

The press echoed their concerns and the debate became truly ignited with an editorial printed in the April 15, 1988 *Wall Street Journal*:

Southern California has been a fertile land for all types of changes in American culture. What it is showing us now is how to wage the war on drugs: crush the consumers. A recent report by the Department of State regarding "principal drug-trafficking countries" resembles a list of all the third world nations: Burma, Egypt, India, etc. But even if we could destroy

---

[85] Report of the National Association of Financial Institutions of Colombia (Bogota, Colombia: September 1985).

[86] Leonidas Gómez O., *Cartel – Historia de la Droga* (Colombia: Grupo Editorial Investigación y Concepto, 1991).

all drug-running operations from Colombia to Thailand, the problem would continue as long as there were domestic production and synthetic narcotics. Until now, it has been too easy for politicians to blame foreigners for the drug problem in the United States. A real solution will only result when more police and more public prosecutors have the will and the authorization to fight this scourge here in the United States.

What followed was a series of editorials in newspapers throughout the United States which put forth their positions on the issue, with some leveling very serious accusations:

For many countries, the anti-drug policies of the United States are pure arrogance. Local families (of other countries) have cultivated marijuana, cocaine and opium for centuries. All of a sudden, they are being ordered to stop. The Americans would never agree to an external mandate of this type.

Who is at fault? The Mexicans who accept bribes, or the Americans whose purchases make them possible? The war against drugs will not be won in the streets of Karachi or Mexico City, but rather in the streets of New York and Los Angeles. If the Americans do not want to pay the cost of winning the war against drugs in the United States, there is no other place where they can win it.[87]

The debate continued in *The Los Angeles Times*:

In 1982, Congress amended the Posse Comitatus Law. The amendment permitted the Armed Forces to share intelligence information with the Coast Guard and the police. This resulted in the arrest of a few drug traffickers, but has not interrupted the flow of narcotics. Like we have said before, the United States

---

[87] *The New York Times*, May 8, 1988.

will not stop narcotics traffic until its legislators discover how to stop the gigantic demand for drugs here in this country. This, of course, is a problem that does not lend itself to quick solutions in an election year.[88]

STUDIES NEEDED, SAYS *THE NEW YORK TIMES*

Irritated by the seemingly infinite death, corruption and crime generated by the illegal-drug industry, a growing number of officials and intellectuals are calling for a debate about what for years had been politically unutterable: the legalization of drugs. However, the majority of politicians and legislators feel it would be dangerous apostasy. It would mean that some highly dangerous substances would be more economical, purer, and generally more accessible; this would provoke, they claim, a sharp increase in addiction. Curiously, there do not exist studies on how the legalization of cocaine and heroin would affect society. For more than a decade, the idea of legalization has been so unacceptable that no one has financed a study on its possible effects.[89]

THE TOBACCO ARGUMENT

Smoking kills over 300,000 people every year in the United States, but we have made the policy decision to treat tobacco as a health problem, and not a criminal problem. The number of people smoking continues to fall because of a conserted public

---

[88] *The Los Angeles Times*, May 12, 1988.
[89] *The New York Times*, May 15, 1988.

education campaign about the health effects of smoking. There is no reason that we could not do the same with drugs.[90]

In 1988, an Associated Press release out of Hague revealed the opinions of a group of experts from the Dutch government regarding the legalization of the use of drugs. They declared themselves in favor of this measure as they thought it would drastically reduce the amount of misdemeanor crimes. However, they admitted it would not be practical to adopt these measures without other nations doing the same. The Academic Council of Government Politics, advised by Prime Minister Ruud Lubbers, stated officially that "of the 20,000 drug addicts in this country, many are German and Italian. If the large European countries and the United States continue with their strict policies of repression, Holland cannot pursue legalization alone." However, at that time Holland had already legalized marijuana.[91]

The debate flares on. The expositions in favor and against legalization continue to enlarge the tapestry of questions and salient points that define both politics.

All of the arguments in favor of legalization seem reasonable and economically vaible. But they only take into account theories, and not people. People become addicted, unproductive, and sometimes dangerous. Drugs kill.

What help are laws? The reconstruction of the individual's character is the problem. The majority of politicians only pay attention to the supply of drugs, and not to the demand. But if there is no demand, their are no sales.

---

[90] *The Washington Post*, May 16, 1988.
[91] Ob. Cit. no 3.

PROHIBITIONISM AND SOCIETY

Francis Caballero is a professor at the University of Penal Law in Paris and the president of the Movement for the Controlled Legalization of Drugs. Caballero favors the liberalization of laws dealing with the consumption of narcotics, maintaining that the legal framework of repression and prohibition which has been in place for more than 20 years has not yielded convincing results. In fact, he suggests, these laws actually promote the growth of organized crime. Prohibition, the professor points out, is an ally of the traffickers, as it assures the high value of drugs.[92]

A gram of heroin in France costs one thousand French francs, 10 times the value of gold. The financial burden this places on its users can certainly manifest itself in ways detrimental to society: "The drug addict, in the search for enough money with which to buy the drugs, is incited to commit crimes ranging from pick-pocketing to prostitution, and even armed assault and murder."[93]

Caballero notes that there is an economic link between activities of organized crime (such as drugs and arms trafficking), terrorism, and state security and sovereignty. Of course, part of this web of illicit economics is money

---

[92] This total value is estimated at between $500 and $700 billion dollars annually.

[93] *Questioning Prohibition: 1994 International Report on Drugs* (International Anti-prohibition League Federated to the Radical Party [IAL], 1994).

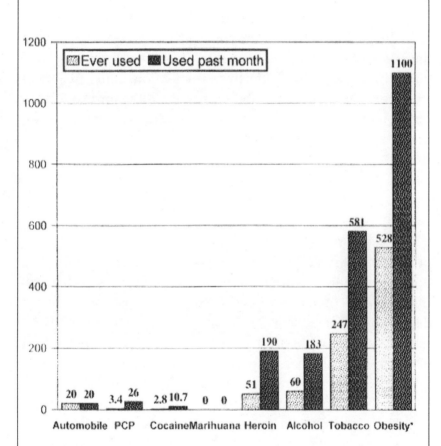

laundering, which has contaminated the banking system and the global economic system as a whole. Meanwhile, the cost of maintaining prohibition continues to get higher and higher.

In Caballero's opinion, the segments of the population which are hardest hit by prohibition are those sectors which are typically victimized by discrimination and racism in the enforcement of these laws. In this way, prohibition can become a tool of repression against certain citizens.

The prohibitionist approach also has a negative impact in the area of public health. That is, with such policies it is more difficult to establish effective prevention and treatment programs. Moreover, prohibition results in the unreliability of drug quality and composition, which, in turn, is a major factor in the high rate of drug overdose deaths.

CONTROLLED LEGALIZATION

The groups under this banner favor an alternative to prohibitionist policy and its repression; that is, they promote a policy of controlled legalization that emphasizes individual freedom and public health. These groups also promote the development of a network of information and research on issues dealing with drug abuse and drug trafficking. As lobbyists for alternative policies, they have proposed the modification of existing treaties, laws and regulations which surround the production, the sale and the use of drugs. Another of the aims of these groups is to overturn the tough anti-drug legislation passed in France in 1970, and replace it with regulations that treat each drug individually, taking into account its particular qualities and level of danger, and do away with automatic blanket prohibition. Also of high priority is their objective to enable citizens who are users of such drugs to be treated in a manner that does not restrict or eliminate their rights as an individual.

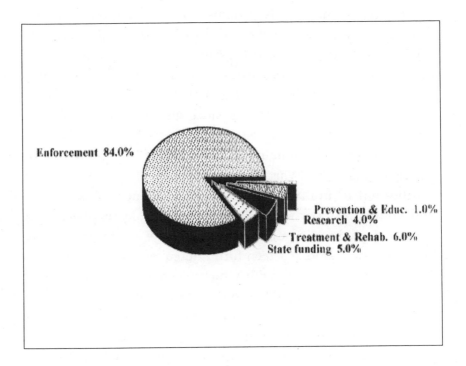

FROM THE LEFT

Dr. Noam Chomsky, Professor of Philosophy at the Massachusetts Institute of Technology and one of the most prominent figures of the American left, has also criticized the existing structure of vigilance. He points to the problematic fact that the United States maintains their prohibitionist stance in order to justify the oppressive policies which they exercise in the Third World. Chomsky refers also to a third world *within* the United States – that is, areas of impoverishment. As the campaign against drugs is planned to be won, he explains, a visible enemy is needed, one which conforms to the needs of the American establishment and is hence defined by that establishment.

Chomsky importantly sustains that drugs are undoubtedly as much a health issue as they are a social issue. However, this duality of focus is largely absent from the United States' approach to the war on drugs. In fact, for Chomsky, this approach is nothing less than a global strategy which produces an *industry of repression*. That is, since the end of World War II, the CIA and other U.S. agencies have been responsible for establishing and maintaining a system of repression. For example, after the War, Mafia involvement was used as a justification to infiltrate and destabilize French labor unions and communist parties in Europe. Chomsky explains that drugs are used in a similar manner to create a common enemy and to create a smoke screen for undercover operations; drugs are the simplest means with which to characterize an enemy and issue accusatory statements. Meanwhile, paradoxically, the United States has their own drug industries which it pushes throughout the world. As an example, Chomsky notes that a U.S. trade representative of the Bush Administration repeatedly proposed sanctions against Thailand for not continuing to buy American tobacco and for not lifting importation restrictions on Virginia tobacco. The sanctions were initially proposed in 1989.

He cites as a comparative example the 1841 Opium War between Great Britain and China. As Great Britain had nothing to sell China, the former obligated the latter to buy opium from them with the objective of addicting them to the drug. The resulting two wars, which are referred to collectively as the Opium War, ended with Chinese society in disarray. Indeed, a good part of the Chinese attitude of denial toward the West can be traced to this conflict.

ALTERNATIVES TO THE PROHIBITION OF DRUGS

Dr. Ethan Nadelmann has studied the effects of the prohibitionist approach on society, and considers the current system hard to justify using a cost-benefit analysis. This is especially the case, he notes, when one considers issues such as privacy, tolerance, and the presumption of personal freedom; these issues become especially salient when one takes into account that the majority of activities relating to drug use are not violent. With this in mind, Nadelmann has formulated questions that would help develop criteria for the creation and evaluation of alternative policies:

> *The serious and systematic consideration of alternatives to vigilant drug prohibition policies requires a considerable amount of intellectual broadmindedness, which is usually absent in political analyses.*
>
> *The development of criteria for such a consideration can be approached using two complementary questions: first, how can we maximize the benefits of the free market and minimize its risks? Second, how can we retain the advantages of drug prohibition, while at the same time minimizing the direct and indirect costs?*[94]

Nadelmann sees advantages to what he calls the "supermarket" model, referring to the free market of opiates that existed through much of the 19th century in the United States. In this period, there was a high rate of consumption of such drugs, but, Nadelmann points out, there did not exist the

---

[94] Ethan Nadelmann, "Pensando seriamente alternativas a la prohibición de drogas," ob.cit. 9.

Federal Financial Analysis of Legalization of Drugs

This Federal Financial Analysis of Legalization comes from Theodore R. Vallance, Former chief of the Planning Brang of the National Institutes of Mental Health. His main professional effort for many years was directed at just this sort of analysis:

Reductions (in millions of dollars)

Direct	*From*	*To*	*Saving*
Law Enforcement	13.203	3.300	9.903
• interdiction costs	2.200	0	2.200
• International anti-drug	768	384	384
• OCDETF [Organized Crime & Drug Enforcement Task Force]	399	40	359
• ONDCP [the Drug czar]	69	17	52
Indirect			
• Victims of crime	842	210	632
• Incarceration	4.434	887	3.547
• Crime careers	13.976	2.679	11.297

Subtotal	
Less increase in prevention research and service	(3.572)
Less increase ini treatment research and service	(2.802)
	22.000
Subtotal	
Plus net income from drug taxes	15.000

Total:	**$ 37.000.000.000**

resulting social problems that we see today. This would indicate an important advantage to this model; that is, this model would allow much of the billions of dollars that are spent each year on trials and prosecutions to be saved, and perhaps spent instead on the prevention of non-organized crime. Nadelmann states that a liberalized drug market would be met with apprehension, to say the least, by various sectors of society, as they would perceive that the spectrum of applicable policy had been tampered with. That is, a law that would guarantee the freedom to consume drugs, just as the rights of free speech, press, religion and assembly are guaranteed, would result in a conflict of values regarding this issue, a conflict that each individual would have to resolve. "The most common fear with respect to the legalization of drugs," Nadelmann explains, "is that those who currently abstain from consuming them, or consume them in moderation, will be transformed into drug addicts in the face of the freedom of access to these substances."

This fear is fueled by the following assumptions:

The only things that prevent drug users from becoming destructive addicts are the high price and the public unavailability of drugs.

Some illicit drugs are more addictive than those drugs that are legal and publicly available.

The imposition of a free drug market would inevitably produce greater levels of experimentation with drugs; and with a wide variety of drugs available, their use and abuse would be fostered as well.

Many people would substitute or complement the drugs which they now take with other drugs that would enter the market.

The imposition of a free market for psychoactive drugs and the greater availability of these drugs would presuppose a greater public tolerance for these substances, thereby nurturing an increase in their abuse.

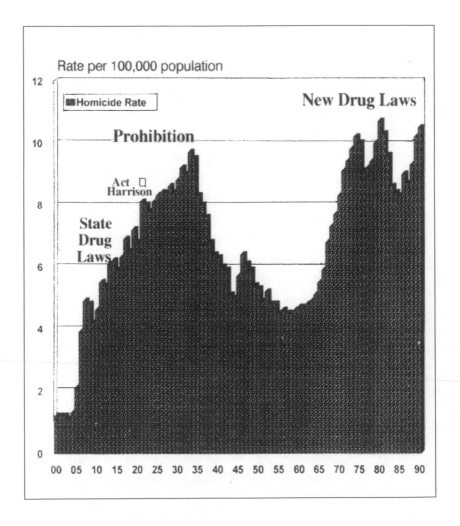

Nadelmann believes that persons who currently smoke cigarettes and abuse alcohol are those most likely to succumb to the regular use of psychoactive drugs if they were legalized. For Nadelmann, these persons would represent a type of personality frontier for this tendency of behavior. However, that is not to say, he notes, that those who do not smoke or drink would never enter into destructive relationships with these drugs after they were made more available.

We need to evaluate which drugs would be most popular in the future, explains Nadelmann, and which persons would use them, responsibly or destructively. An analysis is necessary which focuses on why people use drugs, and more precisely, why they *decide* to use them.

The dominant sectors of global society clearly favor the use of some drugs over others. Alcohol, consumed almost everywhere on Earth, is drunk mainly in the form of beer, wine, or liquor. Coffee, a stimulant beverage, is also found most everywhere, and is especially popular in Muslim society. Coca, also a stimulant, is consumed widely in the Andean regions.

The dominant position of alcohol can be traced to the simple fact that it was discovered thousands of years ago by various societies. This long and broad history helped to facilitate its diffusion and popularize its use. Moreover, the addictive qualities of alcohol and of coffee/coca help to secure the markets that are penetrated.

SOCIAL NORMS VS. LEGAL CONSTRUCTS

. . . *Societies are not totally at the mercy of free markets. Rather, a society retains a potential capacity to create mechanisms of self-protection in order to minimize the risks that these free markets can present.*[95]

---

[95] Ethan Nadelmann, ob. cit. 11.

Availability

Despite being illicit substances in a highly restricted area, illegal drugs are easier to obtain in prisons and in mental institutions than alcohol. An important reason, of course, is that drugs are more easily smuggled into such institutions.

Regarding the alternative of a free market for such drugs, Nadelmann maintains:

> *When we look to modify or steer this policy from its extreme by proposing the concept of a free market for drugs, we suggest that all the basic characteristics of accessibility of a free market be present, and that the framework that emerges resemble a system of "mail order" or specific-request access. This model is based on the notion of permitting adults not only to possess small quantities of any drug for personal use, but also to enjoy the right to be able to obtain such drugs from a reliable, legal source which is responsible for the quality of its products.*
>
> *Such a proposal does not mean to suggest that this right is on a parity with the right of possession and/or consumption. It simply provides useful ethical and conceptual parameters in the formation of alternative drug-control policies.*[96]

This model of access is presented as a potential means to reconcile the existing tensions between individual freedom and the common good. Nadelmann proposes to "fill" the structural framework that this proposal provides with existing anti-drug measures, such as the vigilant limitation to the access of illicit drugs. In developing this proposal, Nadelmann drew advantageously from existing models of alcohol regulation/distribution developed in Canada and Switzerland during the first decades of the twentieth century.

---

[96] Ibid.

TOWARD TRANSITION

In analyzing the different alternatives to the prohibitionist status quo, Nadelmann is careful to distinguish two themes: consumption in and of itself, and the black market. The doctor notes that one should not assume that the black market will die with the introduction of a liberalized drug market, at least not initially. However, the sharing of this market with legal producers will probably produce immediate repercussions on price, availability and the intensity of the legal regulation of drugs.

The production and distribution experience of the traffickers will surely play to their advantage. This advantage will last through the initial stages of market liberalization.

The decriminalization of drugs will have a profound impact on inner-city areas where the practice of selling drugs has rooted itself deeply, particularly within the African American and Latino communities. Nadelmann refers here to one of the principal effects of decriminalization – that is, the reduction in the price of drugs. Of course, as it stands now, the high price/profit margin of drugs is one of the most powerful incentives that lures young people into the business of selling them.

Another impact on this sector, Nadelmann explains, relates to health and health care. Residents of impoverished inner-city areas, whether because of economic or cultural factors, have limited opportunities for adequate health care and/or medical consultation. A fundamental manifestation to decriminalization would be the increased access to medical advice and information. A pharmacist, for example, authorized by the government or by professional agencies, would have an important and growing role as not only a regulator of psychoactive drugs, but as an educator and a medical consultant regarding the preferred and correct uses of the drugs. That is, a society featuring wide accessibility of drugs would have the potential to develop and foster practices of self-protection against various forms of drug addiction and other related dangers.

In such a society, more people would assume a greater responsibility in their relationships with drugs than they assume at present. Furthermore, as medical professionals increasingly undertook the role of regulators, consumers would become safer in their practices.

Nadelmann recommends that available information and education be designed in such a way that it is both easily accessible to and understood by the drug-using public. Toward this end, he suggests four specific goals:

1. Develop an effective manner to determine which categories of drugs are being purchased, both by mail and through direct sales; and assure that the consumers are informed of the risks and of the correct application of these drugs. This task may be carried out by the FDA, non-governmental agencies, or a combination of both.

2. Design a system of information diffusion distinct from systems of distribution, whereby consumers can obtain information on their own, and at no cost to them. This system could be operated through a telephone-based service, as well as through e-mail or other easily accessible forms of electronic media communication.

3. Create an information program which is honest and that truthfully delineates to young people the characteristics of drugs, but in a way that does not stimulate their curiosity to try these drugs.

4. Develop a public health campaign that effectively discourages dangerous or abusive use of drugs without lying, applying fear or demonizing those who use drugs. Current

campaigns discouraging tobacco use and drunk driving are better models in this respect.[97]

The salient issue here is whether legalization can produce a greater spectrum of possibilities, or if its uncertainties are dramatically more numerous than those which persist under the current system of prohibition. Clearly, the model of legalization offers effective means of eliminating or reducing the worst consequences of the prohibition of drugs and represents the best compromise between individual rights and those of the community. Although Nadelmann recognizes that this model presents greater risks than the conventional prohibitionist system, he believes the former offers far more potential to transform the nature of the consumer toward a safer more stable mean.

Addressing the intellectual debate on this issue, Nadelmann considers unquestionable the need to find alternative models to current drug-control systems. He argues, correspondingly, that the acceptable criteria for analyzing the implementation of new measures must be expanded:

> *To limit the questions one asks or the responses one ventures to the official voice of the establishment is to undermine our moral and intellectual obligations as well as our profession and society. Future generations will be harmed or put at risk if today's intellectuals uniformly surrender themselves to the intellectual conservatism that dominates the social sciences and the analysis of public policy.*
>
> *From my perspective, the challenge is to delineate a policy of control that combines a healthy respect for individual rights and personal responsibility with a strong sense of compassion.*

---

[97] The efficiency of the campaign against cigarettes is analyzed in "The Effects of the Anti-Smoking Campaign On Cigarette Smoking," K.E. Warner, *American Journal of Public Health*, number 67, 1977.

> *These values do not necessarily have to be unified or equally present all at once, but it is important that they not be forgotten when the specter of drugs manifests itself.[98]*

The legalization of cannabis was proposed by the State of Alaska in 1975, principally for reasons of public health; that is, this proposal viewed marijuana as a viable alternative to alcohol and alcoholism if left to compete on the free market. In the same manner, Holland justified cannabis legalization as a means to reduce heroin abuse, with the former displacing the latter within drug circles.

More important than the varying levels of confliction and/or (less often) complementation of the different conceptual approaches to the drug problem is the universal recognition of the yet-unshaken existence of *the problem*. This recognition marks an important, new stage at which we must find a point of compromise between existing policy and the anti-prohibitionist alternatives.

Each opinion incites questioning, and each round of questioning brings us closer to the goal of reform. Such questioning and investigation must analyze and justify the reasons for which the current system is to be abandoned for another variant. The goal, simply, is a system which produces the best results, and a system which respects the rights of the individual as well as those of the society as a whole.

Professor Musio, a psychologist and historian at Yale University, explains that the nature of drug use in society is cyclical:

> *First comes a period of growing experimentation, an epidemic wherein drugs are seen as enticing and the chance of danger remote. After such a period, the society becomes increasingly aware of the adverse consequences of drugs.*

---

[98] Ethan Nadelmann, ob. cit. 11.

Finally, a climate of intolerance prevails wherein society distances itself from drugs.[99]

Daniel Samper, a Colombian journalist, categorizes the possible consequences of legalization into two scenarios:

Scenario number 1: The distribution and consumption of drugs are legalized. Drug prices drop drastically. Due to the new condition of legality, millions of citizens decide to try drugs which were previously illegal. The drug Mafias quickly gain control of production and distribution. The number of addicts triples or quadruples. The death rate increases and the number of dysfunctional families/broken homes also goes up. Social services are pushed to their limits. As a whole, the social problem becomes unprecedentedly acute.

Scenario number 2: The distribution and consumption of drugs are legalized. Prices drop drastically. The drug Mafias are ruined. Drug-related crime plummets. Official agencies and health organizations control the quality of drugs and offer help to drug addicts. State-sponsored education programs are stepped up; police repression is toned down. The death rate lowers as does the number of dysfunctional families/broken homes. As a whole, the social problem is reduced to an unprecedented minimum.[100]

---

[99] *El Espectador*, Bogota, Colombia, January 12, 1990.
[100] *Cambio 16*, 1990. The above citations resulted from a summit, convened by this journal, which evaluated the alternative of legalization and considered objections from those who were against this measure.

Charles B. Rangel, Congressman from New York and Chairman of the House Commission on Narcotics, is an outspoken defender of the current system of repression:

With the objective of seeing whether the defenders of legalization could form responses, the Commission on Narcotics of the House of Representatives met for three days with these people, among them Mayor of Baltimore Kurt Schmoke and Professor Ethan Nadelmann. None of those who testified could adequately respond to the following questions:

Which narcotics and drugs should be legalized?

Should narcotics and drugs be put at the disposal of anyone who wants to try them, including children?

Should habitual consumers or addicts be supplied with unlimited narcotics, or, on the other hand, should they have to pay the market price?

Would those who suffer from a strong drug dependence or addiction be able to work? Or would these persons revert back to crime to finance their habits?

Who should supply the drugs – private companies or the government? Should the drugs be sold at cost or with a profit margin? Should they be taxed?

Where should one be able to purchase the drugs? At pharmacies, specialized stores, dispensaries, clinics, or all-night establishments?

Could (legalization) increase consumption of legal drugs which would then be cheaper and easier to obtain? How do you think this would affect the rate of deaths due to drug-related accidents?

Could the legalization of drugs produce an increase in AIDS cases due to an increase in needle-using addicts?

The lack of real answers on the part those who defend legalization make it difficult to identify a conceptual base from which to change national policy. I think we should bury this nonsense and get on with our war.[101]

Nicolás Harman, Latin American Affairs Editor for the British weekly *The Economist,* is in favor of legalization. In fact, he is a primary exponent of this approach and one of the pioneers of the legalization movement:

Those who buy adulterated poison are the poor, those who overdose are the foolish, and those who experiment with dangerous mixtures are the young. Their problem is the nature of medical services. As it stands, if someone feels ill due to drugs, they do not see a doctor or visit a clinic, because to admit to their illness is to confess to their crim.

Modern governments protect their citizenry by regulating the purity of such things as cooking oil, wine and soap. But in the case of illicit drugs, the job of controlling purity and providing dose advice is in the hands of the criminals.

And this is not the worst of it. The addicts, as tragic as their situation is, are only a small minority. That is, many more people are affected by the violence generated by drug trafficking. The war against drugs puts the entire state of Colombia in danger. Similarly, the civil wars in Lebanon and Afghanistan are financed in large part by heroin traffickers. Moreover, as the cocaine market has become saturated in America, the drug trafficking organizations have begun to penetrate Europe. Yet, despite all this, our governments insist on applying the same policies that have failed in America. Consequently, the drug traffic continues to enrich the largest and most powerful criminal organizations the world has ever known.

But there is an alternative: legalize the consumption of drugs. This would eliminate the foundation of these

---

[101] Philip M. Boffey, *New York Times.* Cited from *El Tiempo,* May 29, 1988

organizations' existence. Meanwhile, a taxed legal drug market would channel to the state the profits now reaped by the criminals.[102]

According to Marcos Taradash, a representative in the European Parliament and member of the Radical Party of Italy, the prevailing ideology needs to be dismantled:

> *. . . It is necessary to put a stop to this abstract way of thinking that is indifferent to (prohibition's) results or to its practical application, and rekindle a critical debate of the current government-sanctioned laws and their effects. The concept of legalization does not imply the absence of laws; rather, a system of decriminalization would regulate each and every stage of the chemical production of drugs, their distribution, use, etc. With prohibition eliminated, every adult citizen would have some type of legal access to narcotics, thus drastically pulling down the market value of such drugs.*[103]

For Antonio Escohotado, Professor of Sociology at the UNED in Spain, who sees an undeniable urgency to integrate the scientific community into this debate, also adds to the dialogue:

Trying to prevent drug abuse through prohibition is as logically feeble as trying to prevent premarital pregnancy by forbidding your daughter to come home after 10 p.m. Just as copulation is easily performed before 10 p.m., prohibited drugs can be easily obtained when they are desired . . .

---

[102] *Cambio 16*, April 30, 1990.
[103] "Towards the Dismantling of an Ideology," Marco Taradash, ob. cit. 14.

To change one's state of mind through chemical means is as basic an impulse as eating, drinking and finding a mate.[104]

FEDERAL DRUG ABUSE BUDGET DOLLAR

Reductions (in millions of $)	From	To	Saving
Law Enforcement	13,203	3,300	9,903
* Interdiction costs	2,200	0	2,200
* International anti-drug	768	384	384
* OCDETF (Organized Crime & Drug Enforcement Task Force)	399	40	359
ONDCP (the "drug czar")	69	17	52
Indirect			
Victims of Crime	842	210	632
Incarceration	4,434	887	3,547
Crime careers	13,976	2,679	11,297
Subtotal			28,374
Less increase in prevention research and service			(3,572)
Less increase in treatment research and service			(2,802)
Subtotal			22,000
Plus net income from drug taxes			15,000
Total			37,000
1993 Figures.			

* Theodore R. Vallance, Former chief of the Planning Branch of the National Institutes of Mental Health. The analysis was published in the 7/10/95 issue of National Review. The Director is William F. Buckley.

---

[104] *Cambio 16,* May 21, 1990.

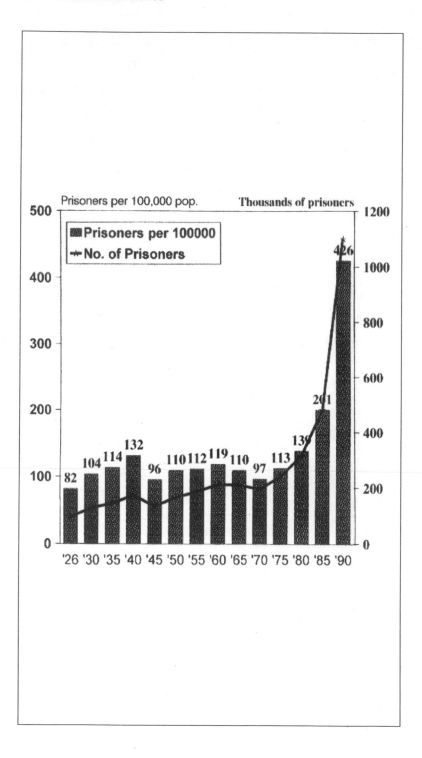

Holland is a country which has pioneered the legalization of drugs. Leo Zaal, Chief of the Anti-Narcotics Brigade of Amsterdam, has the following to say about his brigade's opinion of the legality of marijuana and hashish: ." . .For many years, 250 coffee shops have been authorized to sell 'soft' drugs. This has allowed us to control the criminal element in the city.   We   are   against   the   criminalization   of consumption."[105]

Alan   Parry,   speaking   on   behalf   of   the   drug decriminalization program in Liverpool, England, shares a similar opinion:

> *In Liverpool, we have two policies which apply to drug users. The first one is designed for those who wish to quit. For them we provide the means and assistance necessary to do so. The second is aimed at heroin users. We give these persons medical prescriptions for the drug. We find that pure heroin or high-quality cocaine produces many fewer problems.*
> *The police do not arrest consumers of any drug. We have reduced criminality, the mortality rate is decreasing, and we do not have 'dealers.' There is no drug traffic in Liverpool. We are also observing a decline in AIDS cases among drug addicts. As we provide these drugs in pure form and at no cost, the (illicit)*

---

[105] *El Tiempo*, Conchita Penilla, Bogota, Colombia. Penilla was reporting on a congress organized by the Drug Anti-prohibition League in 1990 in Athens.

drug-dealing industry is dead. Our program is much more advanced than that of Amsterdam.[106]

Emma Bonino, Secretary General of the International Radical Party describes her organization as "the only truly international political party which waves the flag (of legalization)." She continues:

> *The war on drug traffickers is described in unrealistic and inflated terms. As the military well knows, to overestimate the enemy is the best way to deflect criticism in the face of setbacks.*
>
> *I think that few doubts remain with respect to this fact, and that the public perception of the war on drugs is changing. Nevertheless, the cost of prohibition is much heavier in the countries of the southern hemisphere, considering their economies and the significant social problems which affect them. If prohibition were to be lifted, great benefits could be snatched from the criminals and terrorists which threaten the security and democratic rights of the citizens (also, this situation is not very different in my country, Italy).*
>
> *Moreover, the coca leaf, once legalized, would be used for therapeutic and nutritional purposes. For example, the Bolivian government has recognized such qualities in coca tea, and is trying to secure a market for the exportation of this product.*
>
> *In contrast with the countries of the northern hemisphere, it is difficult to imagine that legalization would increase consumption, especially since prohibition has never affected consumption. The use of drugs in the South has completely different cultural origins than those of the North. Nevertheless, few issues link the North and South like this one does.*
>
> *For once, we are not dealing with a zero-sum game, where one party wins and the other loses. With the current system of prohibition, the North as well as the South have much to lose;*

---

[106] Ibid.

however, they would have much to gain if this were to change. It is truly worth the effort to try.

Transnational Radical Party has initiated a global campaign with the objective of overturning the international conventions of 1961, 1971 and 1988. These conventions made illegal the production and consumption of drugs labeled as narcotics.

I will not pay the slightest attention to those who say that this is a lost cause. These are the same persons who predicted our failure in Italy when we were pushing for the legalization of divorce and abortion.

A few months ago we won a referendum. In April, 1993, the Bolivian House of Representatives solicited the modification of those articles in the International Convention which criminalized the production and use of the coca leaf. Specifically, they solicited the elimination of the word "coca" from the list of narcotics. The battle for the legalization of drugs and for the repeal of the current system is, more than any other, a transnational struggle. To adequately continue this fight, we need a transnational, multi-partisan political party capable of affecting public and parliamentary opinion throughout the geographical and ideological spectrum. [107]

The International Anti-prohibitionist League has drafted a document with the objective of revising the International Convention on Drugs. After outlining and analyzing the consequences of a prohibitionist system, the document puts forth a schema for anti-prohibitionism. This schema is founded on the premise that no state can prohibit or punish behavior that does not harm others (a crime without a victim).

---

[107] *Congress for the Compatibility of Narcocriminality Laws,* Buenos Aires, August 2,4, 1993 (Published by the Latin American Parliament).

Next, the document analyzes the issue from a judicial point of view. It considers the overload of the judicial system, prison overpopulation, and the endemic corruption within government and police agencies resulting from drug money. From an administrative point of view, the League points out that the existing anti-drug bureaucracy becomes more rooted each day, and that the unregulated "detoxification" industry is increasingly profitable for private companies who charge significant amounts for their services.

A consideration of economics concludes the League's analysis of the consequences of prohibition:

> *We are critical of the economic effects of prohibition . . . One cannot claim that we need to adapt to a bad or adverse situation in order to avoid a worse circumstance.*
>
> *It is universally recognized that the prohibitionist system is responsible for the particularly elevated drug prices on the "market." This consequence has been labeled as the 'criminality tax,' referring to the monetary compensation that the trafficker reaps for the risk he runs. In this way, the high profit margin provides sufficient incentive for the trafficker to face this risk, and allows him to easily find others disposed to distributing drugs despite the illegality of this practice. Inversely and paradoxically, from the point of view of the consumer, these high prices, far from constituting an obstacle, function as the motor of the market. That is, the high price of drugs which the criminalization tax yields often obligates the consumers, in order to finance their expensive habit, to become involved in the sale of drugs themselves, thereby spreading the marketing of these drugs by yet another level, and frequently leading to the proliferation of more adulterated substances. Therefore, prohibition, by creating an artificial scarcity of drugs, which in reality are not scarce on illicit markets, and by leading to high drug prices, increasingly enlarges the market base for illegal drugs.*

In sum, the economic model created by the commerce of illegal drugs is extremely efficient. As the traffickers cooperate with one another, their monopolistic position allows them to constantly eliminate defects and inefficiencies in their businesses, to optimize their benefits, and to keep demand on an upward trajectory. These are the principal reasons why it is necessary to improve upon the model put in place by the International Convention of the United Nations.[108]

The hypothesis of legalization espoused by the anti-prohibitionist movement can be organized into three thematic categories: medical, commercial, and legal. The medical perspective is the least touched upon under the current system of prohibition. This perspective is based on the right of doctors to limitedly prescribe substances which are currently prohibited. For example, in the case of heroin, doctors would be able to prescribe heroin in reduced doses, and in a non-injected form. From the commercial perspective, the state would have a monopoly for the production and sale of currently illegal drugs in each given country. The state would be able to decide the parameters of drug availability and would maintain complete control over the market. The legal perspective suggests a jurisprudential framework for elements of supply and demand, availability, price, and varieties of drugs produced. Finally, "harm reduction" policies are outlined, providing social and medical solutions for addicts and a means to help reduce petty crime.

---

[108] "Per una revisione delle convenzioni internazionali sulle droghe," Partito Radicale, Liga Internazionale Antiproibizionista (LIA), Coordinamento Radicale Antiproibizionista (CORA) (Rome: Graffiti, 1994).

GROWING SUPPORT

There have been unexpected developments surrounding the issue of legalization. These include the appeal to the Clinton Administration by persons such as Milton Friedman and Joseph McNamara to cease the war on drugs; Gabriel García Márquez's manifesto[109]; the birth of the Movement for Legalization (MLC) in France; Secretary General of INTERPOL Raymond Kendall's pronouncement in favor of the decriminalization of all drugs, as well as similar declarations by a host of other well-known individuals; and an abundance of pro-legalization editorials in prestigious periodicals such as *The Economist*. The international conferences held in Washington and Baltimore in November, 1993, 1994, and 1995 have also been significant.

Perhaps most surprising is the opinion expressed by William F. Buckley Jr., director of the magazine *National Review*, and one of the most important voices within the Republican Party, who characterized the war on drugs as a failure. This significantly shows that an idea once thought solely associated with liberals, progressives and radicals is now being embraced by members of the dominant conservative party. The question now is how long it will take before this notion is accepted by the most powerful members of the party.

---

[109] Published in Spanish in *Cambio 16*.

THE INTERNATIONAL CONVENTIONS

International drug policy is regulated by three United Nations conventions:

The 1961 Convention on Narcotic Substances
The 1971 Vienna Convention on Psychotropic Substances
The 1988 Vienna Convention against the Illegal Trafficking of Narcotics and Psychotropic Substances

The 1961 Convention is a treaty among the member nations of the UN with the objective of preventing and controlling the scourge of drug addiction through internationally coordinated measures. This convention replaced all previous treaties and stipulations regarding international drug policy. The underlying principle of the preamble and written text of the treaty, as stated in Article four, is that "the seizure, use, sale, distribution, importation, exportation, fabrication and production of narcotic substances are exclusively limited to medicinal and scientific ends." The text provides for two complementary spheres of control/regulation: first is the legal use of these drugs for legitimate scientific and medicinal purposes; second is the repression of drug trafficking, abuse and addiction. The former stipulates the prevention of deviancy from legitimate drug use toward illicit use and trafficking. The latter, repressive in nature, lays the foundation to punish and deter traffickers through international penal cooperation.

The control of this illicit market, as stipulated in Articles 2 and 3, shall be through national and international preventative measures which deal with drugs classified as narcotics. Articles 5 and 8 provide that these measures shall be overseen by the Worldwide Narcotics Commission and the International Organization of Narcotics Control. Administration of organizations monitoring national legal narcotics needs (Article 19) and production (Article 20) is also provided for, as is the compilation of regular reports which review the narcotics situation in each UN country.   These instruments allow for policy formation in the areas of production (Article 29), importation and exportation (Article 31) and distribution (Article 30) of drugs which apply solely to medical and scientific needs, that is, state-regulated manufactured narcotics and their retail industries (Article 29).   Drug-particular guidelines which apply to the agricultural production of opium, coca, and marijuana are also included (articles 23 and 28).

The conceptual modification of the Convention of 1961 is the principal objective of the current anti-prohibitionist movement; however, in doing so, it is also the goal of the anti-prohibitionists to change the text of the Convention's articles as little as possible, although there is one exception – the language itself. The 1961 Convention was drafted in English, and correspondingly carries an Anglo-Saxon bent in its terminology and concepts.   Consequently, the anti-prohibitionists feel, the document is not a paragon of international clarity.   For example, the key concept of "narcotic" is merely defined by a list of over one hundred substances classified as such.

The Convention of 1971 is virtually a twin of that of 1961. However, this more recent convention institutes less rigorous standards of international control of psychotropic substances which are produced by the pharmaceutical industry. But in general, due to the similarities between the two conventions,

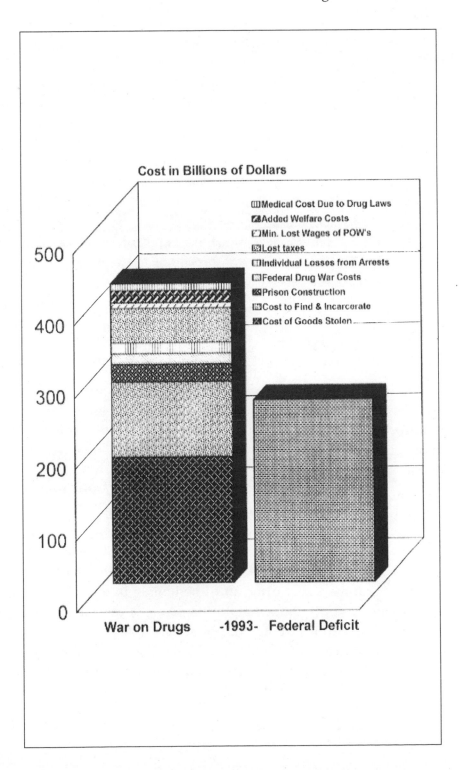

Cost in Billions of Dollars

- ⅏Medical Cost Due to Drug Laws
- ⊿Added Welfare Costs
- ⊡Min. Lost Wages of POW's
- ⊠Lost taxes
- ⊞Individual Losses from Arrests
- ⊡Federal Drug War Costs
- ⊠Prison Construction
- ⊞Cost to Find & Incarcerate
- ⊠Cost of Goods Stolen

War on Drugs   -1993-   Federal Deficit

any modification to the first will most likely be reflected in the second.

The 1971 Convention is merely a corroboration of the principle of a resource economy. However, this is not the case with the 1988 Convention, which is essentially repressive. This convention, adopted on behalf of the 'war on drugs,' and based on prohibitionist logic, is beyond recuperation. The only solution is to simply repeal it. It should be noted that a number of countries have refused to adhere to it due to its excessive rigor. This convention was first applied at the end of 1990, and by 1993, 92 countries had ratified it. In order to invalidate the Convention, it would be necessary for those countries which have ratified it to undertake the process of repealing it.[110]

SOME CONTRADICTIONS

In the late 1950's, England and France produced and distributed opium in their Indian and Indonesian colonies. France has also exploited its Moroccan and Tunisian monopolies of "kif" and of "takouri," traditional names given to the mixture of tobacco and hashish.

In the case of opium, the coexistence of international control with national distribution systems has been possible because the first international conventions do not clearly express the principles of limited medical or scientific use. For example, the 1922 Hague Convention, in its ninth article, provides that the use of drugs must be limited to medical and "legitimate" use. With the help of the United States, the 1931 Geneva Convention, in its fourth article, established more clearly the principle of limited drug use – that is, for medical and scientific needs only – thereby historically modifying the scope of international control. It is precisely the objective of

---

[110] Ob. cit. 25.

the vast majority of anti-prohibitionists to return to the international legal state that existed before these Conventions, when there was no blanket mandate of drug illegalization, and when the problems related to drugs were insignificant compared to what they are now. In addition, according to this anti-prohibitionist camp, such an international environment of drug legality would not hinder the fight against drug addiction outlined in the 1961 Convention.

Furthermore, it must be noted that it is not the objective of most antiprohibitionists to achieve the total legalization of all drugs; rather, the goal is partial prohibition. That is, they believe that currently illicit drugs should not be put on the same level as such substances as tobacco and alcohol. Moreover, drugs such as PCP, or *angel dust*, they maintain, should be prohibited since they present an inherent danger to other persons in addition to the user. For example, PCP can lead to homicidal tendencies, and often to serial killings, as in the case of Sharon Tate.

THE HIGH COST OF CONVICTING DRUG CONSUMERS

Andrés D'Alessio, Dean of the University of Buenos Aires Law School and one of the most prestigious lawyers in Argentina, has publicly declared his opinion against the punishability of drug possession for personal use. Over five years ago, says D'Alessio, a person was arrested after .4 grams of cocaine and .3 grams of marijuana were found in her house. There were also indications that she once had had LSD. It took three years and four months to convict her of the crime of simple possession, which, under Argentine law, is punishable with one to six years in prison (more than torture, embezzlement, kidnapping and usury).

However, a board of appeals acquitted her because of the small quantity of drugs she had possessed. Thereafter, the prosecution moved the case to the Supreme Court, which revoked the acquittal and ordered a new decision, which was again an acquittal. The prosecution appealed again, and the case is once more before the Supreme Court.

This example is especially significant if one considers that 70% of the caseload registered by Argentine federal courts is related to drugs, and 50% of these cases involve possession of less than one gram. Truly, the hunter who wastes his gunpowder on butterflies will come up short in the end.[111]

Let us consider hypothetically, reasons D'Alessio, that it is not a mistake to threaten with punishment those who possess drugs in small, personal-consumption-size quantities. Imagine what would happen if such a regimen of punishment was strictly enforced on consumers of a widely used drug? Such relentless persecution assumes having sufficient means to do so –that is, sufficient police to discover and apprehend the culprits, enough prosecutors to handle the proceedings, ample judges to render decisions in a reasonable time, and enough jails with acceptable conditions to house those convicted to prison. Surely, anyone familiar with the administration of justice knows that such ambitions are unrealistic.

The analysis of such a situation must neither be ethical nor arbitrary, but practical. This situation bears pertinence to the economic law of scarcity: one party cannot produce enough goods to totally satisfy the necessities and desires of a population; that is, they must apply their existing resources as best as possible. They must choose whether to produce butter or cannons.

In Argentina, major terrorist acts, such as the bombing of the Israeli Embassy and of the Jewish Center of Social and

---

[111] Andres D'Alesio, *Clarin*, May 24, 1996. Similarly, in the penal courts, drug cases make up 90% of the load, and the great majority of those are for very small quantities.

Cultural Activities (AMIA), have not been resolved for several years. Meanwhile, judges complain that they are overloaded with cases, that they lack modern systems of computer administration, and that detained major drug traffickers wait for two years to go by without trial, at which time they are set free in accordance with the Treaty of Costa Rica.[112]   This is what happens when the courts are jammed with minor drug possession cases.

John Arroyave Arias, fourth in command of the Medellin cartel, was set free after having been successfully arrested in "Operation *Langostino*" (Operation Shrimp). The operation was named as such because drugs were being smuggled to Europe and the United States inside prawns [*langostinos*]). Meanwhile, as Arroyave Arias went free, Ernie Batista, the DEA agent who had helped in the operation's investigation, was tried; as was Carlos Savignon Belgrano, one of Arroyave Arias' accusers. Moreover, when it came time for Judge Julio Cruciani to oversee the burning of the drugs, another judge had hidden the keys from him.

In another case, Zubieta Bilbao, a major trafficker and money launderer with operations extending into Europe, had been investigated over a period of two years by Judge Roberto Marquevich.   The audio recordings of Bilbao's tapped telephone conversations were stored in huge boxes, a cubic meter each in volume.   Some of these tapes contained conversations of his housekeepers. In Argentina, it is very common for housekeepers to speak *Guarani* or *Quechua*, languages quite common in neighboring Paraguay and Bolivia. As this was the case in Zubieta Bilbao's home, the police had to

---

[112] The Treaty of Costa Rica establishes that no one without an official sentence can remain in jail for more than a reasonable time; in Argentina, this "reasonable time" was interpretted to be two years. This Treaty, ratified by Argentina, was not ratified by the United States.

first transcribe the cassettes in the original language, then have an official certified translator translate the text, and finally enter all the information into the case files, including, for example, conversations the maid may have had with her boyfriend about which movie they should see that night. Consequently, Judge Marquevich ordered that certain tapes which contained conversations that had nothing to do with the case be erased. This would prove to be an important decision.

When Zubieta Bilbao's tanker truck was later intercepted, and discovered to have had a double bottom filled with 120 kilos of cocaine, the truck had just passed over *General Paz Avenue*, an avenue which divides two judicial districts. Therefore, the defense lawyer requested that the case be tried by the City of Buenos Aires rather than by the Province of Buenos Aires. Obviously, the attorney wanted the proceedings taken away from a judge who knew the case well, and given to a judge who did not. His request granted, all the evidence had to be transported in vans to the new jurisdictional office in the City of Buenos Aires. However, when the phone-tap tapes were unpacked and inspected, it was found that some of them had been erased, perhaps, they thought, because some of the maid's conversations may have been fundamental to his defense. Bilbao was set free despite having had confessed his guilt. Bilbao's drugs, at least, were burned. Also, $250,000 in cash was confiscated from his home, along with sophisticated arms and communications equipment. Bilbao was truly a kingpin.

Carlos Capobianco Acha, a Bolivian citizen and provider of coca paste to the Medellin cartel, tried to set up a laboratory in the Province of Buenos Aires when Pablo Escobar began to have problems in Colombia. Capobianco Acha was followed and arrested in 1993 with a 19-kilo bag of cocaine in his possession. The judge of the lower court, Alberto Santamarina, convicted him. But the Appeals Court, presided by Judge

Leopoldo Schiffrin overturned the verdict: "It could not be proven that the bag was his."

When Capobianco Acha was first arrested, the judge tried to take his statement. "I don't have a lawyer." Capobianco Acha said. He was consequently offered a public defender. "No, I will only deal with a lawyer I can trust." A few hours later, Luis Darritchon, a well-known attorney, consultant, university professor, and advisor to the Committee on Penal Legislation of the Argentine House of Representatives, presented himself as Acha's legal representative. This same lawyer assisted, later, in the case of Pascuale Molica, a member of a very famous Italian Mafia family, who was arrested in Buenos Aires.

The Molica Family was involved in various kinds of illegal activities, and they were being investigated by the police forces of many countries. One of the investigations was carried out in Argentina, when a shipment of 500 kilos of cocaine about to be delivered to Italy was discovered by a local trafficker named Juan Luis Pelikán. The operation that prevented this shipment from leaving the country was performed by the local police in cooperation with their counterparts in Italy, Germany, Switzerland and the United States. It was called *"Operación Carbón Blanco"* (White Charcoal Operation). The accumulation of evidence was spectacular. Everyone confessed, and Pelikan's partners, who were arrested in Europe, are all serving sentences. But Juan Pelikan is free, after having spent only two years in prision, liberated as a consequence of the Treaty of Costa Rica. The man who decided to set him free was Judge Leopoldo Schiffrin, who some time later, on a television program, stated that he agreed with the legalization of drugs for personal consumption. However, this highly respected Judge, should be discussing his ideas about decriminalization before the Congress, and not applying them in advance to drug traffickers with huge quantities of drugs.

Argentina's drug problems are intimately linked with its geographical situation: its borders with Bolivia and Paraguay mean hundreds of poor people cross the borders each day, on foot or in small vehicles, transporting small quantities of drugs. This distracts the police, who overlook trucks crossing at other points, carrying serious quantities of drugs.   Eighty-five percent   of the detainees in the jails of *Salta* and *Jujuy* -- Argentine provinces along the Bolivian border- are Bolivians charged with drug-related offenses.   Consequently, the governors of these jurisdictions are constantly requesting funds to house and maintain these illiterate Bolivian aliens. This is the "war on drugs" in action: while the drug kingpins are left untouched, each small-time prisoner costs the government $12,000 per year. The country's annual budget for drug-trafficking prevention and addict rehabilitation is a mere $30 million, which makes the prospects of apprehending any of the *big fish* of drug trafficking seem very unlikely. To make things worse, the drug barons hire the best lawyers while the small time smugglers and street dealers bear the full brunt of the law. While judges slowly wade through a sea of minor possession   cases,   the   leaders   of   international   crime organization die of old age in their mansions.

Epilogue

The Swiss Paradox

An organization called Transparency International has created a system which rates on a 100-point scale the level of corruption within countries. Variables include the level of independence of a country's judicial system and the extent to which the state involves itself in business activities. This organization and its ratings call attention to the abysmal scores of countries closely linked with the laundering of drug money. However, Switzerland has one of the best ratings. Since figures of laundered money are not available, studies of corruption must become even more far-reaching and complex. It seems a joke that the country that launderers the money of all the big criminals and thieves of the world – the home country of the UBS vice president who was caught with $150 million of Pablo Escobar's money and was consequently jailed for a mere 48 hours – should receive such a rating. Is this what Transparency International calls judicial independence? If Pablo Escobar was a criminal, what should we call the person who confidentially safeguards his money?

With the exception of Switzerland, however, everything else Transparency International reports is true. Indeed, it is horrible to live in a country like Nigeria, where the police constantly demand pay-offs and where the bureaucracy is corrupt. But while it is also true that Switzerland is clean and orderly, no one has yet told us exactly whose money is stashed in Confidas. Transparency International must revise its criteria.

From a drug trafficker's perspective, Transparency Inter-national's message seems clear – if you want to produce or traffic drugs, it would be best to go to Nigeria, Colombia or Mexico, where one can easily bribe officials when necessary. After your business is done, the money is collected, and you need a safe and *"honorable"* country in which to put your cash, go to Switzerland. Apparently, in the contradictory case of Switzerland, Transparency International has rewarded a country where the value of transparency has been displaced by that of "discretion," "confidence," and, in fact, a *lack of transparency*.

THE PREVALENCE OF MONEY LAUNDERING

If one speaks of development, investment, growth, education, or the provision of goods and services, one must also speak of corruption and money laundering. It is also true that we can not view corruption in the same way we once viewed it in the past. Today, when we design economy policy, we must factor the consequences of corruption within the currents of investment and within our systems of production.

The Financial Action Task Force (FATF), which includes the principal drug-consuming nations as its members, calculates that between 400 and $500 billion in drug money is laundered each year. This means that the narcotics industry represents between 10 and 13% of all international commerce – this is 1% more than the international trade of petroleum, combustible fuel and lubricants; more than the international trade of foodstuffs, livestock, beverages and tobacco combined;

it represents double the profits of legitimate pharmaceutical companies and seven times the global investment in the development of the third world (which is the origin of the majority of illicit drugs).

The majority of estimates indicate that half of all illicit drug commerce takes place entirely within Latin America. Lower figures, such as those supplied by the FATF, suggest that a minimum of between $50 and $80 billion reach Latin America or is absorbed by that region from illicit drugs.

In Colombia, according to the United Nations, drug trafficking represents between 3% and 13% of their gross national product. Colombian economists estimate that the amount of money repatriated each year by drug traffickers is between $1.5 and $2 billion; this quantity was the approximate equivalent of between 17% and 24% of all legal Colombian exports in 1994. Annual legal private investment is estimated at only slightly higher than this amount, totaling $2.8 billion. About 300,000 families cultivate marijuana, coca leaf, or poppy for heroin; this is about the same number of families as those who produce coffee, which is the most important legal export of Colombia.

In Bolivia, it is estimated that drug trafficking produces about $1.4 billion, more than 20% of their gross national product. According to the United Nations Commission on Narcotics, the resulting overvaluation undermined the development of Bolivia's leather and textile industries, which have faired poorly against cheaper Brazilian and Chilean products.

In 1994, according to the State Department of the United States, Peru produced 165,000 tons of coca, surpassing Colombia and Bolivia to become the largest coca producer in the world. Peru's coca crop generates more than $1 billion annually, in addition to the profits generated by refinement and trafficking. The United Nations reports that the Peruvian narcotics industry represents 11% of Peru's gross national product, making this industrial sector more monetarily significant   that those of mining, construction, fishing, and electricity production.

More and more, Mexico is the country through which drugs pass from Colombia to the United States.   Samuel Gonzales Ruiz, professor of law at the Autonomous University of Mexico (UNAM), estimates that about $6 billion of cocaine annually is sold through the U.S.-Mexican border connection, with about half of that money remaining in Mexico.

It is impossible to calculate the number of jobs generated by drug trafficking, but the Mexican attorney general estimates that in the last seven years, 150,000 persons were incarcerated for drug-related offenses.   According to Professor Gonzalez, farmers in the Mexican state of Sinaloa earn 50 times more from cultivating marihuana or opium than from growing legal crops.[113]

Is money laundering a theme which only involves criminal organizations only, or major banking institutions? Should this theme be dealt with only by the agencies who police this type of crime, or should it be considered by the designers of economic policy?

Vito Tanzi, one of the best-known economists in the world, directs the Department of Fiscal Affairs of the International Monetary Fund; Peter Quirk is an advisor to the Department of Monetary and Exchange Affairs of the IMF.   In July, 1996, the IMF issued reports from these two specialists regarding money laundering.   Tanzi and Quirk, two men as far away from sensationalism as can be, confirm that approximately $500 billion is laundered annually, a sum equal to two percent *of the total annual production* of the world, or equal to two times the gross domestic product of Mexico.

---

[113] José Mairena, *La Nacion*, Costa Rica, April 1, 1996.

According to Tanzi and Quirk, money laundering today is not only a criminal issue, but also a phenomenon that greatly affects financial markets and all that is connected with economic policy.   Consequently, Tanzi proposes the establishment of *universally-accepted* standards of vigilance and information accessibility.   The international organizations of countries that are in compliance would have access to a determined set of benefits; countries that do not comply would not have access to such benefits.   In sum, Tanzi proposes that conditions for international good standing be related to the prevention of money laundering.

Tanzi and Quirk have hit the nail on the head.   Their proposal would prick one of the most sensitive areas for Switzerland, Liechtenstein, Luxembourg, England (and their fiscal island paradises), Uruguay (a country which is striving to become the "Switzerland of Latin America"), and the United States, whose large banks do not comply with the regulations that are in place.

American journalist Claire Sterling, in her book *Thieves' World*, details the globalization of organized crime which has occurred since the fall of the Soviet Union and the unification of Europe. Sterling describes how, in 1993, a Mafia "board of directors" effectively made the island of Aruba "their state." However, Sterling feels that the most significant development in Mafia activity, now and ever, is their gradual usurpation of Russia.

The Sicilian Mafia and its international counterparts – the Russian Mafia, the Japanese Yakuza, the Chinese Triad (with bases in Hong Kong and Taiwan), and the Colombian and Mexican cartels – have constructed, according to Sterling, a system of alliances and territorial division that has made them the among most powerful forces of the world.   The corruption of politicians is merely a manifestation of these new superpowers which now appear inexpugnable.[114]

A NEW TEST FOR THE AMERICANS

In the past, American authorities have spared shame to J.P. Morgan – one of the most prestigious banks of the world – by not divulging the participation of one of that institution's Latin American directors in illegal transactions. In the case of the Bank of Boston, the treatment was only slightly harsher – their Bostonian aristocrat president, William Brown, had to admit the bank's guilt, attributing what had occurred to "human error," and had to pay a petty fine of $500,000. The testimony of bank directors and Treasury Department bureaucrats before the Senate Banking Committee was truly a pathetic display. Now we find the system being tested once again with the case of Confidas. As described, an investment fund was established in Panama, deposited in Switzerland, and directed by the executive vice president of Citicorp. This money belongs to none other than Raul Salinas de Gortari and the Gulf cartel.

If Raul Salinas was telling the truth when he stated that the first remittance was made in the presence of Amy G. Elliott in the Mexican office of Citibank, is it not reasonable to wonder whether the Mexican branch was the *only* branch authorized to receive such "confidential" deposits? Were other Citibank branches in other countries making the same types of transactions with other clients?

The United States has a bilateral agreement with Switzerland. The United States can now, by virtue of this agreement, obligate the Swiss authorities to open the files of

---

[114] Also see Enrique Quintana, "Mafias y lavado de dinero," *Reforma*, Mexico, September 8, 1996.

the confidential accounts of Confidas/Citibank. We shall soon know the specifics of the case. But if not, how will United States functionaries stand before an international conference and declare which countries they believe should be *"certified"* or *"not certified,"* while these same U.S. officials permit the Confidas/Citibank account to remain undisclosed.

The Colombian farmer is in a state of extreme poverty, yet the aristocratic Wall Street bankers are at the other end of the same business. How can we make war on one and protect the other?

If it happens that the sources of the Confidas/Citibank funds are never disclosed, would it not be reasonable to admit that we are all corrupt, perhaps some more than others, and to legalize drugs? It is certainly ridiculous to continue to believe that by fumigating fields in Colombia or Peru that we are fighting drug trafficking. We would only be fighting it if, when the investigations focused on the high end of the social scale, that is, on those who are *discrete, confidential* and *sophisticated*, we pursued these directives with the same rigor. Perhaps the most salient example is the investigation of the Bank of Boston. It makes one wonder if we will always have a valiant general to teach poor farmers a lesson and a stupid bureaucrat to control important banks. It would make more sense if the financial crime unit of the Treasury Department also counted on the services of General McKaffrey. Only then could we say that the politicians believe the war on drugs to be a serious effort, and not just a political exposition. A case in point: Marvin Smillon, a spokesman for the U.S. Attorney General's Office has stated: *"No formal accusation has been levied against Citibank; we do not know when such an accusation will be made or if it will ever be made."*

In late July, 1996, Citibank contracted the services of attorney Robert Fiske Jr. They did so after the U.S. Government widened their investigation of whether Citibank violated banking laws dealing with money transfers. That is, the Justice Department began a criminal investigation of Citibank.

Fiske, an ex-special prosecutor of the Whitewater case, has much experience in these matters. He has defended ex-Secretary of Defense Clark Clifford as well as Washington attorney Robert Altman in the BCCI bank fraud case. Fiske was also an associate at the firm of Davis, Polk & Wardwell between 1976 and 1980.[115]

Walker Todd, an ex-official at the Federal Reserve in New York and the ex-assistant attorney general of the Federal Reserve Bank of Cleveland, explains: *"Bank management of the flight of capital from developing countries is the little secret that we keep in the Unites States. It's kind of like the secret Mexico keeps regarding who killed Colosio."*

Money Laundering represents the institutional acceptance of the Mafia and a *pardon* to organized crime. It is the motor in a vicious circle of demoralization and corruption. Which lifts the moral fabric of our society more – attacking poor farmers or sheltering bankers with unscrupulous laws?

---

[115] See Lauri Hays, "Citibank Hires Fiske in Salinas Investigation, *The Wall Street Journal*, July 30, 1996.

Bibliography

BOOKS

Anderson, Malcolm. *Policing the World.* Oxford: The Clarendon Press, 1989.

Auchlin, Pascal, and Garbely, Frank. *Contre-enquete*, Paris: 1990.

Baldwin, Fletcher N. and Munro, Robert J. *Money Laundering: Asset Forteiture & International Financial Crimes.* Oceana Publications, Inc. 1993.

Beaty, Jonathan and Gwynne S.C. *The Outlaw Bank: a wild ride into the Secret Heart of BCCI.* New York: Random House, 1993.

Block, Alan A. *Masters of Paradise: Organized Crime and the Internal Revenue Service in The Bahamas.* New Brunswich: Transaction Publishers, 1981.

Bresler, Fenton. *Interpol.* Sinclair, 1992.

Butterworths Guide to International Money Laundering Laws. Washington: Legal Publishers Inc., 1994.

Calvi, Fabrizio. *L'Europe des parrains: la Mafia a l'assaut de l'Europe.* Paris, Grasset et Fasquelle, 1993.

Canon, Luis. *El Patron: vida y muerte de Pablo Escobar Gaviria, el zar de la droga.* Bogota, Platena, 1994.

Carberry, Charles M., Abrams, Stuart E. and Berenholtz, Celia G. *Money Laundering: Reporting & Regulatory Requirements.* New York, Law Publishing Co.1993.

Caulkins, Jonathan P. *Developing Price Series for Cocaine.* Santa Monica, CA: Rand Corp. 1994.

Chapman and Hall. *Money Laundering: a practical guide to the new legislation.* Supt Docs, 1994.

Clarke, Thurston and John J. Tigue, Jr. *Dirty Money: Swiss Banks, the Mafia, Money Laundering and White Collar Crime.* New York: Simon & Schuster, 1975.

Comisky, Ian M., and Lawrence S. Feld. *Tax Fraud & Evasion: Money Laundering, Asset Forfeiture, Sentencing Guidelines.* Warren, Gorham & Lamont, Inc. 1994.1056 pp.

Cooper, Mary H. *The Business of Drugs.* Washington: Congressional Quarterly, 1990.

Dombey-Moore, Bonnie; Resetar, Susan and Childress, Michael. *A System Description of the Cocaine Trade.* Santa Monica, C.A. Rand, 1994.

Edelhertz, Allen W. The Nature, *Impact and Prosecution of White-Collar Crime [ICR70-1]* Washington, D.C. National Institute of Law Enforcement and Criminal Justice, Government Printing Office, 1970.

Ehrenfeld, Rachel. *Narco Terrorism.* New York: Basic Books, 1990.

Ehrenfeld, Rachael. *Evil Money: The Inside Story of Money Laundering & Corruption in Government,* Sure Sellers, Inc. 1994.

Escohotado, Antonio. *Las drogas, de los origenes a la prohibicion.* Madrid, Alianza, 1994.

Foerster, Schuyler and Wright, Edward N. *American Defense Policy,* Baltimore: The Johns Hopkins University Press, 1990.

Frieman, Milton and Szasz, Thomas S. *On Liberty and Drugs.* Washington: The Drug Policy Foundation Press, 1992.

George, Susan. *The Debt Boomerang: How Third World Debt Harms Us All.* Boulder, Colo. Westview Press, 1992.

Gilmore, William C. *Dirty Money: the Evolution of Money Laundering Counter-measures.* Strasbourg: Council of Europe Press, 1995.

Gressey, Donald R. *Theft of the Nation.* New York: Harper & Row Publishers, 1969.

Hall, Kermit L. Ed.. *Supreme Court of the United States.* New York: Oxford University Press, 1992.

Hesse, Erich. *Narcotics and Drug Addiction. New York, Philosophical Library,* [c1946].

Illicit Narcotics: Efforts to Control Chemical Diversion & Money Laundering. N. York: Diane Publishing Co., 1995.

Jacobs, James B. *Busting The Mob, United States vs. Cosa Nostra.* New York University Press, 1994.

Kaplan, Marcos. *Aspectos socio politicos del narcotráfico.* Mexico: Instituto Nacional de Ciencias Penales, 1989.

Kegley, Charles W. Jr, and Wittkopf, Eugene R. *American Foreign Policy.* Fifth Edition. NewYork: St. Martin's Press, 1996.

Kelly, Robert J., [Ed.] *Organized Crime, a Global Perspective.* New Jersey: Rowman & Littlefield, 1986.

Kennedy, Michael. *A Simple Economic Model of Cocaine Production.* Santa Monica, 1994.

Kessler, Ronald. *The FBI.* New York: Simon & Schuster, 1993.

Lerner, Michael. *The Politics of Meaning.* New York: Addison-Wesley Publishing, 1996.

MacGregor, Felipe E., ed. *Coca and Cocaine: An Andean Perspective.* Westport, CT: Greenwood Press, 1993.

Madelin, Philippe. *L'or des dictatures.* Paris: Fayard 1993.

Malamud Goti, Jaime E. *Smoke & Mirrors: the Paradox of the Drug Wars.* Boulder: Westview Press, 1992.

Martin, John McCullough and Romano, Anne T. *Multinational Crime: Terrorism, Espionage, Drug & Arms Trafficking.* Newbury Park: Sage, 1992.

McCleean, David. *International Judicial Assistance.* Oxford University Press, 1992.

McCoy, Alfred. *The Politics of Heroin.* New York: Lawrence Hill Books, 1991.

National Association of Attorneys General. *A State & Local Response to Money Laundering Program Manual.* 1993.

Naylor, R.T. *Hot Money and the Politics on Debt.* New York, N.Y. Linden Press/Simon & Schuster, 1987. 463 pp.

Nolan, Jane E., ed. *Global Engagement.* Washington: The Brooking Institution, 1994.

Pace, F. Denny and Jimmie C. Styles. *Organized Crime: Concepts and Control.* New Jersey: Prentice-Hall, 1975.

Painter, James. *Bolivia and Coca: A Study in Dependency.* Boulder: L. Reinner Publishers, 1994.

Pasquini, Gabriel, and De Miguel, Eduardo. *Blanca y Radiante.* Buenos Aires:Planeta, 1995. Intrnational Narcotics Control Strategy Report-1992. Washington, Diane Publishing, Co. 1994.

Perez Toledano. *La otra cara de Caro.* Quintero, Mexico: Publicaciones y Ediciones Oro, 1985.

_____, *The Time of the Assassins.* New York, Holt, Rinehart, and Winston, 1984.

_____, *What to do about Terrorism,* Transcript of Firing Line Program #464. Columbia, S.C., Southern Educational Communications Association, 1981.

Peterson, Virgil W. *The Mob, 200 Years of Organized Crime in New York.*Ottawa, IL. Green Hill Publishers, 1983.

Powis, Robert E. *The Money Launderers: Lessons from the Drug Wars—How Billions of Illegal Dollars are Washed through Banks & Businesses.*

Ragano, Frank and Raab Selwyn. *Mob Lawyer.* New York: Scribners, 1994.

Reeves, Jimie Lynn and Campbell, Richard. *Cracked Coverage: Television News, The Anti-cocaine Crusade, and the Reagan Legacy.* Durham: Duke University Press, 1994.

Renborg, Bertil Arne. *International Drug Control: A Study of International Administration by and through the League of Nations.* Washington: Carnegie Endowment for International Peace, 1947.

Rice, Berkeley. *Trafficking: The Boom and Bust of the Air America Cocaine Ring.* New York: Scribner, 1989.

Sandel, Michael J. *Democracy Discontent.* Cambridge, MA, 1996.

Schroeder, Richard C. *The Politics of Drugs: Marijuana to Mainlining.* Washington: Congressional Quarterly, 1975.

Scott, Peter Dale, and Marshall, Jonathan. *Cocaine Politics, Drugs, Armies and the CIA in Central America.* Berkeley: University of California Press, 1991.

Shannon, Elaine. *Desperados, Latin Drug Lords, U.S. Lawmen, and the War America Can't Win.* New York: Viking, Penguin Group, 1988.

Shultz, George Pratt. *Narcotics: a Global Threat.* Washington: U.S. Dept. Of State, 1987.

Sterling, Claire. *Thieves World: the Threat of the New Global Network of Organized Crime.* New York: Simon & Schuster, 1994.

Varela-Cid, R., Ferraro, L., Crocce, L., Zin, C., Borino, E., Castro, J.,Zaragoza Aguado J., et al. *Narco-criminality.* SãoPaulo: Parlamento Latinoamericano, 1994.

Velasquez Mainardi, Miguel A. *El Narcotrafico y el lavado de dolares en Republica Dominicana.* Santo Domingo: Corripio, 1992.

Weston, Burns H., Falk, Richard A., D'Amato Anthony. *Basic Documents in International Law and World Order.* St. Paul, Minn., 1990.

Wisotsky, Steven. *Beyond the War on Drugs: Overcoming a Failed Public Policy.* Buffalo, NY: Prometheus Books, 1990.

Wolff, Kay. *The Last Run: An American Woman's Years Inside a Colombian Drug Family and her Dramatic Escape.* New York: Viking, 1989.

Woolner, Ann. *Washed in Gold: the Story Behind the Biggest Money-Laundering Investigation in U.S. History.* Edinburgh: Edinburgh University Press, 1993.

Ziegler, Jean. *La Suisse lave plus blanc.* Paris: Seuil, 1990.

ARTICLES

Alcantar, Guadalupe M.; Ritter, Bill. *Los Angeles Times.* June 20, 1985.

Aldrich, Michael. Legalize the Lesser to Minimize the Greater: Modern Applications of Ancient Wisdom. *Journal of Drug Issues.* 1990.

Andelman, David. The Drug Money Maze. *Foreign Affairs.* Jul/Aug 1994.

Arnao, Giancarlo. Italian Referendum Deletes Criminal Sanctions for Drug Users. *Journal of Drug Issues.* 1994.

Bank of Boston.
   Atlanta Journal. Mar 12, 1985.
   Chicago Tribune. Mar 13, 1985.
   Los Angeles Times. Feb 16, 1985.
   Los Angeles Times. Feb 22, 1985.
   Los Angeles Times. Feb 27, 1985.

Bartlett, Sarah; Wallace, David. How Deak & Co. Got Caught in its Own Tangled Web. *Business Week.* Dec 24,1984.

Bartlett, Sarah; Wallace, David. Money Laundering. *Business Week.* Mar 18, 1985.

Bayer, Ronald. Introduction: the Great Drug Policy Debate - What Means this Thing Called Decriminalization? *Milbank Quarterly.* 1991.

Berner, Robert. A Kmart Officer Quits in New Sign of Realty Woes. *The Wall Street Journal.* Jan 24, 1996.

Bertrand, Marie Andree. Beyond Antiprohibitionism. *Journal of Drug Issues.* 1990.

Block, Walter. Drug Prohibition: a Legal and Economic Analysis. *Journal of Business Ethics*. Sep 1993.

Blumstein, Alfred. Youth Violence, Guns and the Illicit-Drug Industry. *The Journal of Criminal Law and Criminology*. 1995.

Bratton, William. Ending the War Against Drugs Could be a Disaster. *Boston Globe*. Dec 24,1995.

Bring Drugs Within the Law. *Economist*. May 15, 1993.

Caputo, Michael; Ostrom, Brian. Potential Tax Revenue from a Regulated Marijuana Market: a Meaningful Revenue Source. *The American Journal of Economics and Sociology*. Oct 1994.

Chaiking, David A. Money Laundering: an investigatory perspective. Spring 1991.

C.I.A. Funny Business.*The New York Times* (Editorial). Jun 8, 1993.

Clary, Mike. Ex-Prosecutor Pleads guilty in Drug Case. *Los Angeles Times*. Jul 4, 1995.

Clayton, Mark. Where World's Crooks Go to Do Their Dirty Laundry. *Christian Science Monitor*. Sep 20, 1995.

Cohen, Laurie; Bacon, Kenneth. Banker at American Express Affiliate Faces Money-Laundering Investigation. *The Wall Street Journal*. Nov 8, 1993.

Cohen, Laurie; Felsenthal, Edward. Bank Emplyees Charged. *The Wall Street Journal*. Dec 22,1993.

Cordtz, Dan. Dirty Dollars. *Financial World*. Feb 1, 1994.

Currie, Elliott. Toward a Policy on Drugs: Decriminalization? Legalization? *Dissent.* Winter 1993.

De-Feis, Nicholas M. Asset forfeiture: How far can the U.S. Courts Go? 1992.

Defins, Philippe. Loi Anti-Blanchiemant: Les Lecons de L'Experience. Aug 1993.

DeMott, John. Dirty Money in the Spotlight. *Time.* Nov 12, 1984.

Dentzer, Susan. E.F. Hutton: Itⓛs Not Over Yet. *Newsweek.* May 20, 1985.

DePalma, Anthony. A $50 Million Payment Fuels Mexican Scandal. *The New York Times.* Feb 1, 1996.

DePalma, Anthony. Drug Traffickers Smuggling Tons of Cash from U.S. through Mexico. *The New York Times.* Jan 25,1996.

Dillon, Sam. An Offering to the U.S.: the Head of a Fugitive. *The New York Times.* Jan 17, 1996

Dillon, Sam. Bribes and Publicity Mark Fall of Mexican Drug Lord. *The New York Times.* May 12, 1996.

Dobinson, Ian. Pinning a Tail on the Dragon: The Chinese and the International Heroin Trade. *Crime and Delinquency.* Jul 1993.

Drage, John. Countering Money Laundering. 1992.

Drug Dealing: Danger Money. *Economist.*Jul 14, 1990.

A Drug Tale of two Cities (Mexico City and Bogota). *Economist.* Apr 6, 1996.

Du-Pasquier, Shelvy; Von Planta, Andreas. Money Laundering in Switzerland. 1990.

Dwyer, Paula. Big Brother Wants to See Your Bankbook. *Business Week.* Sep 16, 1985.

Ex-CIA Agent Suspected in Italian Ring. *The New York Times.*Dec 3, 1995.

Ex-Federal Prosecutor Pleads Guilty in Colombia Cocaine Case *Chicago Tribune.* Jul 3, 1995.

Ex-Prudential Broker is Indicted in Miami in Laundering Case. *The Wall Street Journal.* Feb 8, 1996.

Fegelman, Andrew. Judges Drowning in Flood of Drug Cases Seek Lifeline. *Chicago Tribune.* Apr 15, 1996.

Ferdinand, Pamela. Prostitution Dragnet Targets Escort Services. *Boston Globe.* Mar 27, 1996.

Fialka, John. Cleaning Up. *The Wall Street Journal.* Mar 1, 1990.

Fineman, Mark. Mexican Senate Passes Crime Bill Despite Rights Concerns. *Los Angeles Times.* Nov 3, 1995.

Fineman, Mark; Rotella, Sebastian. Trial of Cash and Land Leads to Raul Salinas. *Los Angeles Times.* Nov 30, 1995.

Fisher, Anne. Money Laundering- More Shocks Ahead. *Fortune.* Apr 1, 1985.

Foust, Dean. *The New Improved Money Launderers: Sophisticated Schemes are Washing up to $300 Billion a Year. Business Week.* Jan 1993.

Franco, Mario de; Godoy, Ricardo. The Economic consequences of Cocaine Production in Bolivia:

Historical, Local, and Macroeconomic Perspectives. *Journal of Latin American Studies.* May 1992.

Frank, Allan Dodds. T-Man Videos. *Forbes.* May 5, 1986.

Frank, Allan Dodds. New Hub for an Old Web. *Forbes.* Apr 7, 1986.

Frank, Allan Dodds. See No Evil. *Forbes.* Oct 6, 1986.

Fried, Joseph. F. Lee Bailey Plans to Return Money to Court. *The New York Times.* Feb 6, 1996.

Gladwell, Malcolm. Bagging a Bumbling Band of Alleged Money Launderers. *The Washington Post.* Jan 4, 1995.

Glynn, Lenny. Trailing Laundered Cash. Mar 25, 1985.

Godwin, Catharine. Determining Mandatory Minimum Penalties in Drug Conspiracy Cases. *Federal Probation.* Mar 1995.

Grinspoon, Lester; Bakalar, James. Arguments for a Harmfulness Tax. *Journal of Drug Issues.* 1990.

Grosse, Robert. The Economic Impact of Andean Cocaine Traffic on Florida. *Journal of Interamerican Studies and World Affairs.* Winter 1990.

Hall, Wayne. The Australian Debate About the Legalization of Heroin and Other Illicit Drugs. *Journal of Drug Issues.* 1992.

Haskell, Robert. Thomas Szasz and our Right to Drugs: Cracking the Constitution. *Journal of Humanistic Psychology.* 1995.

Hayes, Arthur. Seizing Laundered Funds. *The Wall Street Journal.* Jan 25, 1993.

Heffernan, Ronald; Martin, John; Romano, Anne. Homicides Related to Drug Trafficking. *Federal Probation.* Sep 1982.

House Panel Studies Dirty Banking. *USA Today.* Feb 29, 1996.

Ignatius, David. Caught in the Drug War Crossfire. *The Washington Post.* Nov 5, 1995.

Inciardi, James; Saum, Christine. Legalizations Madness. *The Public Interest.* 1996.

Insert Money, Press Start. *Economist.* Feb 17, 1996.

Internal Trade (Nigeria becomes big distribution hub for drugs). *Economist.* Aug 26, 1995.

Intriago, Charles. Bankers Challenge Proposed Wire Transfer Rules. Aug 1991.

Jackson, Robert L. *Los Angeles Times.* Mar 13, 1985.

Jackson, Robert L. Editorial on Federal Investigation of Money Laundering. *USA Today.* Mar 19, 1985.

Jauvert, Vincent. L'Argent de la Drogue en France. 1994.

Jeffress, William H. Jr. The Federal Sentencing Guidelines and Banking Offences. 1991.

Joe, Karen. The New Criminal Conspiracy? Asian Gangs and Organized Crime in San Francisco. *Journal of Research in Crime and Delinquency.* Nov 1994.

Katz, Jesse; Hart, Lianne. Ex Banker Gets 10 Years in Drug Money Scheme. *Los Angeles Times.* Aug 13, 1994.

Kelly, Orr. Banks Caught in Feds⬚ Squeeze on Mobsters. *U.S. News & World Report.* Mar 11, 1985.

Koepp, Stephen. Crack Down on ⬚Greenwashing⬚. *Time.* Mar 25, 1985.

Kohn, Howard. Cocaine: You Can Bank on It. Oct, 1983.

Kornblum, William. Drug Legalization and the Minority Poor. *Milbank Quarterly.* 1991.

Krauss, Clifford; Franz, Douglas. Cali Drug Cartel Using U.S. Business to Launder Cash. *The New York Times.* Oct 30, 1995.

LaFranchi, Howard. Cali Drug Cartel Stretches out Tentacles: Too Big for Bogota, Now Cartel is Eyeing Brazil. *Christian Science Monitor.* Feb 8, 1996.

Langer, John. Recent Developments in Drug Trafficking: The Terrorism Connection. *The Police Chief.* Apr 1986.

Lawyer Admits He Laundered Drug Money. *New York Times.* Sept. 22, 1995

Lee, Li Way. Would Harassing Drug Users Work? *Journal of Political Economy.* Oct 1993.

Legalization: No Answer. *Christian Science Monitor* (Editorial). Feb 8, 1996.

Legalise It. *New Statesman & Society.* Nov 12, 1993.

Lerner, Michael. The Grandma Mafia on Trial. *Newsweek.* Mar 28,1983.

Lernoux, Penny. The Miami Connection. *The Nation.* Feb 18, 1984.

Lewis, Anthony. Prohibition Folly. *The New York Times*. Feb 12, 1996.

Lippman, Thomas. Seychelles Offers Investors Safe Heaven for $10 Million. *The Washington Post*. Dec 31, 1995.

Lubove, Seth. *Cash Capital. Forbes*. Apr 26,1993.

Mac Donald, Scott B. Asia-Pacific Money Laundering. 1993.

MacCoun, Robert; Kahan, James; Gillespie, James. A Content Analysis of the Drug Legalization Debate. *Journal of Drug Issues*. 1993.

Maingot, Anthony. Laundering the Gains of the Drug Trade: Miami and Caribbean Tax Heavens. *Journal of Interamerican Studies and World Affairs*. 1988.

McCarron, John. Finding the Cure. *Chicago Tribune*. Jan 29,1996.

McGrath, Paul. Drugs and Tax Heavens. *World Press Review*. Nov 1985.

Meese, Edwin D. III. *Atlanta Constitution*. Jun 14, 1985.

Meese, Edwin D. III. *Atlanta Journal*. Jun 14, 1985.

Merrill Lynch Brokers in Panama Indicted in Laundering Case. *The Wall Street Journal*. Mar 7, 1994.

Mexico Files New Charges Against Jailed Brother of Ex-Chief. *The New York Times* Dec 4, 1995.

Mexico Reports Say Brother of Salinas is Charged Again. *Boston Globe*. Dec 4, 1995.

Mishan, Edward. Narcotics: the Problem and the Solution. *The Political Quarterly*. 1990.

Mitchell, Chester. Drug Access and Tax Rates: Politics, Efficiency or Justice? *Journal of Drug Issues.* 1990.

Mitchell, Alison. U.S. Freezes Assets of Cartel in New Effort Against Drugs. *The New York Times.* Oct 23, 1995.

Money Launderers on the Line. *Economist.* Jun 25, 1994.

Nadelmann, Ethan. America's Drug Problem: a Case for Decriminalization. *Dissent.* Spring 1992.

Neikirk, Bill; Walker, John M. Jr. *Chicago Tribune.* Jun 19, 1985.

O'Brien, John. Silver *Shovel Mole Took Accardo Money to Laundry.* Chicago Tribune. Jan 15, 1996.

O'Connor, Matt. *West Side Drug King Punished.* Chicago Tribune. Dec 21, 1995.

O'Connor, Matt. *PAC Tied to Gang's Drug Cash.* Chicago Tribune. Feb 2, 1996.

Ostrow, Ronald; Montalbano, William; Malnic, Eric. *Drug Agents Break Global Money Laundering System.* Los Angeles Times. Sep 29, 1992.

Perl, Raphael. *Clinton's Foreign Drug Policy.* Journal of Interamerican Studies and World Affairs. Winter 1993/1994.

Peters, Rebecca G. *Money Laundering and its current status in Switzerland: New Disincentives for financial tourism.* 1990.

Plott, Monte. *Atlanta Journal and Atlanta Constitution* (ATCJ). Jun 22, 1985.

Porter, Bruce. Follow the (drug) money. *Money Laundering Alert.* Sept/Oct, 1991.

Pot Panned. *The Economist*. Feb 19, 1994.

Powis, Robert E.. Money Laundering: Problems and Solutions. 1992.

Raab, Selwyn. Mob Hit? *The New York Times Book Review*. Mar 10, 1996.

Raab, Selwyn. Lawyer Living High Life is Said to Have Ties to Mob. *The New York Times*. Jul 21, 1995.

Rankin, Bill. Firm Accused of Pirating Scientific-Atlanta Boxes. *Atlanta Constitution*. Feb 7, 1996.

Rhodes, William; Hyatt, Raymond; Scheiman, Paul. The Price of Cocaine, Heroin and Marijuana, 1981-1993. *Journal of Drug Issues*. Summer 1994.

Richardson, Martin. Trade Policy and the Legalization of Drugs. *Southern Economic Journal*. January 1992.

Riemer, Blanca; Rossant, John; Dwyer, Paula. The Drug War - European Style. *Business Week*. Oct 2, 1989.

Robins, Lee. The Natural History of Substance Use as a Guide to Setting Drug Policy. *American Journal of Public Health*. Jan 1995.

Ross, Margaret M. Bankers, Guns and Money: Financial Assistance for Terrorism under the Prevention of Terrorism Act. 1991.

Sack, Kevin. 26 Members of Chinese-American Groups in Atlanta Indicted. *New York Times*. Feb 6, 1996.

Safire, William. *Chicago Tribune*. Mar 27, 1985.

Safire, William. *Atlanta Constitution.* Mar 28, 1985.

Sanger, David. Money Laundering, New and Improved. *The New York Times.* Dec 24, 1995.

Short, Lara W. The Liability of Financial Institutions for Money Laundering. Jan/Feb 1992.

Smith, Gladdis. Circle of Influence. *The New York Times Book Review.* Sep 3, 1995.

Stares, Paul. Drug Legalization: Time for a Real Debate. *Brookings Review.* Spring 1996.

Stop Blaming the System. *The Nation.* Feb 23, 1985.

Sullivan, Ronald. New York Presses for State Trial of Clifford. *The New York Times.* Oct 31, 1992.

Symposium: The Anti-Money Laundering Statutes: Where from here? Spring 1993.

Teasley, David. Drug Legalization and the 'Lessons' of Prohibition. *Contemporary Drug Problems.* Spring 1992.

Thies, Clifford; Register, Charles. Decriminalization of Marijuana and the Demand for Alcohol, Marijuana and Cocaine. *The Social Science Journal.* 1993.

Tobin, Mary. *Snaring the Smurfs: The War on Drugs is Heating Up, and the Banks are Playing a Key Role in Efforts to Catch the Launderers of Illicit Drug Money.* U.S. Banker. 1989.

Trying to Shut Down the Money Laundry. *Newsweek.* Mar 28, 1983.

Tutuy, Juan. The Drug Traffickers' Bid for Power. *World Marxist Review.* Nov 1989.

U.S. Lawyer Pleads Guilty to Cali Money Laundrering. *The Wall Street Journal*. Sep 22, 1995.

Van Duyne, Petrus. Organized Crime and Business Crime-Enterpreses in the Netherlands. Mar 1993.

Van Kammen, Welmoet; Loeber, Rolf. Are Fluctuations in Delinquent Activities Related to the Onset and Offset in Juvenile Illegal Drug Use and Drug Dealing? *Journal of Drug Issues*. 1994.

Veiga, Alvaro. Narcotrafico: La Conexion Uruguaya. 1995.

Walker, Ken. How a Medical Journalist Helped to Legalize Heroin in Canada. *Journal of Drug Issues*. 1991.

Walker, William. Efficiency and Effectiveness in Drug Elimination Efforts. *Journal of Housing and Community Development*. Jul/Aug 1995.

Walther, Susanne. Forfeiture and Money Laundering Laws in the United States. 1994.

Warner, Kenneth. Legalizing Drugs: Lessons from (and about) Economics. *Milbank Quarterly*. 1991.

Weilald, S. Cass. The Use of Offshore Institutions to Facilitate Criminal Activity in the United States. 1984.

Weisheit, Ralph; Johnson, Katherine. Exploring the Dimensions of Support for Decriminalizing Drugs. *Journal of Drug Issues*. 1992.

Wessel, David; Davis, Bob. Under a Cloud: Bank of Boston Faces Image Problem likely to Linger for Years. *The Wall Street Journal*. Mar 7, 1985.

Williams, David. Terrorism in the □90s: The skull and crossbones still flies. *The Police Chief.* Sep 1990.

World Wire: Seychelles' Offer Castigated. *The Wall Street Journal.* Feb 2, 1996.

Wren, Christopher. Leading Conservative Voice Endorses Legalizing Narcotics. *The New York Times.* Jan 22, 1996.

Wren, Cristopher. Strategies are Shifting in the Drug War; The Laundering of Proceeds is Becoming an Important Battlefield. *The New York Times.* May 5, 1996.

Yuksel, Mustafa. *Money Laundering.* 1991.

Zanker, Alfred; Scherschel, Patricia. Why It's Getting Tougher to Hide Money. *U.S. News & World Report.* Jun 2, 1986.

Zuckoff, Mitchell. *Boston Globe.* Jun 22, 1995.

Zuckoff, Mitchell. Fugitive Bank Swindler Gets Record 24 Year Prison Term. *Boston Globe.* Sep 13, 1995.

GOVERNMENT PUBLICATIONS

Attorney General's Advocacy Institute, *Money Laundering & Asset Forfeiture Conference* (Miami, FL, 1991).

Bush, George, *Bill establishing a regulatory structure for government sponsored enterprises and other measures. Combating money laundering, regulatory relief to financing institutions, housing initiatives and reducing risk from lead-based paint.* (Washington, D.C. 1992).

Commission on Organized Crime and Money Laundering: *record of hearing II, March 14, 1984.* New York. (Washington, D.C. 1985).

Criminal Division, Money Laundering Section and Attorney General's Advocacy Institute, *Money Laundering & Asset Forfeiture Conference.* (Miami: U.S. Dept. Of Justice, 1991).

Explanatory report on the Convention on Laundering, Search, Seizure and Confiscation of the Proceeds from Crime. (Strasbourg: Council of Europe, Publishing and Documentation Service, 1991).

Financial Investigations: a financial approach to detecting and resolving crimes. (Washington, D.C.: Dept. Of the Treasury, Internal Revenue Service. 1993). 401pp.

Giusti, Jorge, *The economic and social significance of narcotics.* (CEPAL: 1991)

Information Technologies for the Control of Money Laundering, (Washington, D.C.: Office of Technology Assessment, Congress of the U.S., 1995). 144pp.

Kerry, John F., U.S.Senate, *Trip to the U.K. on issues concerning international crime, drug trafficking and money laundering: a report to the Committee on Foreign Relations.* (Washington, D.C.: 1993).

Morley, Charles H., *Tracing money flows through financial institutions prepared by Police Executive Research Forum.* (Washington, D.C.: 1992).

Murphy, T. Gregory, *Uncovering assets laundered through a business...*(Washington, D.C.: 1992).

Reporting Cash Payments of Over $ 10.000. (Washington, D.C.: Dept. Of Treasury, Internal Revenue Service, 1991).

U.S. Congress. Senate. Committee on Foreign Relations. Subcommittee on Terrorism, Narcotics and International Operations. *Andean Drug Initiative: Hearing Before the Subcommittee on Terrorism, Narcotics and International Operations of the Committee on Foreign Relations, United States Senate,* One Hundred Second Congress, second session, February 20, 1992. (Washington, D.C., U.S. GPO 1992).

U.S. Congress. House. Committee on Ways and Means, Subcommittee on Oversight. *Internal Revenue Service undercover operations and enforcement of the money laundering laws...*(Washington, D.C.: 1992).

U.S. Dept. of the Treasury, FinCEN, Financial Crimes Enforcement Network, *Commercial Crimes-United States,* (Washington, D.C.: 1991).

U.S. Dept. of State, Robert Gelbard, *International Narcotic Control Efforts in the Western Hemisphere,* (Washington, D.C. Published by the Bureau of Public Affairs, 1995).

U.S. General Accounting Office, *Money Laundering [microform]: Treasury's Financial Crimes Enforcement Network: report to the Chairman and ranking minority member, Subcommittee on Treasury, Postal Service.* (Washington, D.C. The Office, Gaithersburg, M.D. 1991).

U.S. Congress, House, Committee on Foreign Affairs, *Andean Drug Strategy of the Committee on Foreign Affairs, House of Representatives.* (Washington: U.S., GPO 1991).

U.S. Congress, House. Committee on Ways and Means, Subcommittee on Oversight. *Department of the Treasury's efforts to address money laundering*: hearing before the Subcommittee on Oversight of the Committee on Ways and Means, House of Representatives, September, 20, 1994.

U.S. House of Representatives, Committee on Banking, Fin. And Urban Affaires, Subcommittee on Financial Institutions.., Bank Secrecy Act violation reported by the Bank. *The First National Bank of Boston: hearings, April 3-4, 1985.* iv+573pp.

U.S. General Accounting Office, *Money Laundering [microform] Treasury's Financial Crimes Enforcement Network: report to the Treasury, Postal Service and General Government, Committee on Appropriations.* U.S. Senate. (Washington, D.C., 1991).

U.S. Congress. House. Committee on Government Operations. Legislation and National Security Subcommittee. *International Narcotics: Hearing Before the Legislation and Operations, House of Representatives,* One Hundred Third Congress, Second Session, October 7, 1994. (Washington, D.C.: U.S. GPO 1995).

U.S. Department of Justice, Criminal Div. -Narcotic and Dangerous Drug-Sect.,*Investigation and prosecution of illegal money laundering: a guide to The Bank Secrecy Act.* (Washington, D.C.: 1983).

U.S. Congress. House. Committee on Banking, Subcommittee on Financial Institutions Supervision, Regulation and Insurance, *Money Laundering Control Act of 1986 and the regulations implementing the Bank Secrecy Act: hearings before the Subcommittee on Financial Institutions Supervision, Regulation, and Insurance of the Committee on Banking, Finance.* . .House of Representatives, (Washington, D.C.: 1986).

U.S. Congress. House. Committee on Judiciary. *Money Laundering Control Act of 1986.* (Washington, D.C.: 1986).

U.S. Senate, Com.-on-Governmental Affaires. Permanent Subcom.-on-Investigations. *Domestic Money Laundering: First National Bank of Boston:*(Hearing, March 12, 1985). 220pp.

Webster, Barbara, and McCampbell, Michael, *International Money Laundering: research and investigation join forces,* U.S. Dept. of Justice, (Washington, D.C. 1992).

Wray, Henry R., *Money Laundering [microform]: the use of the Bank Secrecy Act reports by law enforcement could be increased.* (Washington, D.C., The Office; Gaithersburg,M.D. 1993).

INTERNATIONAL BODIES

Gilmore, W.C. (Ed.), Cambridge International Documents Series, Volume 4, *International Efforts to Combat Money Laundering*, (Cambridge: Grotius Publications Limited, 1992).

U.N. International Narcotics Control Board, *Precursors and Chemicals Frequently used in the Illicit Manufacture of Narcotic Drugs and Psychotropic Substances*, (Vienna-New York, UN, 1995).

U.N. International Narcotics Control Board, Report of the International Narcotic Control Board for 1995. Vienna.

U.N. International Narcotic Control Board, Reportr of the International Narcotics Control Board for 1995, (Vienna, NU, 1995).

U.N. Junta Internacional de Fiscalizacion de Estupefacientes-- Viena, Estupefacientes, Previsiones y Necesidades mundiales para 1994. (Naciones Unidas, 1996)

Common Abbreviations

CICAD	Inter-American Drug Abuse Control Commission
DEA	Drug Enforcement Administration
ESF	Economic Support Fund
FATF	Financial Action Task Force
FBI	Federal Bureau of Investigation
INCSR	International Narcotics Control Strategy Report
INL	Bureau for International Narcotics Control and Law Enforcement Affairs
JICC	Joint Information Coorditation Center
MLAT	Mutual Legal Assistance Treaty
NNICC	National Narcotics Intelligence Consumers Committee
OAS	Organizationn of American States
UN Convention	1988 United Nations Convention Against Illicit Traffic in Narcotic Drugs and Psychotropic Substances
USAID	Agency for International Development
USG	United States Gouvernment
kg	Kilogram
HCI	Hydrochloride (cocaine)
mt	Metric Ton
ha	Hectare

INDEX

A

B

M